Radical Poetics

POETS ON POETRY

Derek Pollard, Series Editor
Donald Hall, Founding Editor

For a complete list of titles, please see www.press.umich.edu

Radical Poetics

Essays on Literature & Culture

KHADIJAH QUEEN

University of Michigan Press
Ann Arbor

Copyright © 2024 by Khadijah Queen

For questions or permissions, please contact um.press.perms@umich.edu

Published in the United States of America by the
University of Michigan Press
Manufactured in the United States of America
Printed on acid-free paper
First published January 2025

A CIP catalog record for this book is available from the British Library.

Library of Congress Cataloging-in-Publication data has been applied for.

ISBN 978-0-472-03979-1 (paper : alk. paper)
ISBN 978-0-472-22199-8 (e-book)

For survivors

Acknowledgments

An earlier version of "Painting and Palimpsest: Ekphrasis, History, and Empathy in the Poetics of Natasha Trethewey" appeared in North *American Women Poets in the 21st Century* (Wesleyan 2020) as "Natasha Trethewey's Palimpsestic Poetics."

"A Radical Poetics of Love: Looking for the Love in Invisible Man" appeared in *Of Color: Poets' Ways of Making: An Anthology of Essays on Transformative Poetics* (The Operating System 2019).

"A Poetics of Resistance: On Sor Juana Inés de la Cruz and Women of Action in Early Colonial Mexico" appeared in *Annulet* (Issue 1, April 2021). https://annuletpoeticsjournal.com/Khadijah-Queen-A-Poetics-of -Resistance

Portions of "Muriel Rukeyser: A Study in Imaginative Poetics as Praxis" appeared in *futurefeed* on April 28, 2020. https://future-feed.net/Muriel -Rukeyser-as-Major-Figure

My deepest appreciation to the following people for their support as this book took shape:

Professors and colleagues at University of Denver—Dr. Tayana L. Hardin, for her invaluable, steadfast guidance and stellar scholarly example throughout my doctoral studies; Dr. W. Scott Howard, Dr. Bin Ramke, and Dr. Frédérique Chevillot—for their patience, time, and extraordinary insight; Dr. Eric Gould for a tutorial on Baudrillard that turned to Barthes and helped steer my study more clearly toward the philosophical; Dr. Juli Parrish for excellent early mentorship and pedagogical example; my brilliant, supportive, extraordinary cohort, aka the Golden Cohort: Rowland

Saifi, Emily Pettit, Alicia Mountain, Vincent James, Dennis James Sweeney, Brian Laidlaw, Alison Turner, and especially McCormick Templeman, who read a full draft of this work and offered instrumental advice at a critical moment. Thank you to Erinrose Mager, Ashley Colley, Jessica Comola, and Sasha Strelitz for kind solidarity and strategic moments of mirrored understanding.

This work received research funding support from the English Department and College of Arts, Humanities and Social Sciences at the University of Denver. Time spent in London at the Hazel Barnes Flat thanks to the University of Colorado, Boulder English Department and the Doris Schwalbe travel grant helped enable the completion of an early draft of this work in 2019. Summer research funding at Virginia Tech in 2021, and course releases in fall 2023 aided the completion of this work, as well as the generous support of the 2022 Disability Futures Fellowship from United States Artists and Ford Foundation.

I did not write any of this book at the castle at Civitella Ranieri in Umbertide, Italy, but my fellowship there in September and October 2023 offered invaluable care, healing, beauty, kindness, new friendships, joy, and awe that helped me to approach revisions with new clarity.

I appreciate the ongoing support of my colleagues and students at Regis University and Virginia Tech. Support from my outstanding research assistant at Tech, Dante Fuoco, especially in formatting, citation, and copyright work, helped make the completion of this work possible during the publication process, particularly as I recovered from surgery. I want to thank my friends and family, especially my sister Kim. And, always, I owe much to my son, Tariq, who grew up while I wrote this book, taught himself to cook expertly, and often made sure I ate something, and laughed.

Contents

Digital materials related to this title can be found on the Fulcrum platform
via the following citable URL: https://doi.org/10.3998/mpub.12578382

"How can words have enough space to embrace the world?"
—MAHMOUD DARWISH, FROM *IN THE PRESENCE OF ABSENCE*,
TRANSLATED BY SINAN ANTOON

Preface

Radical Poetics

The world is made of distinct histories and places, but the overlap of experience shared by living things: constant.

For women[1] and queer folks[2] and children[3] and the earth,[4] that experience often involves violence.[5] In addition to physical violence, exploitation and discrimination happen frequently at the hands of men, and in a recent and imperative example in the US in the past couple of decades, mass shootings. Indeed, almost every American mass shooter (exclusively male) had a previous record of committing violence against women and/or queer folks behind closed doors long before they brought their guns into the public sphere.[6] Other men and male-presenting individuals fall victim, too, when they don't participate in such violence—and sometimes when they do—while our culture tends to ignore, minimize, fail to successfully prosecute, and in some cases even reward such acts of violence.[7] Meanwhile, incidences in which women fight back often become gossip fodder or footnotes instead of celebrations of strength.

Why does gender and sexuality still figure so prominently in public and private violence? What is the solution, besides policy shifts around gun control, and what does that have to do with literature? One answer resides in the source of such violence and its widespread acceptance: how we[8] think, how thought translates into belief, how belief extends into behavior, and how behavior leads to the habits and norms that ultimately build our culture. Writers, and literature by extension, have helped to shape culture—and have the power to keep shaping it. Are we going to use that power to repress calls for change, or to enact a powerful transformation? Will we continue to value and define ourselves in terms of dominance and profiteering, or will we shift our priorities toward equity and human connection?

Prevailing Western literary thought has followed Western philosophy since Plato's *Ion*[9] and extended via Descartes and beyond. Ideas such as mind-body dualism offer divisive characterizations of human nature, with the mind topping a theoretical-made-standard hierarchy. Closer to present day, but still on the ancient strategic scale of empire, Paulo Freire calls out this division as part of systemic oppression: "oppressors halt by any method (including violence) any action which in even incipient fashion could awaken the oppressed to the need for unity." He further notes that such systems prefer "*focalized* view of problems rather than . . . dimensions of a *totality*"—since fragmentation suppresses true freedom as well as complete understanding.[10] Literary analysis has adopted and adapted to such divisive beliefs, cutting off the product from the impulse which helped originate it and the medium through which it is delivered. In studying literary theory, I kept asking, "Where is the feeling?" (And feeling, here, refers to the experience of interior human emotion, whether physically translated or not.) I came to believe that instinct and feeling can, through poetry, serve as evidence of the body's thought; in unity with the mind, they form a more complete expression (in practice) and understanding (in analysis) by de-hierarchizing the relationship between body and mind.

I will not spend much time debating dead philosophers or arguing established thought; my focus here is on adding a sense of future possibility, and on creating a practical resource that draws together existing work in this area.

I prefer the term "to create" over "to master," and I use the former throughout when speaking about making and remaking. An overused and little-interrogated term, the word "mastery" infuses the process of artmaking with notes of ownership, dominance, and other implicit violence—ironically, at the same time that Western culture has traditionally characterized passion and emotion as dangerous and violent.[11] But diminishing the importance of feeling ignores the problems of content.[12] Critics and teachers can tout and teach offensive canonical texts without challenging their racist, classist, homophobic, and sexist precepts, maintaining that readers should simply ignore or accept them, never mind the very real harm that these readers' feelings signal and that the texts perpetuate by influencing thought and culture. That approach does nothing to teach readers how to think in an integrated way, taking feeling into account. Instead, it leads to the repression of feelings and a susceptibility to gaslighting—i.e., what you feel isn't what you really feel—and, further, leaves readers ill-equipped to respect and empathize with others' feelings.[13] It leads to fear and denial of feeling—the very thing, even more than thinking, that helps make us human. If we aren't careful, we might move through our entire lives as divided beings who value a false objectivity over true humanity. Resisting prescriptive separation and complacent approaches to analysis, a poetics of self-determination (as part of and related to integrity and trust, love and intuition) reaches toward a reading and thinking practice that translates into a kind of self-knowing which reckons with our living circumstances beyond the text.

Prolific poet, novelist, activist, professor, and scholar Muriel Rukeyser believed that poetry[14] exists as a "useful" tool for understanding and moving through the fear and confusion engendered by the separation of emotion and intellect, the physical and nonphysical, and that by immersing ourselves in poetry we can potentially achieve a sense of wholeness.[15] It may seem naïve or idealistic to think that if we change the way we analyze, think about, read, and write literature we can affect people's lives, but idealism energizes me. I believe we can infuse active, conscious love into our work and our lives, and I feel no shame about that conviction. Walt Whitman believed, for instance, that *Song of Myself* could inspire the kind of unity and human kinship that could stop the Civil War.[16]

Engaging in this work means that the results of such stated intention may not be easily quantified. We can speculate, however, that proofs exist in Whitman's being, in his real-life actions as a volunteer nurse. He put his care for fellow humans into both words and living practice. The proofs do also exist in the text: "Writing and talk do not prove me, / I carry the plenum of proof and every thing else in my face, / With the hush of my lips I wholly confound the skeptic."[17] A canonical text such as *Leaves of Grass* went against stated 19th-century mores in terms of form and sexuality,[18] and still isn't without controversy, of course, particularly with regard to racist themes in his post-Civil War writing.[19] Part of the point of comprehensive analysis: to reckon with and contextualize rather than repeat oppressor habits of erasure; to be deliberate in our expanded understanding of what interferes with a more complete understanding. If we, as writers and thinkers, as teachers and readers, demand and create new structures of thought through our feeling-based actions, we might have a chance to shape culture for the better—whether or not we can measure and attribute that reshaping to something as resistant to measurability as poetry.

Rukeyser believed that science, with its theories and proofs designed to measure and unravel the realities and mysteries of the universe, had a deep connection with poetry. She wrote a substantial biography of the obscure 16th century scientist-explorer Thomas Hariot, and *The Life of Poetry* threads reflections on science throughout. In a subsection of chapter ten, "The Rare Union: Poetry and Science," she writes that "the farther we go along the way we go in each, the more clearly the relationship may be perceived, the more prodigal the gifts."[20] If science and poetry don't represent the union of mind and body, animating spirit and emotion, I don't know what does. But I didn't find a serious engagement between science and poetry on the scientific side until I happened upon a book in a thrift store, its pale pink cover adorned by two dark red cherries entwined at the stem and an all-caps title in burgundy serif font: *A General Theory of Love*.

Co-written by psychiatrists Thomas Lewis, Fari Amini, and Richard Lannon, the book focuses on how love works in human relationships, maintaining—much like poetry does—that the use of such study lies not in fact-finding or proof but in presenting us with practicable approaches to living and behaving with more mindfulness, care, and compassion toward ourselves and other living beings. The authors write: "The investigation of these queries is not just an intellectual excursion: people *must* have the answers to make sense of their lives. We see the need for this knowledge every day, and we see the bitter consequences of its lack."[21] They further link love and intuition to wellbeing: "People who do not intuit or respect the laws of acceleration and momentum break bones; those who do not grasp the principles of love waste their lives and break their hearts."[22] Even though they are scientists, the authors combine scientific knowledge with emotional knowledge, primarily gleaned from case studies ("Human lives form the richest repository") supported by examples in other fields, including poetry: "We searched, in short, for the science of love. Finding no such system in our field, we went hunting in other disciplines."[23]

The first chapter opens with a poem by Denise Levertov that summarizes succinctly the connection between life and poetry. The poem begins: "Two girls discover / the secret of life"—but not in anything scientific; rather, their discovery lies "in a sudden line of / poetry."[24] The authors apply their combined seven decades of practical experience and years of research and set about examining the notion that "[e]very conception of love inevitably depends on a view of the broader totality of the mind."[25] I think Rukeyser would feel incredibly validated by the choices the authors make in *A General Theory*, and their arguments certainly help my own position: "Some might think it strange that a book on the psychobiology of love opens with a poem, but the adventure itself demands it. Poetry transpires at the juncture between feeling and understanding—and so does the bulk of emotional life."[26]

Perhaps, then, one can indeed measure love by its impact, and perhaps a poem is one way to enact such a measurement. But, if poetics also resides at that juncture, can (or should) one even try to measure the impact of a poetics itself? If one cannot or should not measure a poetics, how can one engage in and enact a radical poetics: getting at the root of love, of truth, of intuition, of integrity—and clearly expressing it? It may, in fact, be possible to arrive at a more accurate understanding—one beyond content and structure—by choosing any one or all such terms and searching for how a text engages, enacts, and/or ignores them.[27] Accuracy behooves us not only in academic inquiry but in what that inquiry seeps into: our thinking, which seeps into our behavior, which accumulates into culture-making. A radical poetics acknowledges how thoughts become beliefs which drive human actions which in turn become entrenched as social norms. A radical poetics strives, through literature explicitly, to influence social norms through the same mechanisms by which poetry creates meaning: through feeling-based knowledge, which, given enough repetition, then becomes translated through mind and body as action.

There are three basic prongs to radical poetics, itself based upon the core acknowledgement of poetry as praxis, and their interaction with each other is illustrated in figure 1. Since thinking (poetics),[28] making (praxis),[29] and doing (poetry itself as active agent)[30] are relational,[31] it makes sense to track and examine their relationship further in terms of result—how poetics operates in terms of love or feeling, how it functions with and delivers intuited meaning, and what gives it a sense of whole-

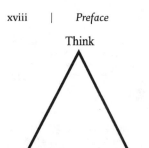

Think

Make   Do

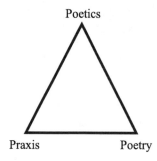

Poetics

Praxis   Poetry

Two stacked triangles illustrating the relationship between the three basic prongs of radical poetics.

ness or integrity. Again, I do not mean romantic or sentimental love, but love for the work—making and reading literature, discussing and teaching it, analyzing and editing it. If we train ourselves only in the mechanics of language during construction and deconstruction but leave out the feeling, where is the poetry?[32] And if poetry provides part of the beauty and mystery of language that produces feeling, how can a text (or the understanding of it) claim wholeness without grappling with the feeling(s) produced?

I start with love as the foundational feeling because of its weight and its familiarity. My essay on *Invisible Man* looks at love—or, more accurately, its absence in the text. Reading Ellison's novel again at the same time I was rereading and teaching Rukeyser's *The Life of Poetry*, I found myself wondering where love resided in the text. The exuberance of poetry existed in the sermons, and that could be characterized as a love for language. However, the novel elides ethical concerns like incest—a glaring choice that demonstrates the novel has no love for women at all.

In fact, women served simply as flat vehicles for male characters' destructive desires and as stand-ins for society's alienating pressures. Due to his race and financial status, the narrator in *Invisible Man* cannot escape participation in the horrific Battle Royale, nor can he escape the fraught episode with the exotic dancer. His forced participation means he cannot then escape what follows such traumatic experiences: the internal and external consequences of violent heteropatriarchal toxicity that manifest as shame, self-hatred, and confusion—all emotions and states of being that keep folks from creating true connection with one another and from even imagining the possibility of that connection, except when it comes to other men. And even those relationships tend toward mentorship and business, not friendship.

And so, without love, the separatist system that renders the narrator invisible remains, and what seems to follow, since the observed realities of force and separation, of harshness and difficulty cannot be successfully overcome, is that one might as well strive for whatever kind of supremacy one can manage to exert.[33] In the narrator's case, that means withdrawing—a refusal to participate that renders the self invisible to that system and to the people who power it. And what a tragedy that is: to give up and go underground in order to live invisibly, to consider invisibility as the safest option. But, as Ellison's narrator discovers, invisibility is an illusion, because we cannot hide from ourselves. Indeed, the use of metanarrative here invites us to speculate that author and character have much in common, with the creative act tethering the two—equating writing about his experience with racism to torture, and explicitly mentioning that "There seems to be no escape" from either racism, or reckoning with its negative impacts.[34]

Ellison's choice to embed what could be construed as his personal authorial position into a fictional narrative may intimate that he needed the layer of imagination in order to deliver the truths about race that the book interrogates. Certainly, the 1950s proved a dangerous time to tell truths that challenged ideas of white supremacy, that documented the widespread damage it causes, and that ultimately indicted America's willful and active ignorance. Though we get glimpses of luminous strength, particularly in the book's sermons, perhaps, in order to publish, Ellison had to cloak those truths in self-hatred and futility, in misery and ruin.

Indeed, the doctrine of dominance can ruin us all, even the ruiner[35] as represented in the novel by Mr. Norton, who, beneath the wealth and propriety that grants him power over others, leads a depraved internal life and a parasitic public one. Ellison uses *Invisible Man* to soundly demonstrate the relational dependence of Black and white Americans, but his premise is flawed because the novel's content and structure show that he still subscribes to hierarchies of race and gender. In our literary theories and in our own creative work, we must reject such capitulations. The absence of the reckoning that love requires can only consign the future to repeat the destructive habits of bloody wars, ignorance, and suppression ad infinitum. The contradiction inherent in canonical works like *Invisible Man*, and in works by other notable writers like Herman Melville and even Rukeyser, is that these texts question the effects of white supremacy because of a feeling of exclusion or a sense of injustice. The glory and privilege, however, still seduce the main characters and sometimes the authors, even if their writing shows that glory and privilege come at great cost to humanity, even if supremacy runs counter to their own marginalization. They seem to want to keep parsing it instead of correcting their baseline perceptions about wealth as power, whiteness as goodness, heterosexual maleness as authority, etc.

Literary analysis can return to those root perceptions and tease apart the contradictions that lie within them. Perhaps cultures around the world have taught people to admire wealth and power because, from time immemorial, wealth and power—whether physical or social—has meant that the odds of survival are greater at the least, and their association with promises of comfort and fame are seductive. However, shouldn't we ask whether wealth necessarily means harming, manipulating, and/or stealing from other people? Is "survival" a justifiable rationale for death-dealing and destruction? We say we value integrity, truth, and love, but observing our glut of movie posters depicting muscular men with guns shows, for instance, otherwise. Looking at American literature through the lens of feeling means that we can better pinpoint the schism between perception and reality.[36] We can look in that literature for the ways language constructs wealth, whiteness, violence, and power as good, aspirational qualities—and further, that poverty, femaleness, Blackness, queerness, and indigeneity are somehow less-than because they imply vulnerability or other qualities we have been socialized to deem undesirable.

Toni Morrison discusses this contradictory and peculiar origin point of American literature in her essay "Black Matter(s)" from her last book, 2019's *The Source of Self-Regard*. She writes that, in works that proudly tout ideals of freedom and justice while simultaneously praising a society that actively enslaves, colonizes, imprisons, disenfranchises, and impoverishes whole segments of the population, particularly Black people, American literature intentionally creates "a vocabulary designed to disguise" that sinister and contradictory practice.[37] My aim with *Radical Poetics* is to dive into that contradiction and its implications by exposing the false root—the culturally enforced separation of emotions from intellect, body from spirit, and all the possible permutations thereof—in order to return to the emotional root of creativity and human connection, which includes trust, integrity, intuition, and love, in terms of both the making of literature and the reading of it. Again, a poetics of self-determination, as a thread running through my own essays, as well as many of the texts they examine, means—through writing and analysis—focusing on generative rather than destructive thinking. It means replacing narrow, uninterrogated cultural training with thoughtful questioning, more humane rhetorical solutions that strive for inclusivity and capaciousness. It does not mean contrariness for its own sake, but insistence on intentional choices based on love, trust, and integrity.[38] It means acting on these principles regardless of others' perceptions and the very real social consequences of such perceptions. We must be as unafraid of and open to the unknown as philosopher and poet Édouard Glissant describes in *Poetics of Relation*: "We know ourselves as part and as crowd, in an unknown that does not terrify . . . Our boats are open, and we sail them for everyone."[39]

In adding to the language and theoretical structure (i.e., intellect) of the seemingly hidden and often-dismissed realm of emotions, I hope to demonstrate the same unity of emotional and intellectual inquiry and expression that I examine. Lucille Clifton's poem "quilting," which stitches together speculated scenes of unknown and known worlds, ends with the lines "do the worlds continue spinning / away from each other forever?"[40] I, too, wondered at the answer to that question, and it occurred to me that cultural practices manufacture the distance between the worlds of emotion and intellect, body and mind, self and other. We must evolve past that manufactured distance to return to the natural impulse to connect, to remain whole.[41] The undercurrent of wholeness-in-difference still exists in literature and in life, as it always has, and that wholeness can drive our inquiry.

How do we begin to discuss emotion and its value within thought, or as a type of understanding, and indeed, how do we articulate its value to understanding? Although I point out the faults of common thought processes and sociocultural practices as necessary, more importantly, I imagine. In concert with the writers I mention, I get to imagine what embracing love, integrity, intuition, trust, and the like makes possible for thought and practice. Clifton has another poem positioned just past the center of her nearly 800-page *Collected Poems*, one that I memorized years ago, and which I relay here in its entirety:

A DREAM OF FOXES

in the dream of foxes
there is a field
and a procession of women
clean as good children
no hollow in the world
surrounded by dogs
no fur clumped bloody
on the ground
only a lovely line
of honest women stepping
without fear or guilt or shame
safe through the generous fields[42]

Like Clifton, I choose to imagine what kind of world or field I dream of inhabiting, which unproductive emotions I can slough off. I get to decide what kind of writer, scholar, teacher, person I am and would like to be.[43] I get to choose how I practice and combine intellectual inquiry and creative process, how much I disclose and what I keep for myself—choices especially relevant to "A Sea of Troubles," an account of the very fraught and personal process of dealing privately and publicly with sexual harassment and assault in literary and academic communities. The Lox, a hardcore New York City–based rap group I listened to quite a lot when I served in the US Navy (and occasionally throw back to when I need a boost of

energy and bravado), has a lyric: "I tell you what I want you to know / f***
what you ask me."[44] That lyric also reminds me that I get to choose what I
imagine and what I say, even when faced with opposition. I choose to do
so alongside the kinds of writers and thinkers who make of that imagination a practice not rooted in an accepted reality but in a possible one; one
where I can move more freely, "safe through the generous fields."

Safety, however, is not without risk, and to make these arguments clear
I've had to balance wellbeing with disclosure, mystery with clarity, having thought a lot about clarity and how to obtain or present that in this
work.[45] I don't know that I have achieved my aim; I don't know whether
more time would help me or shut the whole thing down. One certainty,
however: I have felt a clarity of purpose and inquiry in the process. I
believe both feelings thread through, and I learned to be as informed as
possible while engaging in new experiences simultaneously (i.e., writing
while traveling through Europe, for one example).

Writing while traveling also reminded me to work within my
limitations—physical, linguistic, et cetera. At first, that felt disorienting.
I had to work through some "should" feelings—the disconnect between
how I thought I "should" feel about traveling through and observing
Europe versus how I actually felt. But now, I think that that disorientation was part of the work, too—to get comfortable within the discomfort,
both physical and emotional, to make useful work out of the contrast,
to find freedom in constraint and clarity amid chaos. That process feels
important as I navigate a new life as an academic—a role and label I still
have trouble feeling at ease in accepting as part of that freedom. But I
had help, forebears in thought, even as they warned, as Morrison does
in *The Source of Self-Regard*, "in that freedom, as in all freedoms (especially stolen ones), lay danger."[46] In trying to restructure critical thought
around race in the literary field in a manner that avoids white supremacy,
she faced the prospect of risk when trying to avoid feeling "tethered to a
death-dealing ideology even (and especially) when I honed all my intelligence toward subverting it."[47] We like to believe that determination will
allow us to accomplish anything, and like Morrison, "I want to imagine
not the threat of freedom, but the concrete thrill of borderlessness."[48]

When titling the travel essays I wrote for another project, I chose the
word "peregrination" with that purpose in mind—it can mean traveling
abroad, segmented journeying, meandering and wandering as a for-

eigner, a meaningful sojourn or pilgrimage—containing the hint of both walking and flying, both living and literary.[49] But the word also holds an urgency and a sense of continuance that holds echoes of what Hélène Cixous called for in "The Laugh of the Medusa," an essay first written in French in 1975, the year I was born, and published the following summer: "Woman must put herself into the text—as into the world and into history—by its own movement. The future must no longer be determined by the past."[50] The infinitude of exploration and of an exploratory reading life certainly propels this essay, reflecting the experience of endless striving that so approximates our living.

What if we—writers, thinkers, teachers—showed, in and through literature, that endless striving need not always hold strife or be perceived as solely negative? What if we used idealistic tools like trust (including self-trust), integrity, intuition, and love in order to approximate the process of surviving in a more productive, joyful way for the betterment of humanity instead of self-aggrandizement, "bettering" not as dominance but evolution? Or, perhaps not as evolution but as a more precise way to employ language in service of an evolving humanity.[51]

Roland Barthes reminds us in *The Pleasure of the Text* that "[a] writer is not someone who expresses [their] thoughts, passion or imagination in sentences, but someone who thinks sentences: A Sentence-Thinker (i.e., not altogether a thinker and not altogether a sentence-parser)."[52] A writer both expresses and thinks, engages both feeling and thought. The mind and emotion unify to produce the text—no compelling sentence without imagination, no imagination without thought, no expression without feeling. Barthes attempts to unify process and thought, emotion and creation using the sentence as the vehicle. In my view and experience, that way of making falls in line with a natural way of being, in the sense that making and being are not separate. Instead, both serve as cooperative aspects of the infinite permutations of human experience, emotional and physical, each informing the other. Maya Angelou speaks of something similar in terms of integrity, an existential striving to unify daily life and her creative practice, saying she wants to infuse them with presence and immediacy, taking "responsibility for the air I breath[e] and the space I take up."[53]

We walk around in bodies that contain an electrified charge—whether we call that charge soul or spirit, consciousness or animating force.[54] Why would we want to ignore that? Who profits from that separation, and who gets harmed? The time has long passed for literature and its theories to engage more consciously with those ethical questions on a larger scale, to reject ideas of "purity" manufactured in terms of race, nationalism, and heteronormativity. Sara Ahmed writes that "[e]motions, then, are bound up with how we inhabit the world 'with' others,"[55] and I won't cover her ground—how heteropatriarchal structures use nationalistic love to promote and justify harm, separatism, and discrimination. But her statement connects to Lorde's example, given as early as 1983 in an interview with Claudia Tate in *Black Women Writers at Work*, centering emotion "because we are taught to respect fear more than ourselves," urging us as humans to evolve beyond our silences and separations, to move toward respect and depth of true connection.[56] Emotion as connected to understanding requires engagement rather than mindless programmatics, and if literary theory claims that rigorous engagement with a text leads to deeper understanding, how can we ignore emotion in that process? Can a "new" literary theory dismantle a system of thinking so dominant as to infect nearly every aspect of life on earth?

I believe it already does, because the information already exists in the literature; the work is to focus further attention on both apparent and hidden architectures, tightening already-rooted threads that run toward one another across time and text. And although that might seem like the opposite of an escape—which is another thread woven through this work—radical rootedness is expansive, freely seeking to nourish the living, almost invisibly, under the surface. The roots of a poetics of escape bursts from its container(s), escaping from stagnancy, from harm, from ignorance—and Glissant's theory appears once again, rhizomatic, communicating underground and nurturing what appears above, in relation sans renunciation.[57]

Edward Said, in *Humanism and Democratic Criticism*, definitively calls for escape—advocating for revised methods of thinking and analysis in the field of the humanities, and noting that the revision must be ongoing. He writes that once they mummify into tradition, "they cease to be what they really are and become instruments of veneration and repression."[58] He links humanism with inquiry as a method of shaping culture, and preventing the narrow-mindedness that leads to discrimination and oppression.[59] Regarding the establishment-style pontifications of the prominent literary critic and late Yale professor Harold Bloom, for instance,[60] Said writes that his views on canonical texts lack imagination: "he refuses to engage with other arguments, he simply asseverates, affirms, intones. This is self-puffery, not humanism, and certainly not enlightened criticism."[61] Indeed, Said characterizes the entrenched resistance to reimagining or remaking the Western humanities canon as "bellicose dismissiveness" that fails to recognize the pivotal role of diversity in the innovations and advancements of human cultures and civilizations, ignoring historic and current dialogic and ideological conversations as well as their future possibilities.[62]

Why hold such hostility to complexity and difference? It seems lazy at best, exclusionary and repressive at the mid-level, and violent at worst. It was from reading Said—and later, Saidiya Hartman—that I first began to think of absences in texts, and I found the most glaring absences to have the most connective and human power across the spectrum of literature. Inquiring more deeply into those absences requires an unfamiliar kind of rigor, characterized by feeling. Furthermore, a theory of radical poetics holds that value and rigor lie not just in inquiry but also in a commitment to openness in that inquiry and an alignment not merely to clarity but also to accuracy. Trust, intuition, love, and integrity work together to create openness and accuracy, since they encompass the kind of transformative understanding that poetry strives to create.

Of course, my thinking holds no originality, except perhaps in the collection of texts and terms, and how the particular facts of my existence as a Black woman, an American poet, a single mother, a disabled veteran, and someone who grew up in a working-class family inform my perspective. Over the years, many scholars have decried the mind/body/spirit separation required of so-called objective critical approaches to cultural, literary, and other kinds of social and artistic analysis. A 1985 article from the *Journal of Feminist Studies in Religion* blames Platonic thought and Jungian mind/body-separating archetypes outright, and scholar Naomi R. Goldenberg sets her sights on debunking such separation. She remarks that "theories which separate mind from body are both anti woman and anti life" (*sic*).[63] Setting aside for the moment Platonic thought and Jungian archetypes imagined as subconsciously directing thought and behavior, it is notable that Goldenberg articulates the pervasive influence of separative thought and calls on readers to extend across disciplines: "I hope my critique of the archetype will be applicable to other theories which are based on similar disembodied constructs."[64] Returning to *A General Theory of Love*, Lewis, Amini, and Lannon urge folks to cast off Freud's "long shadow," noting that "his assumptions have endured for so many years that they are mistaken for fact."[65]

Unlike Freudian theories, a radical poetics does not assume fact; it urges the mind toward truth via feeling.[66] Poetics is not a disembodied construct, nor is it a prescription for living or thought, but a mode of inquiry, a method of making and understanding. It is embodied, and applicable to any text, including visual art—one reason I chose to write about the ekphrastic poetry of Natasha Trethewey. Further, this poetics can apply to everyday life, in that we can approach our understanding of relationships and circumstances via these theoretical practices. I use the term practices because this type of poetics serves a practical purpose through repeated application. Lewis, Amini, and Lannon write that "only a delicate admixture of evidence and intuition can yield the truest view of the emotional mind. To slip between the twin dangers of empty reductionism and baseless credulity, one must balance a respect for proof with a fondness for the unproven and unprovable."[67] I don't think people would be as passionate about studying, teaching, writing, and reading literature without poetry, love, or their concomitant mysteries. Love is part of the work, not a suppressible weakness. It is strength, an energetic through-line doing the work of human connection between writer and text, writer and reader, reader and text (figure 2).[68] With that said, the following are abbreviated rationales and applications for the practices proposed herein.

Poetics of Love

Rationale

Love means more than romantic desires or sexual urges. Love means connection: kinship, friendship, allyship, stewardship with the earth. Love means how we feel about what we do, observe, and spend time contemplating, resisting, or aspiring to. Accessing a poetics of love involves paying attention to both its presence and its absence, its success and its failure. Audre Lorde, in her famous essay "Poetry Is Not a Luxury" from

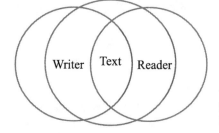

Three overlapping circles illustrating the relationship between writer, text, and reader.

Sister Outsider recognizes the suppression of feelings in our culture at large: "[W]ithin living structures defined by profit, by linear power, by institutional dehumanization, our feelings were not meant to survive."[69] Love, as the most powerful of those feelings, makes sense as a place to start.

Application

In my two and a half decades as a poet and writer, only my doctoral studies aimed to stamp out feeling. Luckily, I had mentors who helped make intellectual room for naming and exploring feeling's relationship to criticality when I articulated that separating them felt alarmingly off-base. Lewis, Amini, and Lannon write that "too many experts, out of plain fear, avoid mentioning love."[70] In asking questions about where love is present and absent in a text, about how love manifests itself in characters' behavior and in the author's formulation of the text, we as readers—and as writers—reject that fear. Instead, we boldly "start to describe emotional life in a way true to known physiology and the life experience of human beings, their passions and anguish."[71] We learn to trust our instincts by expressing the feelings a given text elicits (beyond easy evaluations like good or bad) and questioning the structures and content that invite those feelings. Practicing love and care for oneself, whether as a reader, a writer, or a teacher, is just as important as reading for love and its absence in a text. If a text makes us feel uncomfortable, or triggered, or angry, or jubilant, or inspired, or disgusted—why is that the case? Paying attention to the relationship between content, context, and structure in answering that question can help us to figure out both the meaning within the text and its value (or lack thereof) to us as readers, writers, and thinkers. Similarly, if we do not feel love in a text, is that absence related to our own position as a reader, writer, or teacher? How? Why? This practice of compassionate engagement is not therapy but an education in reading and thinking, an exercise in approaching those activities as a whole person, not merely as a disembodied brain; and are we not all students of human nature, simply by virtue of our being alive and existing among other people?[72] Our relationships with one another and with the earth demand this work.

Poetics of Trust

Rationale

Trust—specifically, who and what garners the trust of readers and peers—depends on a multitude of factors, and sometimes discrimination based on sociocultural factors such as race, gender, ability, and class can influence whether a reader feels they can trust an author or a text. A radical poetics of trust considers the mechanisms by which trust manifests itself in literature and asks us to consider our baseline assumptions as readers.

Application

Accessing a poetics of truth is an exercise in finding the intersection of accuracy and belief—the sometimes-schism between felt accuracy in the present and practiced thinking. In applying this poetics to literary analysis, one can ask the following questions to interrupt ingrained habits of dismissal, as well as of automatic trust. How does the feeling a text produces interfere with what we think we know, and does the author or text do enough to gain our trust in order to change our thinking? If not, why not? If yes, how? Do we trust ourselves enough as readers to make the decision or distinction? What challenges does self-trust face, both internally (i.e., our own imposed barriers) and externally (i.e., the text, habits of explication, questions of authority, etc.)? How does that trust—or the absence of it—affect our perception of a text's meaning or even its worth? Asking such questions clarifies the relationship between reader, text, and author without erasing or ignoring them or the context(s) in which they operate, thus allowing us to arrive at a more complete understanding.

Poetics of Intuition

Rationale

The use of intuition is a valuable and vital way of understanding literature. Outside of common Eurocentric narrative interpretation and literary theory, the role of self-knowledge and inner knowing (or, intuition) in terms of characters' thoughts and actions, including how those thoughts and actions resonate with readers, adds an essential dimension to both critical and creative approaches to understanding and analysis. Intuition— that deep inner knowing that often lacks a scientifically or empirically explainable source—depends upon a high level of self-trust, and a general respect for individual instincts within the culture, and furthermore, of thinking of instinct not as "primitive" or limited to being induced by danger but, to use a familiar phrase, as first thought/best thought. In the context of literary analysis, we can think of instinct as our first impression or first feeling, and that feeling can lead us to a fuller understanding, whether we arrive at that fullness quickly or through deeper investigation. While this book addresses multiple genres, I use the term poetics because poetry is the model I use to describe the methods for such investigation. This is similar to the move Rukeyser makes when she discusses visual art, poetry, film, and fiction in *The Life of Poetry*, a book of essays that greatly influenced my approach and that I treat extensively in the chapter on Rukeyser. Before her time—or in line with ancient times, depending on one's perspective—Rukeyser touched on the relationship between the scientific and the poetic.[73] She also gives primacy to feeling, including intuition, and I continue that line here, taking my cue from Toni Morrison and many others whose work gathers its power from intuitive ways of knowing intrinsic to poetics.

Application

Reading for feeling as physical understanding or as deep thinking instantly felt can include documenting the performance of intuition in terms of possible authorial prescriptives, characters' behavior, and/ or the reader's surrender to knowing. It can also include intuition as one of several ways of knowing that exist within and beyond traditional academic or literary modes. Accessing a poetics of intuition requires a respect for and comfort with engaging in mystery. In a September 6, 2019, episode of *Science Friday* on NPR, Dr. Annette Lee, an indigenous scientist from South Dakota, describes the growing movement to incorporate Indigenous or "native ways of knowing" into scientific inquiry, ways of knowing that are "just as valid as what [people] been taught from a Western worldview."[74] Lee states that "science is not separate from culture. Science comes from culture."[75] She also notes that she believes "spirits, dreams, and intuition are tools for building scientific knowledge" and what she calls a four-part way of being: body, mind, heart, and spirit.[76] Western science forgets the latter two, which leaves a gap in knowledge.[77] My essay on the poetics of intuition focuses on indigenous literature in no small measure because intuition figures so prominently in the content and structure of the works discussed—indeed, it is inextricable. That is not to say that it is absent elsewhere, but intuition feels openly integral to identify in the examined texts and thus likely to provide strong examples of my approach for the sake of future applications.

In many ways, applying a poetics of intuition is both the easiest (if you don't have to explain it) and the hardest (if you must delve into explanation) poetics to theorize. How do you add theoretical and practical structure to a mysterious way of knowing in a field, indeed a culture, that prizes material proof over feeling? And more, that privileges certain facts over others, including feeling-facts?[78] How do you reconcile the explained and unexplainable?[79] One way, one that I tried while rereading Ralph Ellison's novel *Invisible Man*, is to simply treat intuition as a valid metric. In the reading process, I proceeded to record and track instances of epiphany and behavior that occur as a result of characters intuiting from the environment, circumstance, action, or other characters sans (or disguised in) dialogue. Another way is for each reader to employ their own intuition in reading a text, but to do it consciously. We might do this already, and intuition can sometimes manifest as a physical reaction.[80] At the same time, while I consider intuition a strength of mine, I realize not everyone has the same level of attunement. This method is not singular. It is simply one more way in, another access point, and not everything is for everyone—which is what led me to writing theory in the first place. My way of combining thinking and feeling didn't fit, and I felt diminished when I tried to force myself to conform or comply—a state of being I resisted.

Talking about intuition in literary analysis in a critical context seems like folly. No proofs in the text at first, just impressions. Risking being wrong, or being right in a different way; daring to create a record of feeling as an analytical method—it would hardly seem out of bounds to encounter resistance to *my* resistance. And yet, tracking the evolution of one's feelings toward a text may, in fact, be a useful critical lens; it may also prove useful to self-understanding—adding an awareness of one's thinking and feeling process, which can be useful to everyday life. I believe that learning to use—or regain a connection to—our intuition more consciously can enrich our modes of literary analysis—and, should that exercise cloud our perceptions (as is entirely possible), we have a written record of how that happened. That may, in turn, show us our own biases, as well as how to avoid them in the future.

Poetics of Integrity

Rationale

Integrity can mean wholeness; it can also mean decency or goodness—the antithesis of corruption. For too long, albeit for reasons related to the threatened and actual violence discussed at the beginning of this preface, integrity has been portrayed in literature and culture as naïve. Although we are socialized through fables and militaristic stories to strive for and respect honor, honor can ignore wholeness, working as it often does to reinforce governmental or military power structures. But what if the characters in our literatures were rewarded for behaving with integrity instead of being jeered, tortured, or killed for it?[81] What if our literature imagined integrity not as an unattainable ideal but as central to who we are as humans, vital to ending entrenched violence and violent patterns of thought and behavior? Yes, integrity can mean disobedience to unjust or unethical instructions; that doesn't mean, however, that we must reproduce ad infinitum the negativization of integrity we insist or believe is intrinsic to realism.[82] What if instead we operated from a different assumption: that integrity, rather than an endangering trait, is instead connected to our survival?

A radical poetics insists that we push past obsolete thinking and imagine more, imagine better, choose the humane over the inhumane in critiquing and creating the worlds in our literature—to model questions of integrity that more richly, imaginatively, and accurately portray possibility. Building on a poetics that embraces intuition, a poetics of integrity would require us to push toward a holistic understanding of the text with honesty, curiosity, and care. It would mean our risking naiveté. For my part, I'm willing to risk foolishness in the name of joy—and yes, as I perceive it, there is joy in integrity because other than what exists in the text itself there is no façade to peel back. Like Muriel Rukeyser, I want a poetics—i.e., a theory, a practice—that spills into everyday life.

Application

As with love, accessing a poetics of integrity may involve finding where integrity is not and performing an analysis of the effect of that lack. Additionally, a study of integrity may remind us that analysis doesn't always have to mean breaking down a text or pulling it apart. It can also involve a holistic approach in which we not only include but *start* with the feelings that lead to reflection that in turn lead to deeper understanding. What if our experience of the text is all one process, with feeling as the unifier? Hopefully, as readers we commit to reflecting on our first impression in order to deepen our understanding of the text. I define impression here as the unified thought-feeling that creates a pathway to the interior of a text. Conditions for this understanding on that pathway should be accessible and adaptable to different folks, even as they are singularly human.[83] That means explicitly and automatically designing our lesson plans, classrooms, buildings, and evaluations with disabled folks in mind. Instead of viewing the practice of inclusion as one that requires extra paperwork, scheduled separations and forced changes, we can learn how to foreground impression-based understanding as it relates to how readers feel upon encountering a text. That means close attention, flexibility, deep consideration, and empowerment—changing the relationship between students and teachers from an adversarial one to one of trust and mentorship. As teachers, we can help students create reading conditions that allow them to clearly identify and use their own feelings to help articulate their thoughts about a text. As bell hooks advocates in

Teaching to Transgress, we can treat our students not as passive minds to mold, but as thinking/feeling human beings making active, aware connections between literature, the world, and themselves[84]—another exercise in wholeness.

Poetics of Self-Determination

Rationale

For me, the personal is entangled in the poetics of self-determination, created in resistance to control, to patriarchy, to authority, to joy, to death, to difficulty—it can be positive or negative, but I resist giving over to harm. Sometimes resistance means I resist the control of others; sometimes it means I resist aesthetic control and surrender or escape into abandon. Resistance and escape are often linked. Resistance and self-determination and survival are often linked, and in practice these concepts lean collective for oppressed groups, not individual. Cixous writes about them in terms of escape—echoing Morrison, which I discuss later— through the metaphor of flight, speaking of the "double meaning" of the French word for flight, *voler*, and comparing women to birds: "[F]or centuries we've . . . lived in flight, stealing away, finding, when desired, narrow passageways, hidden crossovers . . . [taking] pleasure in jumbling the order of space, in disorienting it, . . . dislocating things and values, breaking them all up, emptying structures, turning propriety upside down."[85] In the tradition I have created for myself, a living tradition ever in motion, I resist destructive and death-centered critical texts. I embrace the work of poets younger than I am, braver, undeniably fierce and confident and unashamed and alive. It is a process I do not want to escape, a process and active choosing—literary self-determination—that sustains me.

Application

I will stay close to the personal in the following application exercise— but that application is no less practical for being so aligned. Briefly, and beyond analysis, in considering what sustains you, as a poet and/or a reader of poetry and other literary texts, I suggest keeping conscious of what enlivens you as you read, and what kind of language feels most electric. Make a list in your mind or on paper or electronically—or all the above—if that helps concretize the items on that list in a useful way. Your list can include authors, texts, images, lines, sentences, scenes, questions, structures. Use both intellect and feeling in doing so; in other words, trust your intuition. Once you've begun to make such choices, you may find you resist anything that tries to deaden that living energy in your work and in your reading and in you. Practice with a single poem if it feels too difficult to start with a book; exercise care—i.e., keep stakes as low as possible when practicing. If you fail, try again when the impulse calls you.[86] Repeat as necessary.

Addendum: Poetics of Motherhood

I began to write poetry seriously in August of 2000 when my son was an infant. I started taking online classes, since I was still on active duty in the US Navy, and one of those classes was Introduction to Poetry. The instructor asked us a question in the discussion group: What is poetry? I wrote naively that it could be anything you want, that poetry is an expression of what you feel. He said I might revisit that definition by the end of class, and, of course, he was right. I learned the mechanics of poetry quickly, and, after overcoming an initial passionate aversion to the I-centered lyric, became obsessed with writing and reading poetry. In addition to assigned texts, I began to seek out more poetry, walking to the nearby bookstore as my son took naps—leaving him with my mother. She never rushed me or hurried me home; she loved that I had found something I loved, that I was learning something, and she never questioned whether I could be both a working parent and a student at the same time. She just helped me make it happen.

Thus, I can't talk about a poetics of love without mentioning motherhood, and when I realized mothers appear in most of the texts discussed in *Radical Poetics*, I decided that it needs its own entry. Motherhood is fierce, in its presence and its absence, in our rejection of it as much as in our embrace, whether we succeed in committing to the life-altering responsibilities it demands or whether we fail.[87] I believe that mothering and writing are natural companions. They both require everything you have to give in order to survive, to continue to thrive. They require more energy and generosity than you can imagine. They require faith and strength of mind, determination and endurance, humor and a sense of self-forgiveness, continuous learning and adjustment, and a willingness to fail and to start again.

Rationale

Without mothers, we would not exist. Yet, many cultures often dismiss, denigrate, abuse, ignore, shun, and manipulate mothers and confine them to domestic spaces. Why? Do we want to diminish the creative power inherent in the making of one human inside another? Is that why law, over the centuries, has had to legislate the power of the paternal? Examining the depictions and treatment of mothers in texts that are not necessarily "about" mothers might give us a clue.

Application

How do mothers figure in texts? The mother character—or her/their absence—can lead us to an understanding of how love operates, whether explicitly or as a subtext. By extension, since mothers often serve to indicate the formation of emotional life, observing how a text and/or author treats the feminized realm of feeling can offer other clues to the concerns addressed in poetics, the concerns of form, content, and style. Scholar and writer Alexis Pauline Gumbs, in her introduction to the anthology *Revolutionary Mothering: Love on the Front Lines*, writes imperatively of the need for unapologetically nurturing solutions to building community, that we must collectively "demand a society where people help to create each other instead of too often destroying each other . . . and look at the practice of creating, nurturing, affirming and supporting life that we call mothering."[88]

With Gumbs's imperative in mind, several questions spring up. How do mothers do their work? Is it characterized by repetition, or is it haphazard? How do they show up for their children? Do they make sacrifices or demand them? How does their presence or absence, their action or inaction, shape the emotional choices of the characters? Does the text deny feeling or embrace it? How, in the absence of a mother or maternal figure, do characters mother themselves?

Perhaps we can also rethink the authority of mothers not as absolute in the context of their roles as the people who carry and/or nurture us to/ through life, or as a dismissible vessel for progeny, but as collaborative; not as subservient to paternal authority but as concomitant. Even more radically, if we think of children as sentient, willful beings who, despite their dependence upon adults, exert some authority over their own lives, perhaps we can care for them as a society and culture with more respect and support.[89] Perhaps we can replace control, neglect, and domination with critical thought, patient redirection, and thoughtful choice. In that vein, we might also think of our readers and students not as receptacles for our teachings but as partners in an ongoing process of learning and making. Instead of promoting or forcing obedience, we can cultivate attention and trust for the benefit of all involved, using love and integrity, trust and intuition to guide us forward: "The way is before us, and culture is the future as well as the past."[90]

Conclusion

Now that folks around the world are, more than ever, taking action to reshape that world into a more equitable one when it comes to the earth and to each other,[91] we need to understand how to create new systems of thought,[92] to avoid replicating prior systems that are linked to sanctioned discrimination and violence. That doesn't necessarily mean we strike the current canon; on the contrary: it means that we recognize how white supremacist capitalist heteropatriarchy, to crib bell hooks,[93] threads itself into our literature, thus our thinking, thus our culture and behavior. It means that our modes of analysis do not ignore bias in literature, and instead consider how bias works formally, examine through feeling not as subconscious habit but as willful propagation, as active choice, as a foundational given. I return to and side with Edward Said, who criticizes Eurocentric forms of humanism that refuse stubbornly to evolve, and urges reinvention toward more complexity, fuller awareness, and aromantic remembrances.[94] Said believed that we can do the work of revision, incorporating all humans regardless of nationhood, financial status, or other external Western definitions of worthiness.[95]

Said's belief does not claim newness. Recalling 18th century scientist Giambattista Vico's concept "sapienza poetica," Said's advocacy of creativity—rather than rigidity—recognizes its presence in previous models of thought.[96] A theory of radical poetics similarly returns to such roots, and widens them, emphatically, as these current times feel like our lives depend upon a fundamental shift away from constrained thinking to capacious inclusivity across time, geography, race, class, gender, aesthetics, and beyond.

As Rukeyser pointed out, through feeling we can get at the resistance to recognizing such foundations as integral to our systems of thought. Through poetics we can analyze how feeling works structurally. I am less (although not *not*) interested in the scientific, choosing instead to focus on the practical application of the theoretical. In other words, I would like to unite the theoretical and the practical to create usable, repeatable, and customizable frameworks for reading, writing, and talking about literature inside and outside academia.

This proposal is not objective. I am interested in shifting the field of literature and literary studies toward systems of thought and analysis that include the full range of knowing—feelings as knowledge, useful to understanding ourselves and useful to understanding and communicating with others. I believe that building on the bedrock scholarship and creative work of Sara Ahmed, Lucille Clifton, Toni Morrison, Hélène Cixous, and many others is vital to my own continued participation in the field of literature and the humanities. Combining creative and critical prose gives me a freer and truer space in which to write, to think and feel, to make what I make in line with the poetics I discuss.

A Radical Poetics of Love

Looking for the Love in *Invisible Man*

To love means to open the door to connection. When writers work toward the opposite of detachment, toward encompassing unruly feelings through a process of definition and inclusion that allows us to create abundantly and to invent freely, a kind of solidarity with language occurs. That solidarity fosters an acceptance of emotional articulation via an imaginative process of examination, which allows us to question what we think we know from the perspective of how it feels to know it. To feel is not a weakness, but a strength.[1] This essay advocates for critical engagement based on radical love, rooted in womanist thought.[2] If it's true that any worthwhile exercise has at its root a desire for deeper understanding and connection, and if criticism's main motive is inquiry, then the radicality I'm proposing resides in a wider questioning—intellectual, physical, and emotional.[3]

Although a radical poetics may ultimately fall short of such completeness, such a thinking practice may also move the conversation further than lines of inquiry that aim to exclude because it centers on the capacious notion of love, where "we are each other's / business" in the Brooksian communal sense, where "we are each other's / harvest."[4]

If one aspires toward the collective good in a humanist rather than in a Marxist way, then what happens to the reader's ego when the text triggers an investigation of once-fixed ideas? Where does it go when set aside? And what impact on one's thinking and making does such a setting aside have? Perhaps we might make an equation featuring time, experience, prior reading, and the unquantifiable element that is awareness/consciousness in order to answer these questions. But one size does not fit all. Which seems to bring us to one of Tina Turner's songs: What's love got to do with it[5]—with writing, with poetics? For our purposes, what does it mean to read critically for love?

We can start with definitions. A radical poetics of love defines love as a form of self-love, both in terms of the specific and the broadly applicable self, but also as a love of future-making, of possibility, even if—or precisely because—it seems futile. Far from a fetish for the foolish, it rejects the recklessness of cynicism in favor of a future that, if it's possible to imagine, we can create as a new reality—if we pay attention to how we feel when we read and write, radically and rigorously. Rigor in the context of a poetics of love means inquiry, for certain—no less thorough, diligent, or exhaustive in its investigative questioning—but inquiry that starts from a place of care, inclusion, and expansion. Rigor mortis describes the stiffness of a dead body—but a poetics of love assumes and operates from life and aims to function as part of a whole self, with a natural and unforced flow.

Indeed, if we understand that the mind is a powerfully creative living instrument, and given that the brain is part of the body—which is also a creative living instrument—then we know that thinking and feeling occur on the same plane in conversation with each other as part of creativity. To ignore that, even in literature and literary criticism, is to ignore humanity—and thus to be at cross-purposes to that literature. This plays out in Ralph Ellison's *Invisible Man*. When the narrator's body transforms into a metaphorical negative space, the body's absence results in a grotesque existence comprised of unmediated observation, a terrorism of consciousness, a hyper-lucidity sans outlet. But that energy must have somewhere to go, even if it's outside the body and mind, outside a specific place or geography, vented out into the larger universe, creating a connection that has everything to do with the intersections of time—how it repeats itself in us, linking the past, present, and future in an endless loop.

In his essay "On the Mimetic Faculty," Walter Benjamin points out that "in the remote past the processes considered imitable included those in the sky. . . . Allusion to the astrological sphere may supply a first reference point for an understanding of the concept of nonsensuous similarity."[6] If we look at *Invisible Man*'s astrological chart using the publication date for the calculations,[7] we see eerie parallels to what we already know, emphasizing a wholeness that exists alongside—and permeating—the artificial boundaries we impose whenever we feel compelled to separate one thing from another. Besides having several planets in bombastic fire signs like Aries and Sagittarius, the ascendant is in Gemini, and the ascendant in astrology dictates how the individual appears to the world. For *Invisible Man*, that means interest in "intellectual activities, humanism, and abhorrence of violence, constant doubt of all mental concepts, hesitancy, and academic interest."[8]

The resemblance of the chart to the novel is uncanny. And although astrology may not necessarily be destiny, it often offers explanations that feel correct. And what does such apparently esoteric knowledge have to do with a radical poetics of love? Arguably, that you can't really love yourself if you don't know who you are, and that astrology—by connecting human nature to the position of planets and stars—provides another insight into the self. What does that have to do with literature? Maybe nothing. Maybe everything. Ellison, in an audio interview conducted in 1983 and re-aired on NPR in 2014, recalled that when he read novels and translations he felt more concerned with the meaning of the text and connected with the characters on a human level.[9] Our aims as writers, then, are not separate from our aims as humans: connection, understanding, knowledge, and, yes, love—of self, of others, of the world—for which the body is an important key. Significantly, *Invisible Man* begins with an enumeration of the characteristics that make up the narrator's identity, from visceral body to interior consciousness; serving to characterize his invisibility as externally imposed: "I am invisible, understand, simply because people refuse to see me."[10] That sets the tone for what Ellison's novel asks: How do we reconcile a material self with the material world's negation of that self? What do we lose when we lose a self? What do we gain when we lose a self that has been imposed on us? What does the truth cost us to know? Must it be our very existence?

Speaking to Hambro, the narrator questions the specious way other characters—particularly men in authority—have shown through their actions that they've used him for their own gain, all while constructing an illusion in language that they were helping him (505). To extend the narrator's line of questioning, I also wonder: Is it possible to implement a more humane alternative to absurdly inhumane social systems, and can literature play a role in that implementation? I suggest that it is, because literature asks these questions of us ("us," as in readers, writers, teachers, thinkers—as in human beings) by showing us the truth of who we are and of what we tolerate, of what we accept and of what we don't, of what we hate and of what we love—and how we're able to do both.

Now let's return to the original question posed in this essay: Where is the love in *Invisible Man*? The nihilism at the heart of the novel at first appears to have no love in it. In considering a radical poetics, reading for love is part of reading generously: What do the characters love? Does that love have substance, or does it merely replicate what the characters are told to love, a surface type of repetition, a mechanical habit born of cultural or familial programming? Does Ellison show love for the story, for language, or for individual elements of the novel's construction? Those questions assume that love, far from being a frivolous concern, lies at the heart of the discourse on textual construction, literariness, aesthetics, and the relevance of a work to the larger human story within the field of literature.

If a radical poetics exists or can exist within that field, how does beauty function at the intersection of love and poetics? In terms of *Invisible Man*, beauty is not only in the story but in the language of the text, in how it has been formed and crafted by the author. Even when the narrator's story consists of harrowing and horrible scenes arguing the opposite of beauty, the language demonstrates arresting aesthetic qualities and conjures images that resonate far beyond the tumultuous era in which Ellison wrote into the raging tumult of our own historical moment. Passages like the one early in the book describing the "hole" where the narrator lives let the reader ruminate on appearances, both visual and cultural, even if beauty most often functions within the narrator's world as an illusion and a danger, using light as a metaphor for conscious awareness of his place in the world—a world that cannot see him, but he exists anyway, and loves the literal-metaphorical light that that realization creates (6).

Thus, at the intersection of the love the narrator expresses, the beauty with which Ellison expresses that love, and the difficulties and traumas the content presents the reader, there is a literariness that has retained its compelling quality, that connects seemingly disparate ideas and makes room for the simultaneity of contradiction.

And because a radical poetics embraces contradiction, it looks not only for the presence of love but also for its absence. In this case, there is notably no love for women in *Invisible Man*. There's lust, fear, a mild and somewhat fond appreciation—but no love. The dancing white woman at the beginning is sinister and seductive, representing an oft-repeated idealization that is a bit heavy-handed, even if Ellison deploys it in service of an uncomfortable historical accuracy. A womanist[11] reading of the text, however, demands attention to the male narrator's conflicted feelings toward and rather simplistic depictions of female characters.

The women in the novel are not referred to or discussed in true human terms, and thus they become thin archetypes. We have the nurturing mother figure in Harlem, Mary (again, a little heavy-handed in terms of symbolism, since she shares a name with Mary, mother of Jesus); we have the stripper/whore at the Battle Royale, dehumanized and roughly caricatured (19), and later, the wealthy (and married) seductress, who calls emotion "primitive" (413). One could argue that the novel isn't about the women, but the narrator's interaction, or lack of interaction, with them is central to his situation, his character. The women function as tools used to show the narrator's state of mind, to move the story forward, to symbolize the dichotomy of desire and repulsion, of what's possible and what isn't. While the narrator's fear of his desires takes center stage, the women's desires appear nonexistent, incidental, or merely speculated upon— often ungenerously. Particularly glaring is the blonde dancer, introduced at the beginning of the novel and described by the narrator, who is beset by contradictory feelings at the sight of her naked form, in terms both reverent and "exotic"; he voices how he feels seduced and repelled by her, both loving and violent at once (19). One cannot, then, put a poetics of love fully into practice without accounting for love's counterpoint, fear— and fear's fraternal twin, violence.

Setting aside authorial intent and concentrating on the text itself, how do fear and violence operate in a novel? A radical poetics would point to a fear of love or attachment on the part of one or more of the characters (the spiritual implications of which I will set aside for the sake of brevity). Thus, the common American trope of the alienated man, for example, for whom women serve as symbols of the "American Dream" (or nightmare) and function as props to plot rather than as complex individuals with their own identities, arises from a fear of love as much as it does from a struggle against a rigged system. This often means that more than half the population continues to be silenced or suppressed in literature because of women's portrayal as complicit, accessories in a system that men created—thus reinforcing a destructive loop. This also means that, until we know these women as the complex characters they are, we won't know the whole story, either of the postmodern or of our own history.

Significantly, *Invisible Man*'s Black women characters hold the loudest silences. The extended detour at the Trueblood property again highlights the absence of love, especially for women, and exposes just how deeply destructive that absence is. Trueblood's daughter Matty Lou's silence and unintelligibility, along with Trueblood's inscription of dream and memory onto his act of incestuous sexual violence toward her, exemplify the historical—and still rampant—justifications for the abuse of women. Furthermore, Trueblood embodies Mr. Norton's insinuated fantasy of raping his own daughter, which, structurally, the side trip is designed to illustrate. The scene isn't meant to decry the abuse Matty Lou suffers; rather, it serves to demonstrate Mr. Norton's barely bridled lechery, centering white maleness in a way that undermines the novel's apparent purpose of making visible the humanity of an invisible man. Indeed, the narrator's reckless desperation to be like Mr. Norton doesn't only take depravity for granted but recognizes it as an imperative of those in power.

By contrast, Matty Lou's power is in her endurance, her survival. Writing to Black women and girls in an article that appeared in *Essence* magazine in May 1985—a generation after the appearance of Ellison's novel—Toni Morrison recognizes and elucidates their living presence: "You had this canny ability to shape an untenable reality, mold it, sing it, reduce it to its manageable, transforming essence, which is a knowing so deep it's like a secret."[12] In the context of the novel, Matty Lou and her mother hold the family together, not Trueblood, who endangers them in public and in private. Still, the world they inhabit forces them to hold their tongues to avoid further/future harm.[13] In a futuristic American (or indeed human) narrative, women must exist as more than markers of occasions or sidebar plot devices. If we as literary scholars, critics, and professors are to call works like *Invisible Man* canonical and continue to study them, we cannot in our analyzing or our teaching ignore the absence of love dramatized by the flattening and silencing of women characters, Black women characters in particular. Morrison's letter again: "What doesn't love you has trivialized itself and must answer for that."[14] We can be critical of the American imagination and its products—with love. We don't have to accept it the way it is. But we don't have to dismantle the canon in its entirety, either. We can simply widen, reconfigure, and recontextualize what's included in it. Inclusion, after all, is simply another word for accuracy—and another positive aspect of rigor.

To return to the subject of detours, we can't ignore the role of narcissism in *Invisible Man*. The narrator's self-interest and self-obsession are staggering, and they could easily be considered his fatal flaw—indicative of his ignorance of any true kind of love, especially love of the self. He cannot crawl out from the depths of his self-concern, his obsession with what he believes to be a chance to elevate his station in life, choosing to connect to the incestuously licentious but wealthy white patron, Mr. Norton (39). The narrator is desperate for all the wrong things, albeit with a desperation born of the basic need for survival: acceptance by white benefactors and the precarious privileges that that entails. Importantly, he also wants respect. He wants validation as an orator, as a scholar, and, at the most elemental level, as a man and a human being—an ontological state he simply cannot arrive at in a society that functions completely counter to his desire by denying his humanity. Indeed, without the inner knowledge and conviction of who he is (knowing himself to exist as a person among other people, as opposed to being confirmed as a person by others), he enacts an erasure of himself that mirrors his invisibility to the white benefactors he so ardently and repeatedly tries to impress. Though he cannot recognize or articulate it himself, his pursuit is also a pursuit of love—he wants to be loved and accepted. Yet, he doesn't even know how to love himself.

Invisible Man tells us that the absence of love distorts our very humanity, and that the damage of such an absence is often total and inescapable. In the Trueblood section, for instance, Mr. Norton's insistence that his fate is tied to the Black students at the college generally,[15] and to the narrator in particular, isn't an exaggeration—though it does end up being an inversion, as it is Norton's words that lead to the narrator's expulsion and that seal his fate. The narrator's misunderstanding, or slow understanding, of that fact speaks to his youth at the time, but it also highlights his misguided identification with Mr. Norton. Not only does the encounter with Trueblood upend such identification, it also uncovers deep fears and insecurities and further exposes his precarious position as a Black student vulnerable to the whims of white benefactors. The pretending or masking he is forced to endure during the violent Battle Royale, Ellison makes clear, would be for naught if he were to make even one misstep outside the ring.

What, then, is the purpose of enduring brutality and suffering under such absurd and persistent conditions? And what's more, can a person be visible if they are not truly seen? One possible answer: Not if they are invisible to their own selves. Mr. Norton's comic interchangeability with the other veterans at the Golden Day shows that, he, too, carries a certain invisibility. He represents more than himself: he represents the oppressor, the absurdity of racism, the pain it inflicts, the traumas it engenders, the chaos it creates. As Edna, one of the Golden Day prostitutes, points out: "These old bastards don't never git enough. They want to have the whole world" (88). Although his inebriated state makes Mr. Norton vulnerable to the Golden Day inhabitants' scrutiny and commentary in a way that his usual sobriety would prevent, his whiteness still protects him from any real life-threatening consequences. His invisibility, such as it is, is only temporary.

The narrator, on the other hand, tries to intellectualize his feelings while he becomes invisible so that he can integrate his traumatic experiences into memory and continue to function and to strive. While it's unclear how much Ellison knew about trauma victims, the elaborate scene at the Golden Day strongly suggests that he knew something about Black existence as shell shock, as a kind of grief for enduring violence you cannot escape, as an awareness that the world actually is so absurdly brutal that the only option you have is to give up or to redirect the world from your sight. But instead of doing what the veterans do, drinking themselves into oblivion, the narrator has to find a way to reconcile himself to what is happening apart from his rage—conscious of settling into the harsh reality by force, rather than choice (572).

A radical poetics would seek to revise this erasure—of Blackness, of being—toward an empowered self-awareness that overturns the narrator's pathological examination of the self in terms of the monolithic whiteness presented in *Invisible Man*. This would be self-love as self-actualization, made possible by focusing on the here-ness of the self as self—formed under pressure, made powerful by its attention to that ontological formation, and existing outside of any institutionalized system keyed to the destruction of the individual for the sake of that system's preservation.[16] If, rather than being lured by the Communist group's flattery, for example, the narrator had instead remained with the Black folks in Harlem, in Mary's welcoming boardinghouse, he may have been able to visualize and actualize himself as a man and as a vital part of a community. As Audre Lorde writes in *Sister Outsider*, "It is not the destiny of Black america to repeat white america's mistakes. But we will, if we mistake the trappings of success in a sick society for the signs of a meaningful life."[17]

But *Invisible Man* also asks, do African-American characters avoid erasure only by existing outside of white-dominated spaces? Is that the only place true visibility is possible? We see segregation's ideological pollution in the college's culture, with Dr. Bledsoe fiercely guarding the carefully built and delicately positioned world of the university he runs, which has been made to appear acceptable to the surrounding monolith of whiteness. *Invisible Man* presents the problem of integration as both individual and collective, highlighting how difference factors into the nature of existence. If we agree that so-called nonwhite people are, indeed, people in the exact same way that so-called white people are, then why don't culture and society behave in a way that upholds this fact? In mathematics, we have givens in an equation. If the givens don't sync up between different systems of equations, then whatever the problem is can't be solved. Until an ontological agreement occurs—that Black people exist and are human beings—then it seems the problem of integration cannot be solved either. Our thinking about humanity in terms of problem-solving is misguided. Why can we not accept what we do not control or understand?

Perhaps clues reside in the ways our brains are constructed, in how—and what—we feel, think, and surmise. Perhaps answers, in literature, reside in the symbolic, which imbues the ordinary with extraordinary meaning. And yet, even as we consider a radical poetics of love in the context of literature, it also asks us to think beyond literature: Can the symbolic translate into action, into positive change?[18]

Ellison's frequent use of symbols that make the case for Blackness as local and global, national and international, personal and political might have just such an effect—it certainly has for me. During the eviction scene, for example, the narrator describes the belongings of newly displaced elderly inhabitants and recounts being overcome by deep and chaotic emotions. The vivid portrait of the elderly couple's belongings, a poignant list of personal treasures, being removed by white workmen and placed on the street shocks the narrator still (271–72). One object calls up the colonialist, racist spectacle of the World's Fair; the commemorative plate is important here, as it symbolizes a witnessing of and a participation in a world that largely seems incapable of doing any better by Black people than forcibly removing them from their homes in the name of profit and degradation—mirroring the reasoning behind the abductions and violent displacement of Africans during the slave trade.[19] But community's rallying around them in the eviction scene also demonstrates that love is Black, and that both love and Blackness tend to be met with state regulation and violence, a fact that animates the fear the narrator speaks of.

Invisible Man thus maintains that the repudiation, ill treatment, dismissal, and persecution of Black people, of their bodies and belongings, means that the broader world will remain crueler and lesser for the ferocious incompleteness such repudiation perpetuates. I return to June Jordan's essay in *Revolutionary Mothering*, which connects it all:

> And because we coexist on a planet long defiled by habits opposite to love, it seems to me that the task of surviving and/or the task of providing for the survival of those who are not as strong as I am, is a political undertaking: Vast changes will have to be envisioned and pursued, if any, let alone all, of us will survive the destructive traditions of our species. Enormous reversals and revisions of our thinking patterns will have to be achieved, somehow, and fast. And to accomplish such lifesaving alterations of society, we will have to deal with power: we will have to make love powerful. We will have to empower the people we love so that they can insist upon the validity of their peculiar coloring or gender or ethnicity or accidental economic status, so that they can bloom in their own place and time . . . beautiful and free.[20]

A radical poetics acknowledges that love cannot exist without consummately human readers who recognize that both beauty and horror exist, that both the created thing and the world in which it has been created exist. Separating the two might seem an admirably clinical approach, as a surgeon operating on one part of the body in order to assess its function and correct any malfunction. But the surgeon must also account for the rest of the body, how it reacts to a part of it being violated—for surgery is a violation, a cutting into a whole body, despite its reasoning that the excision and/or invasion is for healing purposes. The body bears scars, it changes, it remembers the trauma, it heals, but that healing takes time, and the body sets the pace. Love exists in allowing it to do so. Thus, the binary created by apparent or stated opposition holds a certain deception if we believe beauty and horror coexist—and love allows for that truth, especially when it comes to the body. As a symbol of both wholeness and emotion, and as the physical site of feeling, whether that feeling is pain or pleasure, injury or healing, violence or love, the body carries the self through experience; love exists in that acknowledgement as well.

Importantly, by the penultimate page of the novel Ellison's nameless narrator does arrive at love—albeit a conflicted love marked by the hardships he's suffered: "And I defend because in spite of all I find that I love. In order to get some of it down I have to love . . . So I approach it through division. So I denounce and I defend and I hate and I love" (580). Ellison then has the narrator compare his own humanity to that of his formerly enslaved grandfather's, instead of rejecting or feeling ashamed of his lineage, or trying to deny the stigma that slavery can engender. The narrator flips his past script: he is, despite being hated and invisible in American public spaces, a person full of love, full of light, just as his grandfather was a person whose vast humanity—which the narrator admits he can only aspire to approach—was never lost to the degradation of slavery. Words matter, and the truth matters, and the narrator's acknowledgement of his grandfather demonstrates huge love and respect for someone who did not receive it in proper measure during his lifetime. If only the narrator could have extended that love to women; had he done so, he might have had a chance at visible wholeness.

To employ a radical poetics analysis means not shying away from painful or difficult truths. Rather, it pushes those truths out into the open, where they can be examined earnestly in the hope that that examination hastens an evolution toward the practice of loving and positive change. A love-based poetics has no shame. It does not worry about appearing foolish. Rather, it lays itself bare in the name of transparency and progress. It avoids using apparent or supposed weaknesses, disparaging so-called vulnerabilities to win arguments or to dominate. A radical poetics insists there be no domination, no contest whose only goal is winning. And yet, I want to be careful to acknowledge that even this insistence, tendered lovingly as it is, might simply be another form of domination: one poetics taking pride of place over others. True to its own axioms, though, a radical poetics of love acknowledges the contradiction and embraces the wholeness that such simultaneity manifests.

Not-So-Invisible Crossroads

Race, Gender, Disability, and Class
in 19th-Century American Literature

An intersection, or a crossroads, relates to the junction at which two or more roads meet. From its very beginnings, the United States (and its literature) has existed at such a crossroads—of race, of class, of gender, of disability—an incontrovertible fact, despite sustained efforts by the dominant culture to promote a myth of separatism that serves to perpetuate and further entrench such dominance. The stories of able-bodied, often privileged white males and male characters populate the established canon of 19th-century American literature, a fact that has helped to define ideas about what and who America is, at home and abroad, historically and in a contemporary context. But the way these same stories depict women and people of different races, classes, and abilities requires deeper scrutiny. However peripheral such interventions may have seemed at first, history has shown—just as our current historical moment continues to show—that de-centering and interrogating whiteness in literature is vital to recasting America's literary origins and creating a canon at once more inclusive, more representative, and more accurate.

This chapter traces depictions of race, gender, and disability as they intersect with each other in American literature in the 19th century, using Herman Melville's final novel, *The Confidence-Man: His Masquerade* (1857); Frances Ellen Watkins Harper's novel *Iola Leroy* (1892); Harriet Jacobs's memoir *Incidents in the Life of a Slave Girl* (1861); Kate Chopin's short story "Désirée's Baby" (1893); and Mahkatêwe-meshi-kêhkêhkwa's[1] narrative *Life of Black Hawk, or Ma-ka-tai-me-she-kia-kiak: Dictated by Himself* (1833) as primary source material. I chose these texts in order to draw a line between truth and fiction to see how fiction and nonfiction relate to each other in the reader's imagination as it connects to the writer's intention. Further, and more importantly, all five books deal with race, class, gender, and/or disability, either without being aware of the relationship between them or by taking that relationship for granted—or, as in the case of Jacobs's and Mahkatêwe-meshi-kêhkêhkwa's texts, speaking to these issues within the context of a true account of the writers' lives. Covering themes and movements in these works as they engage with the philosophical, social, and cultural shifts that were taking place at the time—particularly within violently colonized spaces—exposes the hidden dialogue between those individualized identity markers, particularly in public in terms of how they navigate the world or are treated by others, but also what that simultaneity means for the interiority of certain characters. In order to add to our understanding of how our culture came to divide identities so starkly according to physical identity markers, and advocate for a more cohesive approach to addressing identity in literature, examining the places where story and history meet and overlap feels vital.

In that overlap, we find the shaping of a cultural imaginary through language. Toni Morrison, in *Playing in the Dark: Whiteness and the Literary Imagination,* talks about the inextricable relationship between language and imagination when it comes to race.[2] I am interested in how those complications work to reinforce one another in 19th-century American literature, thus creating an interconnected web of bias that helps to reify an oppressive cultural belief system from which it seemed nearly impossible for anyone to escape. In other words, rather than ignore or minimize race—and I would add to that gender, class, and disability—I want to highlight them, to get at the root of exclusionary behavior and destructive bias, self-destructive bias included. Some attention will be paid to the importance of intersectionality as defined by scholar and attorney Kimberlé Williams Crenshaw in order to address concerns related particularly to Black women in several of the texts. I will draw on works by Crenshaw, Morrison, Saidiya Hartman, Jessica Cantiello, and Nazera Sadiq Wright as both models and critical support for arguments with regard to the ways early American literature has helped to shape modern American consciousness.

In her article "Demarginalizing the Intersection of Race and Sex: A

Black Feminist Critique of Antidiscrimination Doctrine, Feminist Theory and Antiracist Politics" (1989), Crenshaw defines intersectionality in terms of naming the combined effect of racism and sexism on Black women, and "underscores the need to avoid filter[ing their experiences] through categorical analyses that completely obscure their experience."[3] Because I do not have a much better term for describing what I am doing in this chapter, I want to acknowledge my debt to Crenshaw at the start. Intersectionality, as she defines it, draws on the persistent real-world need to address Black women's concerns—in court, in the workplace, in relationships—as they are female and Black in a system that refuses to account for that doubly marginalized status. For the purposes of literary analysis, centering the experiences of marginalized peoples and considering the writer's approach to depicting them offers the opportunity to undo a similar and long-standing kind of erasure and denial. Because literature's role in culture-making is so profound, no more so than in the United States during the 19th century, putting intersectionality at the center of critical inquiry alongside a fluid, holistically-oriented analysis has the potential to recast long-held assumptions about whether people of the time, especially thinkers and writers, participated in white supremacy out of choice or out of ignorance, and if the latter, whether they chose that ignorance in order to gain or consolidate their perceived rights or privileges. Even when the violent enforcement of supremacist beliefs is acknowledged, the claim of white innocence persists as a rationale to preserve the perception of the morality of white people who were complicit in slavery—as indeed most law-abiding citizens were, since enslavement was a legally sanctioned industry—and who did little or nothing to challenge the systemic biases that persist today. That claim continues to have a diminishing effect on scholarship and classroom discussions and to close down the difficult conversations that might lead to real repair.[4]

Indeed, that denial has played out recently with the virulent backlash against journalist Nikole Hannah-Jones's *1619 Project*,[5] which has sparked anti-critical race theory legislation that is under review in several states.[6] Instead of participating in a potentially restorative reckoning led by the people descended from those most harmed by America's deeply-rooted legacy of racism and slavery, folks like Newt Gingrich doubled down on a false narrative that continues not only to perpetuate harm but also to deny historical fact: "The NY Times 1619 Project should make its slogan

'All the Propaganda we want to brainwash you with.'"[7] Once again, so-called "conservative" pundits, politicians, and parents are focusing their energies toward conserving the same stale fables that mythologize abled, heterosexual, patriarchal whiteness as the center of power and morality.

It is past time to look at the actions of white people in positions of power, rather than simply continue to consume the spectacle of everyone else's suffering.[8] When discussing their acts of cruelty toward enslaved people in Jacobs's memoir, Toni Morrison writes of practitioners and defenders of legalized human trafficking in *The Origin of Others*, "[W]ho are these people? How hard they work to define the slave as inhuman, savage, when in fact the definition of the inhuman describes overwhelmingly the punisher."[9] Indeed, such depictions of enslaved people are a diversionary tactic meant to draw attention away from the violence that enslavers enact, defining an "other" in negative terms in order to affirm a narrative façade of baseline normalcy by comparison.[10] Normalizing slavery, colonization, the subjugation of women, and the marginalization of disabled people has been central to the perpetuation of each of these systems of brutality and continues to undergird social structures and practices today. How much different are the attitudes of literary scholars from those of 19th-century slaveholders and other wielders of institutional power if American literature continues to be whitewashed, the context of racial supremacy ignored or conveniently glossed over?[11]

Consider the work of Herman Melville. Unwilling to look past racial inequity and injustice, Melville chose to place interracial interactions at the forefront of much of his fiction. Despite such close attention to the built-in conflict that race invites into a text, Melville's work, and indeed 19th-century American literature overall, repeatedly fails to undermine the systems of oppression. *The Confidence-Man*, a satiric short novel published in 1857 and set on April Fool's Day, contains practically every permutation of human interaction, with blatant stereotypes making for rich possibilities in terms of critical analysis. We have a "grotesque Negro cripple";[12] an "Indian-hater" (1004); various swindlers, speculators, and problematic women; and the stranger—described as a deaf-mute, later suspected of being the mastermind behind all the con games aboard the aptly named steamboat *Fidèle,* which is bound for New Orleans.

At the heart of the novel's conflict: Trust. How well do we know each other? And, knowing that we live in a world in which people do one another harm, how can we trust anyone around us? Melville's greatest accomplishment in *The Confidence-Man* might be his revealing the one con that underlies all the others: how "the illusion of power" is constructed "through the process of inventing an Other."[13] He uses the language of prejudice to point out its insidious absurdity. From his position of privilege as a white man, Melville would certainly have been privy to many malignant conversations about race—which he certainly reproduces in the novel. But he takes pains to use the word "good" to describe many of the white characters, particularly the "good merchant" (858) who harangues "the Negro cripple" as the latter panhandles via an exaggerated performance of his Blackness and disability. Indeed, Melville repeats the word "good" in dialogue and descriptions throughout the novel to draw attention to the problematic nature of the term, showing that the common habit of calling people good often covers a multitude of sins:

> [C]onsidering that goodness is no such rare thing among men—the world familiarly know the noun; a common one in every language—it was curious that what so signalized the stranger, and made him look like a kind of foreigner, among the crowd . . . was but the expression of so prevalent a quality. (877)

We see this in the scene in Chapter 3 that features a Black disabled character—named Guinea, just in case the reader might require further racist titillation—who must resort to beggarly minstrelsy for survival. Melville describes the character as follows:

> [O]wing to something wrong about his legs, [he] was, in effect, cut down to the stature of a Newfoundland dog, his knotted black fleece and good-natured, honest black face rubbing against the upper part of people's thighs as he made shift to shuffle about, making music, such as it was, and raising a smile even from the gravest. (849)

Such exaggeration, done in the name of satirizing—since the authenticity of the performance in terms of both race and disability becomes a central question—still seems to do little to examine and overturn bias toward Black people in the white imagination, nor disabled people generally.

Instead, the conversation among the other, abled white passengers turns toward existential performance, once again centering whiteness and using Blackness emblematically:

> "Does all the world act? Am I, for instance, an actor? Is my reverend friend here, too, a performer?"
> "Yes, don't you both perform acts? To do, is to act; so all doers are actors."
> "You trifle.—I ask again, if a white, how could he look the negro so?"
> "Never saw the negro-minstrels I suppose?"
> "Yes, but they are apt to overdo the ebony; exemplifying the old saying, not more just than charitable, that 'the devil is never so black as he is painted.'" (874)

If, as Saidiya Hartman writes in *Scenes of Subjection: Terror, Slavery, and Self-Making in Nineteenth-Century America*, "both minstrelsy and melodrama (re)produced blackness as an essentially pained expression of the body's possibilities,"[14] then Melville cuttingly uses aphorism to intimate that minstrelsy has more to do with the performance of whiteness as a disguise for unconscionable wrongdoing. I will come back to melodrama later in discussing Jacobs's and Harper's work, but Melville uses it here to challenge ingrained prejudices using those very same prejudices against the characters who hold them—and, by extension, 19th-century readers of the same racist inclinations who still considered themselves to be essentially "good" people,[15] people not unlike those who echoed the bigotry so often on display in—and in support of—the Trump White House.[16]

Melville's mission to debunk the myth of the good continues with the chapter on John Moredock, the soldier and "Indian-hater." Melville definitely takes the opportunity to lampoon transcendentalism in this section, calling out the hypocrisy of whites celebrating nature while despising other peoples—Black indigenous folks specifically—for whom such celebration has been an integral part of their culture for countless generations. The character of the judge, after listing the crimes whites accuse Indians of, notes that such "histories . . . are almost full of things unangelic as the Newgate Calendar or the Annals of Europe" (996). The judge further pronounces that "[t]he instinct of antipathy against an Indian grows in the backwoodsman with the sense of good and bad, right and wrong. In one breath he learns that a brother is to be loved, and an Indian to be hated" (996). Melville uses Moredock's tragic family history—his family killed by "a band of twenty renegades from various tribes, outlaws even among Indians" (1004)—to expose and debunk popular excuses for the colonization of America through the oppression and murder of indigenous peoples. Ever the ironist, Melville wants to make it abundantly clear that just as white settlers were swiping indigenous peoples' lands with broken treaties, they simultaneously accused Native Americans of that very same behavior: "want of conscience," "lying," "double-dealing," "blood-thirstiness," "diabolism" (996). Melville saw the hypocrisy of his time clearly and wrote about it in novels like *The Confidence-Man*. Given the reviews of the novel at the time, his readers were apparently not as willing to entertain the idea that such hypocrisy existed, because to do so would have required action-based evolution on their part.[17]

In *Playing in the Dark,* Morrison writes about reading not as she'd been trained to do as a student, but as a writer, and therefore as a more critical and culturally aware reader: "I have to place enormous trust in my ability to imagine others and my willingness to project consciously into the danger zones such others may represent for me."[18] But even with such imagination, a writer's work—Melville's for one—can remain both subversive and problematic. Melville's characterization of Guinea reinforces stereotypes even as his satire critiques the prejudice that produces them. Yet, his career-long fascination with people of color tells us he knows that something is wrong; he just cannot divest himself of the desire for power enough to join in a total mutiny against the system of wealth and station that eludes him at best, rejects him at worst. By writing Guinea in such dehumanizing terms still serves the baseline humanity of the white characters, questioning the nature of goodness and trust, yes, but without upending racially hierarchal systems of belief.[19]

Indeed, one could argue that the American colonizers and their descendants took a page from their British forebears and defined their worth according to class, replacing the royal class system with a racial one. Further, that Guinea is disabled—and that that fact gets elided in most analysis or accepted as the joke that "The Confidence Man" makes of it—strikes me as such an important issue because of that extra layer of vulnerability. His physical dependence on the whims of people who have been socialized to ignore or hate him because of his race is near absolute and appears inescapable; what greater horror could there be? All the while, Melville's story maintains a cheery tone, amplifying the sheer absurdity of Guinea's existence. The constant questioning of whether or not Guinea is actually disabled is a central plot device, one that echoes the way disabled people are treated today—as if they are faking, as if their presence in public is unwanted or surprising, as if their bodies are worthy of negative scrutiny, of pity or disdain rather than respect and inclusion.[20]

Since we're so accustomed to looking at a single or a primary focus in analytic modes, to discuss disability may feel uncomfortable or out of place; for precisely that reason, I insist on including it. Disabled folks experience a level of suffering that has nothing to do with their physical or mental ailments—a cultural and social one that has for too long been minimized. Literary criticism will benefit from consistent re-imagining of language to undo the practiced underlying harm that language does in reifying the perception of disabled people as less-than, as other, to be hidden or doubted or made fun of. Literary analysis will benefit from fuller and more complete attention to the impact of this long-ignored sociocultural factor.

Melville's long sentences and lighthearted style—one gets the sense that he is laughing as he writes—contrasts with the very serious questions the novel poses. His ability to laugh, however, even bitterly, is a kind of warped, privileged thinking[21] that can imperil groups targeted for ridicule. Melville's admirable attempt to identify prejudices as absurd still centers whiteness and still uses damaging stereotypes. The reader—even an imaginative one—is left to wonder what it would be like had Melville not, to the degree that he did, internalized the unreadiness and unwillingness of his readers and critics to embrace characters of color and female and disabled characters on par with the white, male, abled ones they were accustomed to.[22]

Frances Ellen Watkins Harper's *Iola Leroy; or, Shadows Uplifted* and Harriet Jacobs's *Incidents in the Life of a Slave Girl* offer sweeping, poignant portraits of the relational and philosophical complexities of that same period, even if their condemnation of slavery cuts through those complexities with a moral certainty very much in keeping with our own. Both books were written with antiracism (Harper) and antislavery (Jacobs) in mind, and both use melodrama to appeal to readers' emotions. While Melville made use of raucous stereotypes, Harper and Jacobs had to meticulously dismantle them, presenting portraits of Black people that affirmed their humanity and feeling, rather than capitulating to the notion, as Melville does in describing Guinea (with yet another crass amputation metaphor) of helpless hopelessness: "it was improbable that a Negro, however reduced to his stumps by fortune, could ever be thrown off the legs of a laughing philosophy" (902).

Harper shows us the ignorance of such beliefs through the title character, whose mother is Black. Iola's skin is light enough for her to pass for white, and she believes she is white until her father dies and her mother's Blackness is brought into court by white relatives in order to strip the Leroy family of their property and sell them into bondage. Iola's initial naiveté about slavery disappears when she herself is enslaved. In chapter 12, subtitled "School-girl Notions," Iola defends slavery to her abolitionist-leaning Northern school mates: "Our slaves do not want their freedom. They would not take it if we gave it to them. I don't think these abolitionists have any right to meddle in our affairs. I believe they are prejudiced against us and want to get our property."[23] Little does she know that the attorney Bastine is watching her, calculating her monetary value: "She would bring $2000 any day in a New Orleans market" (85). When confronted with the tragic anecdote of two Creole girls who died of shock when they discovered they were part Black, he is unaffected: "I can't help that . . . business is business" (85).

This scene shows the intersection of race, class, disability and gender on multiple levels. First, with regard to disability, it must be said that the Creole girls who die of shock show the deadly impact of enslavement on mental health. Money makes Bastine immune to the suffering and risk of death that his intervention is bound to inflict. With money as motive, class and skin color thus serve as deciding factors in the fates of several characters in the novel, but particularly Iola's. Harper does an excellent job of portraying how vulnerable Iola is despite her light color and her being a "beautiful creature" (85). In fact, both of these characteristics operate against her. Nor can she be saved by her class, which is dependent on her father. He cannot protect her from the greed of racist relatives who capitalize on her misfortune when he dies. The confluence of factors dictating Iola's fate demonstrates the double-bind free Black women found themselves in during slavery. Even when her own body reads as white, the facts of Iola's femaleness and of her mother's race render her legally powerless.

Upon learning of his family's terrible fate, Iola's brother physically goes into shock. All the news hits him at once, sending him to his sickbed for months; and, while it appears that trickery saves Iola from a similar disabling collapse, it is worth noting the difference between his tenderly administered recovery at school and his mother's anguished suffering in the South. He is attended to by a white administrator and doctor, while she only has the kind support of her slaves and is ruthlessly routed in her grief by her husband's relatives and Judge Starkins. Tragically, as she hovers at the edge of death, her youngest child, Gracie, succumbs—a death portrayed in the novel as a blessing: "[S]he, too, was stricken with brain fever, which intervened as a mercy between [Gracie] and the great sorrow that was overshadowing her young life" (82). Thus, disability and illness in *Iola Leroy* are tantamount to destruction, particularly when they happen to Black women. The mother's illness leaves the family vulnerable to predators, and death is a mercy because an enslaved child suffers a fate worse than death—a characterization that presages Morrison's novel *Beloved,* which is based on the true story of Margaret Garner, who killed her children rather than see them sold.[24]

What does it say about our society that we treat ill people so predatorily? It doesn't seem to register that, rather than protecting folks who are physically disabled, we take on a fear of becoming physically vulnerable because of that absence—that active withholding—of protection.[25]

In the case of *Iola Leroy*, aligning the appearance and morality of the main character as closely as possible with a protected class (i.e., white women) seems to be Harper's primary method for trying to attain protection through empathy. But there is a danger of even fictive testimony regarding the experience of slavery.[26] The stories of suffering being relayed—in the case of *Iola Leroy*, based on Harper's personal experience and research—will not necessarily be used for social change, but rather for the reader's entertainment. The novel risks sensationalizing the very real abjection and torture enslaved people experience by conflating the main characters' morality with that of white American notions of propriety—feeding the sense of spectacle rather than humanity.[27] Indeed, worth noting in this context is the reliance in much 19th-century literature on historical or factual information to add weight and consequence.

In discussing the "Indian question" in *Iola Leroy*, for instance, scholar Jessica Cantiello points out that Harper often revised work in progress to include new knowledge based on new political events,[28] and Melville certainly relied on news for content.

If writers present us as we are through a combination of reported facts and fictive imaginings, issues of race are much more important to our nation and national character than the popular and oft-repeated "melting pot" analogy would like us to believe. Speaking to this in Harper's work, Cantiello writes that "Harper's references to civilization, savagery and barbarism reflect civilizational discourse and scientific racism in regard to African-Americans, but these keywords were also central to Indian policies and discussions of the Indian question at the same time," showing Harper's knowledge of how white American treatment of the two communities intersects.[29] That the novel's position ultimately allies itself with white notions of civilization—meaning in this case that Native Americans must remain "lesser," "other" in order for African-Americans' character to appear positively distinct—is extremely unfortunate, compromising to Harper's position as it is, even if perhaps perceived as unavoidable given the persistent negative biases toward indigenous peoples at the time.[30]

Hartman maintains that we must turn to archives to find what's hidden, to recast narratives of oppressed peoples outside of the dominant, and often erroneous, narratives about them—and the people who have oppressed them.[31] Harriet Jacobs's *Incidents in the Life of a Slave Girl* operates under such reclamation, being one of the most important books directed against slavery when it was first published—under the pen name Linda Brent to protect Jacobs from her former slaveholder—in 1861. In *Black Girlhood in the Nineteenth Century,* Nazera Sadiq Wright points out that it's particularly the "Childhood" chapter in Jacobs's memoir that compellingly "makes a political statement about slavery's violent impact on all women."[32] Jacobs takes pains to describe her childhood in idyllic terms in order to make the death of her parents and the wrenching away from innocence that followed that much more dramatic and affecting. The chapter begins, "I was born a slave; but I never knew it till six years of happy childhood had passed away."[33]

Wright again notes that Jacobs's depiction of the innocent beginnings of her girlhood, and its subsequent shocking corruption, meant to show how her life progressed not only in age, but character, making her endangerment feel more urgent—especially if her story could impel white women to empathize with her vulnerable state.[34] Before Jacobs can appeal to the sentiment of such women, who have the power to help abolish slavery, she must first humanize her character: she must help her readers get to know Linda, even identify with her through her—and their—feelings. She must deconstruct stereotypical and debasing notions of just who an "enslaved black girl" is and what she is capable of thinking and feeling as she interacts with others. Wright observes that on southern plantations, girls may get to play, but their recreation can only "function as brief respites that magnify slavery's miseries. Enslaved black girls' play accentuates this ironic aspiring: their vulnerability and resistance convey slavery's sadism."[35] *Incidents* has high stakes, and like much of the literature of the time, borrows from theater and uses melodrama to depict them.[36]

The most melodramatic element is the ongoing battle between Linda Brent and the lecherous Dr. Flint. Flint deludes himself and tries to gaslight Linda repeatedly, constantly confronting her with the threat of sexual violence when she fails to believe that being his concubine would be the best deal she'd get in life: "[H]e told me I was his property; that I must be subject to his will in all things. My soul revolted against the mean tyranny. But where could I turn for protection?"[37] Linda's staunch resistance, even while being in a position of such vulnerability, contrasts with Flint's determined wrongdoing, making her a sympathetic heroine and him the unconscionable villain: "Dr. Flint swore he would kill me, if I was not as silent as the grave . . . and he did not wish his villainy made public."[38] He cultivates public propriety, then, while privately terrorizing an underage enslaved girl—performing immoral private domination, and guarding the appearance of upstanding morality as justification for legalized domination in public.

Another form of domination, reproduced by way of the sinister nuances of white-passing, appear in "Désirée's Baby" by Kate Chopin.[39] Perhaps the benefit of a generation's removal from the legality of the institution helped Chopin's 1892 short story to so succinctly encapsulate the racist power dynamic between Black and white Americans during slavery. Multiple instances of foreshadowing set up an unexpected overturning of expectation, using place and setting to extend the idea of the people in her story—and the land they inhabit—somehow being cursed. The first instance is the house where Désirée, a beautiful and white-appearing orphan of questionable origins raised to young womanhood by a kind and childless white woman, goes to live with her new husband Armand Aubigny, a wealthy planter. Armand's estate is sprawling but dilapidated: "The roof came down steep and black like a cowl, reaching out beyond the wide galleries that encircled the yellow stuccoed house" (149). Any brightness that the color yellow implicates gets dampened by what weighs it down, surrounds it: "Big, solemn oaks grew close to it, and their thick-leaved, far-reaching branches shadowed it like a pall" (149). Désirée's mother has "a shudder at first sight" of the house, which she describes as "a sad looking place, which for many years had not known the gentle presence of a mistress" (149). Thus, the dimming feels physical and psychological, memory/past and present eerily coexisting, both haunted.

And when Armand falls in love with Désirée, he does so violently: "the way all the other Aubignys fell in love, as if struck by a pistol shot.... The passion that awoke in him that day, when he saw her at the gate, swept along like an avalanche, or like a prairie fire, or like anything that drives headlong over all obstacles" (148). And yet, practically speaking, that love cannot overcome all obstacles. Indeed, despite the love he harbors for Désirée, Armand treats the enslaved people forced to work on his estate with unrelenting violence. The zeal with which he inflicts that violence stands out as a stark contrast to his adoring feelings for her, and spill over into their marriage after they have a child. Since her origins are in question, he presumes—once their baby becomes darker in color—that she has hidden African lineage. He then begins to brood, becomes crueler than ever toward his slaves and freezes out his wife.

When Armand withdraws his love, Désirée's distress escalates to suicide: she carries herself and her baby into the swamp to their deaths, despite her mother writing to tell her to come home and to bring the baby. Désirée cannot abide her own mistaken Blackness, and so, not unlike Armand, whose brutal torture of enslaved people on his plantation smacks of self-hatred, she destroys it. But while his hatred is directed outward, hers rushes inward, toward herself and the nameless child she has given birth to. Thus, Blackness appears as a kind of sin, one befitting the punishment of death—but only because the strictures of law and social practice decree it. Feeling, though, cannot be legislated, even if it can be influenced.[40] The love between Armand and Désirée is real, but shame interferes and their love atrophies, showing how racism destroys lives and creates a legacy of destruction that is visited upon generation after generation, as we see when Armand accidentally discovers, reads then burns a letter that ends the book—one his mother wrote to his father before she died:

> He read it. She was thanking God for the blessing of her husband's love:— "But above all," she wrote, "Night and day, I thank the good God for having so arranged our lives that our dear Armand will never know that his mother, who adores him, belongs to the race that is cursed with the brand of slavery." (158)

In another instance of foreshadowing, Chopin hints at this outcome when she describes "Armand's dark, handsome face" (151). Readers, however, likely don't realize the truth until we reach the story's shocking turnabout ending.

"Désirée's Baby" shows the devastating effects of racism on relationships. No one can escape the tragedy of it. Notably, Chopin does not write that race is the curse. She chooses instead to demonstrate through her characters' behavior and their fates that slavery is the curse perpetrated upon a race. Even though his mother is buried "in France, and she having loved her own land too well to ever leave it," she and Armand are connected by blood (157)—and, I would argue, law and circumstance. Armand cannot escape her Blackness, nor can he escape his own. It is a part of him, whether he desires it or not. His wife's name, meaning desired (désirée) in French, is another reminder of this, as it represents the whiteness he desires, but he then destroys once he has it. Cruelty poisons his life, just as it poisons hers and their child's, and poisons the home in which they live—to the detriment of the health and wellbeing of all involved. The curse of racism damages and dooms everyone and everything it touches in "Désirée's Baby." And yet, Armand Aubigny lives on with his misery and guilt for company, slavery continues, and the house still stands— upon land that remains a horrific site of death and harm.

Chopin thus suggests that geography is another key factor in racial, sexual, and class conflict—an observation that is particularly harrowing in the case of indigenous peoples in America. Mahkatêwe-meshi-kêhkêhkwa's *The Life of Black Hawk, or Ma-ka-tai-me-she-kia-kiak: Dictated by Himself* (1833)⁴¹—the first native autobiography translated into English and published in the United States—depicts the interaction between his people and white settlers in a continuous, unbroken narrative. There are no chapters, no section breaks, no transitional markers. He presents Sauk ways of knowing as ways of being, from the crane dance—"This national dance makes our warriors" (48)—to deep-seated beliefs about the sacredness of the land: "My reason teaches me that *land cannot be sold*" (56, emphasis in the original). He does not privilege the views of white Americans over his own, and he makes no apology for his steadfast refusal to do so, despite the devastation wrought upon his people and his family as a result.

Like *Incidents in the Life of a Slave Girl, The Life of Black Hawk* begins with nascent idyll: "I was born at the Sac Village, on Rock River, in the year 1767, and am now in my 67th year. My great grandfather, Na-na-ma-kee, or Thunder (according to the tradition given me by my father, Py-e-sa,), was born in the vicinity of Montreal" (9). He thus places himself first in the landscape, and then within a familial lineage. He then connects the people to the land by way of ritual and custom, finally bringing us to the prescient moment that would lead to the historical present Mahkatêwe-meshi-kêhkêhkwa is writing about: "Montreal, where the Great Spirit first placed the Sac Nation, and inspired [my father] with a belief that, at the end of four years, he should see a white man, who would be to him a father" (9). Mahkatêwe-meshi-kêhkêhkwa's story importantly provides a primary source, albeit one that has been translated, a firsthand account of the confrontation between the Sauk—including their ways of knowing, of seeing, and of being—and the white settlers, soldiers, and government representatives whose motives and actions history shows us were often treacherous and self-serving. When describing the difficulty of surrendering territory as white settlers encroached more and more violently and in ever greater numbers, Mahkatêwe-meshi-kêhkêhkwa moves from political concerns to personal ones:

> When I called to mind the scenes of my youth, and those of later days—and reflected that the theatre on which these were acted, had been so long the home of my fathers, who now slept on the hills around it, I could not bring my mind to consent to leave this country to the whites, for any earthly consideration. (62)

The phrase "bring my mind to consent" implies both physical and mental effort; he cannot reconceive his position, just as he cannot bear to relocate to a reservation, away from what he knows as the "home of my fathers." In reference to the treaty of 1804, which ceded Sauk/Fox lands east of the Mississippi to whites, who then reneged on remunerating the Sauk and Fox peoples as promised, Mahkatêwe-meshi-kêhkêhkwa bitterly observes, "How smooth must be the language of the whites, when they can make right look like wrong, and wrong like right" (57).

Discussing the matter of truth and language with regard to white Works Progress Administration (WPA) interviewers and transcribers tasked in the 1940s with documenting the testimony of survivors of 19th-century enslavement and legalized human trafficking, Hartman writes that even those efforts to shed light on social ills can serve the dominant narrative.[42] With this in mind, how does literature—as and adjacent to historical documentation—serve to perpetuate erroneous beliefs and false American myths? Conversely, how does it reveal the truth behind the myths that literature (and law, and social custom, and culture) may present? As this chapter has shown, we can look to 19th-century American literature for some answers, particularly in relation to today's political and social environment and the clashing of cultures that creates as many opportunities for connection as for conflict.

Criticism of American literature as a field has tended to characterize intercultural interactions in early American literature through a masculinist, Eurocentric lens, despite rich and varied evidence that women and people of color influenced the shaping of that literature—whether as creators of or characters/figures in the texts. The works examined here confirm that intercultural interactions and narratives about them existed from at least the 19th century and that the inscription of whiteness as the overriding norm ignores the voices of those writing themselves in the face of it. Further, the elision of disability and the reflexive use of it as an othering device deepens social and racialized harm. These texts—and so many others—show that it took acts of deliberate and systematic erasure to silence those voices and to whitewash the canon. It will take acts of deliberate and systematic revision to heighten the accuracy and the historical diversity of American literature, hopefully providing a more balanced sense of the 19th-century zeitgeist, both creative and cultural. Let us not forget that our love[43] as writers and readers, as students and scholars for a given text and/or a given author is a powerful force in shaping literary and critical discourse, and that our questions about language and its shapes, its shaping powers within texts, is instrumental to that process.[44] Provided our questioning originates in generosity and a spirit of inclusion, our criticism—informed by a radical poetics—will move us away from the periphery, away from narrowness, and away from other hierarchal qualifiers toward a more equitable, a more deeply felt mode of inquiry that highlights context as much as it does content and structure.

A Poetics of Resistance

On Sor Juana Inés de la Cruz and Women of Action in Early Colonial Mexico

Just as it does today, life in 16th- and 17th-century colonial Mexico for women[1] of all ethnic backgrounds varied greatly according to race and class. But what they dealt with in common, however, was a social and cultural upheaval that significantly shaped and changed the face of the entire Atlantic World, literally and figuratively. They confronted expansions and shifts of not only colonial empire, but of the laws, rules, and customs which governed their daily lives. To address issues of gender alongside those of race and class as placed in the context of power themes in the Atlantic World is to give a more inclusive view of the far-reaching effects of colonization. It is a view in human terms, to be sure, moving away from the representation of women in terms of what was done *to* them versus what they did *for* themselves, and their families. That shift in perspective advocates for an examination of women from their points of survival and resistance, rather than victimization. In my mind, that is a radical enough shift that to shape a poetics of resistance—via poems by Sor Juana Inés de la Cruz, and by reading between the lines of archival documents à la Saidiya Hartman—is an effort worth beginning to undertake.

Feminism is not new, and neither is resistance. A poetics of resistance accounts not just for the larger movements documented in history, but the unheralded episodes of resistance—ones that occur internally, that we document in diaries and kitchen conversations, in bedtime conversations with our children, in toxic workshops and workplaces, in our personal relationships and in traffic, in reading racist passages in Flaubert and

Stevens. Resistance does not have to be armed or organized. Resistance is a type of thought that leads to behavioral change that leads to action. It is a refusal to accept harm, a refusal to perpetuate harm; imbued with and related to love, trust, intuition and integrity, resistance holds a power that has nothing to do with hierarchies or money. It deals strictly in the human. For the purposes of this essay, I briefly call attention to how African, European, and Native women in early colonial Mexico resisted various oppressions through language and the law. They navigated the fluctuating lines of power between race, class, and gender not passively, but actively. Their lives and work provide examples of how average women asserted themselves, resisted instances of exploitation (whether financial, social, or sexual) and protested or maneuvered through oppressive conditions.

Poet Sor Juana Inés de la Cruz (1648–1695), for example, used her writing to expose hypocrisies of the Catholic church, men, and society on gender issues, specifically. A famous writer in her time and still an important figure in literary history, de la Cruz, daughter of a mestizo mother and Spanish father, learned to read at the age of three[2] under her grandfather's tutelage and proved to be a child prodigy. Despite enforced social and legal limitations on her race, gender, and class, she became a sought-after figure in elite Mexican society. Later in her life, she advocated for the education of women and girls, making that part of her work as a Hieronymite nun. *Juana Inés*, a 2017 Spanish-language Netflix series captures her spiritedness and her queerness, her resistance to suppression and devotion to knowledge acquisition, and her ability to find solace and strength in writing.[3]

Take de la Cruz's "Poem 281," where she describes the *Virgén de Guadelupe*, a figure still revered in Mexico and other parts of Latin America today, as in alignment with indigenous beliefs about her representation and consistent with the Bible's characterization "black and comely."[4] de la Cruz explicitly chooses to equalize race and gender, writing against the typical portrayal of Blacks and women during that time. Another poem, "Poem 92," or "Satira Filosófica"[5] takes men to task for their treatment of women, stating that men accuse women of the very same ills they themselves practice, and indicts them for seducing women to such actions in the first place:

Hombres necios que acusáis
a la mujer sin razón,
sin ver que sois la ocasión
de lo mismo que culpáis:[6]

Foolish men accuse
women without aim,
without seeing you cause
the same harm you blame. (My translation)

Her strong voice adds weight to the notion that women participated vigorously and vocally in opposing race and gender bias, even five centuries ago. "Poem 92" parallels Frances E. W. Harper's mid-19th-century poem "A Double Standard":

Can you blame me if I've learned to think
Your hate of vice a sham,
When you so coldly crushed me down
And then excused the man?[7]

Harper goes on to elucidate the deception and its cost:

Can you blame me that I did not see
Beneath his burning kiss
The serpent's wiles, nor even hear
The deadly adder hiss?[8]

And, again, that sentiment is in parallel with de la Cruz's third stanza, which follows:

Combatís su resistencia
y luego, con gravedad,
decís que fue livianidad

Fighting her resistance
and then, with gravity,
you say it was lightness (My translation)

While Harper's subject dies, however, de la Cruz's direct address to men never loses its strident focus, the penultimate stanza demanding that men "Dejad de solicitar," or "stop your soliciting" (my translation, i.e., leave women alone), then ending with an argument that manages to both allude to scripture and echo a lawyer's closing remarks:

Bien con muchas armas fundo
que lidia vuestra arrogancia,
pues en promesa e instancia
juntáis diablo, carne y mundo.[9]

I'm armed with proofs of what
your arrogance deals—
now in promises and appeals
you fuse devil, flesh and world. (My translation)

Hers is not a timid voice. A poetics of resistance asks that we do not censor such justified anger, but acknowledge and enjoy and examine it as part of a literary lineage and as part of a feminist lineage that stretches back further than even de la Cruz.

But to look further back asks us to search the archive. One such instance of resistance occurred on the heels of a successful 1608 revolt by Angolan chief Yanga. The uprising resulted in the incorporation of a free town in his name a few years later near Veracruz, Mexico, which still exists today. It is also where, in 1612, a group of enslaved women of African descent participated in a plot to attain freedom. Seven women were among the thirty-five executed when the plot was discovered.[10] At the time, women of African descent could bypass their imposed status by virtue of their skin color if they were mixed race; some fair mulattos passed for white in secret. Some of those women petitioned the audiencia—a sort of colonial tribunal or appellate court—to declare them white—"que se tengan por blancos"—and a very few could purchase the title of *blanco*, regardless of their actual skin color.[11] More broadly, children of enslaved women and Spaniards could also have their freedom purchased by the father.[12] Even when relegated by law and evolving custom to lower-status castas, then, Black women, when able, used whatever means at their disposal to reject the limitations imposed upon them by colonial racial, social, legal and financial restrictions. A poetics of resistance acknowledges that persistence in the face of continuous rejection as evidence of humanity and dignity. It further centers women's efforts at agency, even or especially when legal systems and social strictures deprived them of it, as a common human and creative practice.

In different and less violent ways, European women in colonial Mexico also endured gender restrictions and strict social expectations that they sometimes resisted. As depicted in Alexandra and Noble David Cook's *Good Faith and Truthful Ignorance: A Case of Transatlantic Bigamy,* Doñas Catalina de Vergara and Beatriz de Villasur both fought to preserve their rights to be seen as virtuous women, using the Spanish court system to protect their interests. The fight also had to do with maintaining their financial well-being.[13] Neither of the two Doñas let their bigamist hidalgo/conquistador husband, Don Francisco Noguerol de Ulloa, exploit their finances or sully their reputations without a fight. In another case, in the very late 17th century, criollo Josefa Sánchez de Aldana sued Don Martin Cacho for not following through with marriage after an exchange of gifts and sex. After "le entregué mi cuerpo" ("I gave him my body"), de Aldana stated, Don Cacho married someone else and her father sent the resulting baby away; the suit was to restore her good name.[14] That there are such cases where women fought to preserve notions of propriety that were crucial to a woman's reputation at that time shows also that women of various racial backgrounds and classes did resist exploitation and asserted their rights. And, they used existing legal and social systems to assert their claims to them.

In the case of indigenous women, one particular story stands out as such an act of resistance to subjugation. Describing an incident noted in a primary source in which a Mayan woman successfully resisted a Spaniard's advances, Matthew Restall writes that "often the very ideology or system that subordinated women paradoxically gave women value [. . .] the Spanish (and male Maya) association of male dominance with colonial (or political) dominance made the Maya woman's sexual resistance all the more potent."[15] In this case, noted in an early 17th-century legal document, the unnamed indigenous woman's steadfast resistance even in the face of his vehement advances shocked the Spaniard enough that he backed down.[16] That she then sued the Spaniard illustrates that native women made use of the Spanish legal system when necessary to protest offenses against them.

Women's legal and extralegal resistance continued into the nineteenth century. In her article "Lessons of Gender and Ethnohistory in Mesoamerica," Irene Silverblatt outlines a late eighteenth-century incident in a Maya village called Ixil, in which Maya women collectively opposed colonial policies that prevented traditional burials. The women literally "laid siege to the community church and held government and religious authorities hostage" in order to "forcefully [express] defiance of (resistance to) the policies of institutions they could not otherwise affect directly," and Silverblatt notes that the "women's lack of access to official political life could sanction their engagement of male-dominated structures in extralegal ways."[17] Silverblatt also discusses nuances of sexual violence during the period, examining the nature of resistance and subordination in relation to choices of survival. Her article shows that native women proactively sought to preserve their rights, despite the overwhelming presence and power of the colonizing Spaniards. Stepping outside legal and social structures, women organized. "One of these riotous women 'took the voice,' making it clear that release was contingent on the community being able to bury their dead properly."[18] To take the voice means to name in public the transgressions against them, and they worked toward solutions both within colonial systems, and by means they themselves devised.

Women in early colonial Mexico did not unilaterally accept ill treatment; they resisted it with the means available to them, from legal action to poetry to forceful protest. Their survival often depended on perceived submission and deference to men, but women devised many ways to live and fight and thrive as much as they could with the resources, knowledge, and choices available to them. A poetics of resistance intentionally seeks and holds awareness of the entrenched undercurrent of historical resistance that has ebbed and flowed within wider public view. It acknowledges resistance's constant presence, demonstrating that women along intersecting lines of race and class pursued self-assertion during a time of explicit establishment of those lines. The record of such resistance continues in the fact of their survival as well as in extant poems in the literary-historical record. Women—and particularly women of color—were, have always been, and continue to be more than mothers and workers and sexual companions, and further, they demanded to be valued and respected in whatever role they served in societies, communities, and families. Their contributions overlapped politically and culturally to help shape the Atlantic World, and their resistance helped them retain some of the humanity and dignity of populations that imperialists seem(ed) so determined to exploit, brutalize, deny, and destroy.

Painting and Palimpsest

Ekphrasis, History, and Empathy in the Poetics of Natasha Trethewey

Natasha Trethewey's books are part of a critical and creative conversation about one of the most important issues facing the world—that of self-definition, particularly in the midst of the labyrinth of traumatic external impositions known as racism. Her work addresses many layers of the conversation, examining Southern US histories and 16th-century casta paintings, a white man's serial photographs of mulatto women, the lives and deaths of unsung Black soldiers, her mother's tragic death, and the aftermath of Hurricane Katrina.

Trethewey's keen attention to the unfolding narrative—the very Southern slow reveal; the borrowing from an oil painter's layering and the photographer's aperture; the unmistakable, variegated and yet indefinable music of Blackness itself—creates deep parallels in the work between content and craft. Often, her line breaks leave just enough tension and interest to propel the narrative forward, but each line holds a beautifully self-contained image or story to be reflected upon solo. On both micro and macro levels, her work is palimpsestic, asserting the speaker's memories and observations while erasing what may have previously been accepted—i.e., misconceptions—in order to reassert and redefine a situation, an image, a memory, or a history more intensely with each additional stratum.

The repetition and, at times, meandering pace that tends to characterize Trethewey's work can belie the calculation and focus beneath it. Reading *Thrall,* published in 2012, José Ortega y Gasset's 1956 classic *Dehuman-*

ization of Art and Other Writings on Art and Culture comes to mind in terms of both approach and outcome, fitting because ekphrastic pieces are so integral to the collection. Trethewey seems to use the same techniques painters use in delivering these poems, relating the story/image while creating a relentless way of seeing beyond the surface. Ortega y Gasset writes:

"Painting tends to become planimetric, like the canvas on which one paints . . . Instead of painting objects as they are seen, one paints the experience of seeing."[1] He writes that such a planimetric surface renders "figures" as well as "objects" as other than themselves, turning the subject matter into something that belongs less to the world at large and more to the world and action the painting creates, making them "subjective states through which and by means of which things appear."[2] Through the sensory detail in her content and "planimetrics of form," Trethewey does the reverse—heightening the visibility of the people and characters in her poems, while at the same time exposing the machinations taken for granted in what they suffer through cumulatively, from major tragedies to daily microaggressions.

In that context, "Miracle of the Black Leg," based on several 16th-century paintings by Juan Patricio Morlete Ruiz and others, as well as a carving by Isidro de Villoldo, is one of the strongest poems in *Thrall*. The opening lines depict a never-ending abuse, the act captured in Villoldo's painting applied as continuously in language:

Always, the dark body hewn asunder; always
    one man is healed, his sick limb replaced,
placed in another man's grave: the white leg
    buried beside the corpse, or attached as if
it were always there. If not for the dark appendage,
    you might miss the story beneath this story—
what remains each time the myth changes.[3]

The image, depicted in the poem's fourth section with the most literal language, shows the opulence amid the grotesque abuse and the clear stratification of the two men. The amputee left alive on the floor to witness the surgical collage highlights the macabre way the "the men [are] bound one to the other [. . .] in a story that's still being written."[4] Indeed,

Isidro de Villoldo, *The Miracle of the Black Leg*, Spain (1539).

the awareness in the final section means ongoing cultural violence is no accident: "Always, the dark body hewn asunder; always"—the absolute "always" used twice, leaving no argument as to the simultaneous history, presence, and currency of the facts. We may think of Mary Turner, the woman lynched by a racist mob in Georgia in 1918, her unborn child sliced from her hanging body and crushed under the boots of his mother's killer.[5] Or of James Byrd, Jr., dragged through rural Texas streets until all that was left of him was, as poet Lucille Clifton wrote, "a man's head hunched in the road."[6]

More recently, we may think of Trayvon Martin, the seventeen-year-old shot in the chest with a hollow-point bullet by a neighborhood vigilante in Florida in 2012, while walking to his father's house from the store, armed only with candy and iced tea.[7] Such endless examples implicit in the first line of Trethewey's poem begin in the gloomy past but go beyond the 19th-century painting, bleeding into the present, and indeed the future as we continue failing to decisively end such violence—"always / one man is healed, his sick limb replaced, placed in another man's grave"—the truth buried in gruesome and unnatural ways, the "sick limb" of racism placed quite literally in the graves of those dead because of racist murderers. But the fact that this poem exists means that such truths do not remain silenced, despite the apparent anonymity of the figures it depicts. Text resurrects, even in its incompleteness: "the black leg is at once a grafted narrative, a redacted line of text." Trethewey's poem gives the leg and the man from whom it was taken elegiac due, inserts a version of that redaction which does justice to the abject offenses of history.

As *Thrall* progresses, the poems become more personal, concerned with reckoning historical offenses alongside familial ones. Like "Miracle of the Black Leg," "Knowledge"[8] details the cutting of a body via the autopsy, this time of a woman, "young and beautiful and drowned" (line 8), and rather than a bedroom, occurs in "a temple of science over which / the anatomist presides. In the service of beauty" (lines 12–13). After the discussion of objectification, something opens besides a body: "The anatomist's blade opens a place in me / like a curtain drawn upon a room in which / each learned man is my father" (lines 28–30). Fear, violation, indignation—the speaker as both witness and the body on the table dissected. This sort of metacognition, wherein the speaker recognizes herself as having been abused and powerless, delivers an important characterization that goes beyond the stated offense of the father stating, "I study / my crossbreed child" (lines 31–32). It speaks to the parent's ability to implant a narrative in their child's head that can define how they see themselves, discourage self-discovery, and thus spur a reactionary search for something that feels truer. "Knowledge" feels caught in a loop wherein the speaker is left at the mercy of "the dissector—his scalpel in hand like a pen / poised above me, aimed straight for my heart" (lines 39–40).

In contrast to the imaginative ekphrasis in the two previously discussed pieces, "Taxonomy" uses more explanatory or literal language. Trethewey devotes the whole of section 3, subtitled "De Español y Mestiza Produce Castiza," to the hierarchy of miscegenation, in short-lined quatrains and couplets that naturally slow the pace. The white space feels like an exercise in erasure, but the lack of density means we must sit with the terms and only the terms. Some readers—and I admit, I at first counted myself among them—may tire of the many referents of darkness to "taint" in section 4, "The Book of Castas"—"of stain: blemish: sullying spot: / that which can be purified, / that which cannot—Canaan's / black fate. How like a dirty joke" (lines 14–17) and wordplay "Call it the taint—as in / T'aint one and t'aint the other" (lines 22–23), or take issue with easier or cleverer choices earlier in the poem: "one hand a shape / like the letter C. See" (page 34, section 1, lines 35–36).

In fact, in a 2012 review in *The New Criterion*, critic and poet William Logan skewers *Thrall* for just such choices. Among other insults, he bemoans what he sees as simplicity and repetition: "if she can't think of a better adjective, she chooses 'dark.'"[9] Logan laments Trethewey's attention to issues of racial oppression; he refers to the casta paintings as "portraits displaying the bewildering variety of mixed-race children," taking issue not only with the content but the "bland, passionless verse," wherein "the images are already like encyclopedias."[10]

While Trethewey serves the subject better in "Miracle of the Black Leg," which dramatically examines the ruthlessness and brutality of the illustrated act, an assumptive thievery immortalized in gold and paint, stating the more obvious in an effort to contain and cohere to the larger themes can be necessary. It's telling that Logan doesn't engage "Miracle," or any of the other poems that depict more explicit atrocities, other than to call "lurid" the tripartite poem "The Americans"—its first section being subtitled "Dr. Samuel Adolphus Cartwright on Dissecting the White Negro."[11] His non-participatory dismissal and stated bewilderment smack of the same kind of disengagement and lack of compassion that has made real conversation about race difficult.[12] It is the same wall of blatant bias, unconscious or not, that has traditionally confronted Black women writers from Toni Morrison to Ntozake Shange, the same "self-puffery" Edward Said calls out Bloom for in *Humanism and Democratic Criticism*.[13] Even a possible connection to Trethewey's personal poems about her father are cast aside and infantilized as the whining of an "oversensitive [daughter], so quick to view the world through the narrow lens of race, that soon she loses the reader's sympathy."[14] One might argue that, far from aiming to elicit sympathy, Trethewey's clarity and repetitiveness means to educate and elucidate instead.

A group interview, "Interchange: Genres of History," from a 2004 issue from *The Journal of American History*, finds Trethewey discussing her motivations for choosing her subject matter as part of an interest in "public history and/or cultural memory" that includes people discriminated against because of their race, gender, and/or class.[15] She knows that the topic can cause some readers—and critics, as we have seen—to reject the work outright, so describes her technique as invitational, with that invitation embedded in "vivid imagery" that helps them to not just confront racism and oppression, but "experience the emotional context."[16] She rejects the notion of readers "as distant observers who are told what to think or feel about the historical material I am presenting," preferring to recreate a feeling-experience that honors the human subjects of her poetry: "This is, of course, all about empathy."[17] Thus, it would be a mistake to reject wholesale the perceived or actual literality without approaching the content with openness to new understandings and different points of view, as well as trust of the writer. Even when, on occasion, some of the language in *Thrall* seems too literal, Trethewey accomplishes her aim clearly and deftly. Rather than depicting race, gender, and class as solely political topics—a limited view—her poems acknowledge the deep personal cost of how politicized identities affect how real people live, love, and are treated both publicly and intimately.

In the same interview, Trethewey makes plain that, as with most stories that capture public imagination, she writes about her "own experience," mining her "personal history, within the larger context of public history."[18] Her personal narrative is most contextualized by public history in her 2010 book *Beyond Katrina*, a hybrid text of poetry and nonfiction prose, which together offer a winding narrative that details histories of Gulfport, Trethewey's corner of Mississippi. She focuses on the devastating effects Hurricane Katrina had on her family, effects that the individual towns and people, including her brother, still contend with. The prose makes special notice of the man-made damage done by corporations—even as many of her poignant memories include them:

Gulfport is me at the Woolworth's lunch counter [. . .] listening to the sounds of shoes striking the polished tile floor of Hancock Bank, holding my grandmother's hand [. . .] me riding the elevator of the J.M. Salloum Building—the same elevator my grandmother operated in the thirties.[19]

Trethewey points out how connected the people are to the agents of their own destruction when she reveals how the casinos eroded the coastline, making the area that much more vulnerable to hurricane damage, lamenting Governor Haley Barbour's decision to allow onshore gaming while recognizing the people in the area could sorely use the jobs the gaming industry provides (58). Likewise, the poems reflect the bind between the South and its inhabitants, taking a wide sweep across the Mississippi landscape and through centuries, decades, and moments with a simultaneity and overlap that is admirable. "Theories of Time and Space" has a circular arc, a cinema pan:

You can get there from here, though
there's no going home.

Everywhere you go will be somewhere
you've never been. Try this:

head south on Mississippi 49, one-
by-one mile markers ticking off

another minute of your life. (page 5, lines 1–7)

The general "there" and "here" from the first line, then "everywhere" and "somewhere" in the third, draw the reader into the narrative. Delaying specificity until the third stanza destabilizes expectations, and along with the second person usage becomes an invitation to "Try this: / head south on Mississippi 49" with the speaker, even with "one-by-one mile markers ticking off / another minute of your life."

Now that we're moving along the road, the poem instructs further, offering a sense of futility: "Follow this / to its natural conclusion—dead end" (lines 8–9). We're all headed there, aren't we, toward death? Except meanwhile she's got us in Mississippi, "at the coast, the pier at Gulfport where / riggings of shrimp boats are loose stitches / in a sky threatening rain" (lines 10–12). In those lines one can feel the blues strung up with the storm, leading us to the "buried terrain of the past" from which "you" cannot escape, weighted with that familiar "tome of memory" (lines 15–16). Indeed, memory seems impossible because of—which photographs symbolize and make material: "the photograph—who you were—/ will be waiting when you return" (lines 20–21). The lack of punctuation at that final line of the poem denotes a continuousness. You can't escape the past, and you can't escape who you are; both have got to be dealt with.

During a panel discussion at the 2012 Dodge Poetry Festival, "Conversation: In the Path of the Storm," Trethewey, along with poet Patricia Smith (author of the award-winning Hurricane Katrina–based poetry collection *Blood Dazzler*), talked about Katrina as "a human event."[20] She said that one has to let go of wanting to be an insider, or approved by insiders, in order to tell the story that needs telling. Trethewey discussed George Orwell's *The Road to Wigan Pier* as an influence, how she realized she couldn't help but impose outsiderness because she no longer lived in the area and wasn't there during the storm, but challenged herself not to "otherize" Katrina victims.[21] This is important to mention because in her poetics, Trethewey walks the tenuous line between subject and speaker with a certain grace, confronting outsiderness while sometimes safely removed physically but not necessarily emotionally, and sometimes the other way around. The prodigal daughter as an adult must come to terms with histories both personal and cultural in a way that allows a moving forward only once the speaker has finished mucking through memory, the inescapable past, and its very apparent effects on the present. Unlike Smith, who powerfully takes on personae of Katrina victims (and Hurricane Katrina herself) in the majority of her book, Trethewey's speaker tends to hold the same singular voice and maintain a certain self-concerned observational distance that is nevertheless melancholy, grieving not only for a personal past but its public surroundings. In section 6 of "Congregation," subtitled "Prodigal," she writes:

Once, I was a daughter of this place:
daughter of Gwen, granddaughter
of Leretta, great of Eugenia McGee.

I was baptized in the church
my great-aunt founded, behind
the drapes my grandmother sewed.[22]

Names are important, lineage is important—the work of women's hands made material and embodied, as part of living. The word "once" calls up both fairytale and memory, letting readers know the past's presence isn't so distant—lines 10–12 in the fourth stanza imagining the self as palimpsest for story and memory, of place, of incidences, and of ancestors: "Still a girl, I put down the red flower / and wore a white bloom pinned to my chest—/ the mark of loss: a motherless child." The white bloom symbolizes innocence and grief, the two intertwined in the speaker's memory. Then, moving back to the present by lines 17 and 18 of the sixth stanza, the speaker asks: "What is home but a cradle / of the past?" The cradle image denotes perpetual infancy, as if the past is constantly reborn through memory, held and nurtured by home with its complicated connotations—possible refuge and escape, care and neglect, love and loss, joy and bitterness. Home, in this poem, is a place where random landmarks like "the sign / emblazoned on the church marquee" hold more meaning than was likely intended during their conception and construction: "Face the things that confront you" (lines 24–25, 32). For Trethewey's speaker, that means not only the death of her mother and the racist violence of the south, but her own relationship to all of that. She is a "pilgrim" but an uncertain one, returning to the church as observer rather than participant: "I stood there, my face against the glass, / watching" (lines 33, 42–43). Despite an invitation from a congregation member, despite family connection, she remains trapped in betweenness:

I got as far as the vestibule—neither in,
nor out. The service went on. I did nothing
but watch, my face against the glass—until
someone turned, looked back: saw me. (lines 49–52)

The longstanding connection of the speaker to the people and the places shows through in the details, but so does her disconnection. Just as the child speaker hides "behind / drapes my grandmother sewed" and with

"a white bloom pinned to my chest" at her mother's funeral, feeling sin-
gled out as "a motherless child," as an adult she cannot mend that breach.
Both the poetry and prose of *Beyond Katrina* talk about feeling apart from
a place that is so much a part of her. Instead of shying from the complexity of those feelings, though, the work constantly addresses it, unravel-
ing the endless stitch of the internal and external machinations threaded
within it.

Reviewing *Beyond Katrina*, scholar and Dillard University professor
emeritus Jerry Ward says that Trethewey "accomplishes the yoking of
narrative and metanarrative and explores the devastated but recovering
'physical landscape as well as the landscape of our cultural memory.'"[23]
Native Guard also dives into Mississippi history and personal memory;
"Theories of Time and Space" first appeared as the opening poem in the
book, setting the tone for the recollection of a Southern experience rid-
dled with habitual fears, making hurt both expected and accepted. Small
and large hurts have happened and not happened so many times that it
becomes one continuous act of psychological violence, the warped normalcy of it captured, aptly, in a pantoum titled "Incident." A harsh reality
unfolds in what should be a celebratory time, turning it into a new kind
of normal:

> We tell the story every year—
> how we peered from the windows, shades drawn—
> though nothing really happened,
> the charred grass now green again.[24]

No attempt at forgetting here, though a minimization in "nothing really
happened." But the pantoum lends itself to the re-inscription of memory,
the haunting image of the cross burning on the front lawn "trussed up
like a Christmas tree" (line 6) just as haunting with each retelling and
restating.

The twisted angels in the fourth stanza exude a quiet and incendiary
hate that clashes with the holiday reflection, ingrained childhood images
of godly and innocent protectors—"white angels in their gowns"—
recast into something to hide from, to be wary of (line 10). The holiday
emblems become characterized by fear ("the wicks trembling in their
fonts of oil"), destruction ("charred grass"), and the narrative delivers

the speaker's acceptance of that ("Nothing really happened"). The apathy with which the family was greeted when confronted with the cross-burning—"No one came. / Nothing really happened"—plays on both sides of the racial fence. That "no one" and "nothing" echoes not only the impunity oppressors enjoy, but further, enforces the silencing of Black victims, who are still frequently urged to "get over" racially oppressive acts and forgive those who commit violence against them and their communities.[25] Beginning and ending with "We tell the story every year" implies both warning and remembrance. To forget, to not tell the story, is to deny both history and reality, a denial Trethewey makes it her mission to avoid, and not just with personal histories.

The formal qualities of "Elegy for the Native Guards" also put Trethewey in conversation with literary traditions and historical personae. Rather than intersecting with family, though, "Elegy for the Native Guards" tells a forgotten story of Trethewey's native Gulfport. The speaker addresses the "black phalanx" of Union soldiers who served in the Civil War in Mississippi—"tokens of history long buried," their names absent from the honorific "plaque" at the fort she visits.[26] In recounting this "half reminder" of their existence—a harrowing existence, to be sure, detailed thoroughly in the book's title poem—Trethewey ultimately shows the civic and human responsibility both to stake a claim to the "weathered monument" (line 6) where "fish dart among their bones" (line 20) and to celebrate the experiences and sacrifices of all Americans. Indeed, "God's deliberate eye" (line 24) watches not only over the ruined monument, but also over those who have neglected it. The palindromic rhyme scheme (ABCCBA) that Trethewey uses reads the same backward and forward, suggesting that the history of the Native Guard continues to be disremembered in the moment of the poem's composition. Thus, like the "casemates, cannons, the store that sells / souvenirs," the poem itself joins other "tokens of history long buried" (lines 11–12). Further, the monument to Confederate soldiers who also died there serves as another palimpsest—a partially erased surface upon which Trethewey can write the lives of the Native Guard. In inscribing and describing the *Native Guard*'s missing history onto a monument already memorializing "some of the dead," the speaker's detailed and layered seeing becomes an enhanced remembrance (line 6).

A more recent poem by Trethewey, "We Have Seen," performs a

reverse architectural ekphrasis, with its speaker looking outward from a church. The act of seeing a building and understanding its meaning and function in community and history is described from inside of the building, framed by the church's choice of east-facing windows with the depiction of a protective Christ figure in stained glass.[27] The poem could serve as a distillation of Trethewey's palimpsestic poetics that both sees and sees beyond "the ruined tableau" (line 18)—in this case, the bombing of the 16th Street Baptist Church in Birmingham, Alabama, on September 15, 1963, as stated in the headnote. Though the speaker is unable to change what happened, the poem nevertheless provides the reader with an alternate understanding of the tragic and yet politically galvanizing event that killed four little girls. History might allow for this alternate understanding imaginatively or continue to deny it through repeated brutality. Trethewey invites the reader to imagine an alternate history in which the girls live: "If you could look beyond it—/ the palimpsest of wreckage" (lines 18–19). She uses photographic language to describe the figure who captures the scene on camera, a painterly snapshot of someone who used his lens to make the moment bear eternal witness to that terrorist act (lines 27–30). Once again, she layers an event, palimpsestically, with a fictional photograph, masterfully linking history with imagination and fact with a futile longing for a possible safer future for Black parishioners. But even the images of Jesus are not spared: "his body left nearly intact / but faceless, after the blast" (lines 37–38).

"It is commonplace that the landscape is inscribed with the traces of things long gone," Trethewey writes in *Beyond Katrina*.[28] With both land and memory as palimpsestic surfaces, the parallels consistently drawn, her oeuvre contains carefully tended and boldly asserted personal and political histories, rendered with a fiercely intelligent attention to those whose lives have no national monuments, whose existence risks being dismissed or forgotten, calling to mind sacrifices of all Americans, "God's deliberate eye" not only watching over the ruined monument but those who have neglected it.

If *Thrall* uses the casta paintings as an entrée into an examination of her own mixed-race heritage, then similarly, *Bellocq's Ophelia* might also be considered "in thrall to a word"—specifically, mulatto, in particular its connotations to the depicted women but also in a larger sociocultural context relating to the complexities of race within the male gaze, while imagining the interior and daily lives to accompany the often mournful faces in Bellocq's photographs.

In his essay "Seeing and Using: Art and Craftsmanship," poet and Nobel laureate Octavio Paz maintains that "the act of seeing is transformed into an intellectual operation that is also a magical rite: to see is to understand and to understand is to commune."[29] If that is true, then the pattern Trethewey succeeds most in imagining into those places where it seems the poet discovers a truth in the process of the writing, the poem having taken on a life of its own. Supposing a conflation between the observer and the observed means that the speaker's fictive imaginings blur the lines between feelings and a sense of the historic, bringing the subject's presence to life in a visceral way. "Vignette" is representative, with the photograph as delicate palimpsest for history, history as source for story, and story as imagined memory. Trethewey takes the woman out of the photograph via conjecture, away from the sitting and Bellocq and into the interiority, where he nonetheless "waits / for the right moment, a look on her face / to keep in a gilded frame, the ornate box / he'll put her in."[30]

The poet Edward Hirsch gives his take on ekphrasis in an interview, noting the expansion of the definition of poetry via ekphrasis, and describes a relational evolution of the genre made possible in part "by the . . . cross-fertilization of the arts."[31] If, as art critic and curator Nicolas Bourriaud maintains in *Relational Aesthetics*, "[a]rt is a state of encounter,"[32] then Trethewey's "Vignette"[33] (and perhaps *Bellocq's Ophelia* in general) depicts that encounter in a way that becomes a new encounter between text and reader via photograph. Such a Russian doll of literary art—poems encountering photographs which encounter their subjects—cannot be anything but complex, despite the deceptively simple language in the poem. "Vignette" looks at what Bellocq interpreted photographically and imagines it beyond surface impressions to speculate on what the subject, once a living woman, might see, "stepping out/of the frame, wide-eyed, into her life" (lines 34–35). That kind of layered understanding is part of the power of ekphrasis. As Paz notes in "The New Analogy: Poetry and Technology": "Poetry is time unveiled: the enigma of the world translated into enigmatic transparency."[34] The enigma in the poem is the woman in the photograph and not her image, "how / Bellocq takes her, her brow furrowed / as she looks out to the left, past all of them" (lines 30–32). The transparency Trethewey speculatively creates unquestionably situates that woman in the world—a world that would deny her thoughts and dreams voice, would deny her life's validity or downgrade its value simply because of her race and gender and circumstance, asking us to "imagine her" (line 33) both in her time and in our time in history. Using ekphrasis, Trethewey unveils the possible inner life of an enigmatic persona, thus fleshing out and giving import to someone whose anonymity heretofore mostly served the photographer. She finds a medium to incorporate history and empathy, a portrait of a portrait, a moment captured in situ with a figure who reaches forward in time to speak through both image and history-infused imagination of a life.

The most compelling pieces in *Bellocq's Ophelia* are those in which much is at stake; variations from the subtlety of gesture and straight description of the photographs widen the lens, so to speak, bringing us into the very real danger of skin and gender in the early twentieth century. The section "March 11" from "Letters from Storyville" uses persona, with the speaker compelled to recall the Southern atmosphere of racial violence ("news of another lynching where you are / dredges the silt of my memory") when news of the 1911 Triangle Shirtwaist fire appears:

Such things come as less and less
a shock. Everywhere there are the dead and dying—
disease taking them slowly, or violence with its quick
and steady hand. In the paper today, tragedy
in New York City—a clothing factory, so many women

dying in a fire. The place they worked, locked up tight,
became a tomb. I live where I work. Will I die here
too? I read that some chose a last moment of flight,
leaping nine stories to their deaths. Others stayed
inside, perhaps to be burned clean
in the fire's embrace, to rise again through the flames.[35]

Trethewey's poem highlights the illusion of human separation, using the lens of death to demonstrate the connectedness that most hierarchical cultures, including America's, deny with economic and ethnic divisions, but which comes vividly alive in Western artwork.[36] Perhaps that is why Trethewey chooses to do so much ekphrasis, and marry it with memory; the image divulges its secrets in immediate ways, the truth of their messages felt incontrovertibly, however subjective that truth. The persona in Trethewey's poem further helps the reader to identify with the fear of failing, dying ("will I die here, too?"), of succumbing to circumstance beyond one's control. The epistolary address creates an intimacy that calls Édouard Glissant's characterization of Middle Passage to mind, of how the "original victim floating toward the sea's abysses, an exception," is yet part of something larger, "something shared," which holds familiarity: "Relation is not made up of things that are foreign but of shared knowledge."[37]

Glissant is talking about "the first uprooting" of displacement, of the Middle Passage, but in many ways the violence Trethewey depicts and the human connections that cannot help but be made, despite and in the midst of it, suggest that without reckoning with that first uprooting, violence will continue. The poet, ever hopeful, finds the language for the beauty of survival alongside the hideousness of brutality. For Trethewey, narrative holds space for that dichotomy and crystallizes the truest feeling of that holding inside the reader's imagination, and transfers that feeling to them. As Muriel Rukeyser wrote in her introduction to *The Life of Poetry*, "The work that a poem does is a transfer of human energy,"[38] and Trethewey accomplishes that by uniting the mechanisms of story and image, both literally and technically.

One of the powers of ekphrasis lies in its ability to layer an image with story, and it is not easy to do well. A poet can too quickly give in to the urge to remain in the top layer of the literal. But story is the way deeper. Bourriaud writes that "art and psychic life are interwoven with the same agencies,"[39] something Trethewey's poetry performs as the subjectivity of art, history, and memory coincide. Rita Dove, in her introduction to Trethewey's *Domestic Work*, offers a quote that fits all of the latter's books: "'People are trapped in history,' James Baldwin has said, 'and history is trapped in them,'" noting Trethewey's "challenge: to bear witness and give face to the legions of nameless men and women who cooked, scrubbed, welded, shoveled, hauled and planted for an entire nation."[40]

Like Gwendolyn Brooks did for the "nameless" in Chicago, whom she did name, in poems like "The Anniad" and "The Ballad of Chocolate Mabbie" and many, many others, Trethewey elegizes those "Whom the higher gods forgot / Whom the lower gods berate"[41] with sharp visual attention and an eye for the subtle that has developed further since, such as with the formal pieces in *Native Guard*. In contrast to the more visceral and stark images and the ballad-esque lyric approach of Brooks, she addresses the daily gorgeousness of people who might go unnoticed in a culture that values flash and opulence, that sees only those with the kind of beauty that is mass advertised, and even then, only their outsides generally, not their character. Trethewey's lyrics weave slowly and softly, carefully document snapshot moments rather than unfold in a dialogic spin; the music of them feels less songlike and more compositional, gestural—like the photograph.

As Hirsch pointed out, "The more that poetry encounters the other arts, the more it becomes conscious of what it can and cannot do, what is boundless in it and what is limited in it in terms of what language can do."[42] Indeed, about Lorna Simpson's photographs, whose famous works depict enigmatic domestic scenes (stills from the 1997 film *Interior/Exterior* being of note) and Black women with their backs turned, artist Coco Fusco writes that she "admired [Simpson's] work's elegance and sense of restraint. Those enigmatic and alluring black female figures with their backs turned or their faces out of frame came to stand for a generation's mode of looking and questioning photographic representation."[43] The same could be said of Trethewey's work, wherein gesture takes on the same kind of role it does in painting, capturing the full meaning of a moment, and making the object emblematic.

Another poem from *Domestic Work* does just that with an everyday object for Black women—the hot comb, an iconic but dreaded instrument that gets heated on a stove in order to straighten coiled or curly hair. "Hot Combs" finds its aliveness through the senses: "At the junk shop, I find an old pair, / black with grease, the teeth still pungent / as burning hair."[44] Then, she begins to connect it to her own memory, an associative leap backward in time:

[. . .] *Holding it,*
I think of my mother's slender wrist,
the curve of her neck as she leaned
over the stove, her eyes shut as she pulled

the wooden handle and laid flat the wisps
at her temples. *(lines 5–10)*

The vivid physical gestures are familiar and delicate, particular to Black women, and imbued with love: "The heat in our kitchen / made her glow that morning I watched her / wincing, the hot comb singeing her brow" (lines 10–13). But the speaker's depiction of the mother also acknowledges the visceral pain and risk of injury that accompanies the act of pressing one's curls straight, as well as the perspiration-inducing effort required: "sweat glistening above her lips, / her face made strangely beautiful / as only suffering can do" (lines 17–19).[45] The self-immolation present in "Hot Combs" may seem trivial to some, but in capturing that moment Trethewey extrapolates upon a history of pain that plays itself out in the grooming process. The poem has Trethewey's signature child-hood reflection from a very adult point of view that understands the painful contortions racism imposes on the body and the mind. In particular, Black women contend with damaging standards of beauty that her own mate and/or community subscribe to, straightening one's hair even if burning hair and tender parts of the skin (typically the back of the neck, forehead, or behind the ear) in the process.

While "Hot Combs" is not overtly ekphrastic, the portrait of the commonplace object, used to transform Black women's hair from its natural state to one closer to white women's hair texture via an often painful ritual, serves as an instrument that allows Trethewey to showcase the pervasiveness of racism's effects, from the very small gesture to the very significant violence. Even the making of beauty for Black women is a small violence, the poem seems to say ("I watched her wincing"; "her face made strangely beautiful/as only suffering can do"). The object itself becomes slightly menacing, even as it bears witness with its "black with grease, teeth still pungent/as burning hair," and contrasts with the delicate rendering of the mother's "slender wrist." The need to look more like a white person, to heat the hair in order to, has encroached upon the mother's body and the speaker sees the effort, the "eyes shut," the "sweat glistening on her lip," watching more than just the hot comb "singeing her brow." One can extrapolate that the dance between pain and beauty in an effort to groom oneself into fitting into an external paradigm not meant for the mother in the poem parallels Black efforts at integrating into white society. You can go through the motions, but there's a good chance you might get hurt, and at the very least, such a practice will leave its mark.

Domestic Work, comprised of incisive textual portraits of ordinary women rendered extraordinary by their particularities, their strength, "their dailiness" as Trethewey writes, in action, such as in "Gesture of a Woman in Process": "hands circling," and "the white blur of her apron / still in motion." Still, her poems move beyond ekphrasis to become stand-alone textual portraits—visual, tactile, revelatory, qualities even more pronounced in *Bellocq's Ophelia*. The complexities and contradictions of the dramatic tragic mulatto story re-envisioned by an eye that sees not only outward, but inward; the external as gateway and mask simultaneously.

Then in *Native Guard*, the linguistic elevation into legend of Black Delta soldiers makes evident the irony of fighting for a land one isn't safe to be in, entwined with personal tragedies, connected by national racial conflict, perpetuated and inflicted by and upon its citizenry of all colors. Trethewey's collections embody that tumultuous brew, where "[w]hat matters is context—[. . .] how suddenly/everything can go wrong."[46] The respite is often not a respite. What is asked even of God may have an answer too devastating to beg for. As in *Beyond Katrina*, where Trethewey tackles the way the tragic hurricane and its aftermath affected her home state of Mississippi, which, with all the attention on New Orleans, went somewhat neglected in terms of aid, media coverage, and recovery.[47] The devastation serves as an entry point into before, during, and after in the slow motion of a page that mirrors the lasting moment it describes.

As a figure painter might work to transfer her internalized impression of an imagined or actual body onto canvas to create a kind of filtered representation, Natasha Trethewey works to extract language from interiority, transform it into physicality and then to the atmospheric where readers may experience its weight. Trethewey's poems are muscled and elegant, meant to experience aloud. Refined style creates contrast and tension with raw emotion, restrained only by the forms she chooses. Restraint can be overrated in these extreme times we live in, but her courage content-wise trumps any timidity the word restraint implies. In other words, binding to craft leaves the poems unfettered and uncluttered by device. As in Lucille Clifton's work, clarity marries complexity on narrative levels, but in ways that belie any surface attraction or accusations of simplicity. "It is commonplace that the landscape is inscribed with the traces of things long gone,"[48] Trethewey writes in *Beyond Katrina*. With both land and memory as palimpsest, the parallels consistently drawn, her overall oeuvre contains myriad important discoveries, carefully tended and boldly asserted. Undoubtedly, her poems' fiercely intelligent attention to humanity, place, emotion, and history mark Trethewey as one of the finest stewards of collective memory in contemporary letters.

Poetics of Intuition, Love, and Integrity

Black Time and Geographic Space in *The Blue Clerk*

If intuition means understanding through feeling, Dionne Brand's *The Blue Clerk* manages to deliver, through the music of vivid scenes and imaginative sentences, a narrative wholly steeped in such understanding. With a series of prose poems called Versos, she deals with the archive as extant, active architecture requiring constant tending: archive as memory and its fractal echoes, as conceptual architecture, as secretly inherited knowledge and hidden territories, as evolving grammar or set of rules for negotiating the consequences of enforced absences. Brand frames the archive via the book design conceit of the left-hand pages,[1] creating an extended metaphor for envisioning presences of the past while giving voice to possible futures, and never ignoring the events of the present. The effect results in an analytical continuity that feels simultaneously happening in the moment and in the eventful but unfixed past, while stitching itself into a future Black existence characterized by complex multiplicity. The characters of the author and the blue clerk converse seamlessly in a dialogue sharpened by awareness, a clarity that wounds and heals at once. The result is a radical integrity which has at its core a unity between love and intuition. Situating that unity within discussions of the book's use of black time and geographic space further acknowledges Brand's habit of making time represent space and vice versa, with geography standing in for time.

Before I get into explication, however, I want to review a few baseline assumptions. First, I use the word *radical* intentionally, since its first definition simply means *of or going to the root or origin*. Brand is interested in definitional radicality, as in defining the root significance of certain words and how they function, starting with the structural basis of the book in versos. Latin for *reverse*, as in the reverse side of the right-hand page in book design, verso in Brand's usage indicates a commitment to reversals of documentation inseparable from the official record. Indeed, repetitive usage identifies them as official for the book's purposes, as vital to the completeness of the document they are contained in. That document or documents in which the verso plays its role exists in the archive. Particularly, if the living *body* becomes archival (or neo-archival, to invoke Erica L. Johnson) in Brand's poetic, critical memoir *A Map to the Door of No Return*, the living mind and body come together with the living *world* with the archive—and all of it becomes part of the blue clerk's patient accounting.

In *The Blue Clerk,* Brand uses the narrative as an attempt at mirroring or, to return to the term verso, reversal. As Johnson writes: "Brand structures something as intimate as personal memory and identity as an intervention in the archive."[2] So, just as the archive intervenes in her own memory-work in *A Map*, Brand's blue clerk intervenes in the archives, resulting in an enhancement of both—archive and memory benefiting and challenging each other. Indeed, if the blue clerk is the work itself, Brand situates the imagined archival text within the larger archive of cultural memory: "The clerk, despite the weight of things, loves her work, or, one might say, because the clerk is a creation of the work she is indefinable from the work or, better still, the work is the clerk."[3] That kind of radical eclipsing of separation can only have at its root an obsession with the same origins Brand maintains too much has been made of,[4] even if the goal is to redefine those origins, to root them out, or destabilize their connotations to the point of unity. Interest in lexical accuracy is core to radical poetics, with the apparent destabilization actually serving to create the kind of "deep knowing" Toni Morrison describes in her May 1985 letter in *Essence* referenced in my first chapter.

The Blue Clerk begins with a "S T I P U L E," defined in an italicized subtitle: "*A small leaf-like appendage to a leaf,*" signaling that not only that opening stanza but the poems within the book overall form an organically connected structure. S T I P U L E begins with the blue clerk pronouncing, with regard to silence: "I have left this unsaid. I have withheld. What is withheld is the left-hand page. [. . .] I have withheld more than I have written. Evergreen and deciduous. Incurable. And uneasy, and like freight" (3). The withheld information has tree-like qualities—alive, rooted in the earth, but then uprooted, perhaps carried across land or sea, cut down to be used in production. That violence and its resultant damage are "incurable"—as is the damage done by displacements of peoples across time.

Following that poem, the clerk delivers the stories of several women, both anonymous and known, most of whom are in the process of moving around geographically, whether that travel comes from adventurous intention or necessity: "a woman leaving by boat" (15), "a woman who did not want to be in the world, or the world she was dragged into, who noticed right away the fatal harm but who gave birth to a woman who wanted to be in the world true and absolutely whole and therefore lived with ghosts since that world could not happen yet" (18); "a great-grandmother, Angelina, who fled in a pirogue across the four Bocas del Dragón. From the ragged coast of one island to the ragged coast of another" (20); "there is always a girl on a bicycle because the author cannot ride a bicycle" (25). Brand weaves the women's stories with the author's and the blue clerk's, having the effect of populating the world of this book with a glut of often unnamed (but never nameless) women who might be considered background elsewhere, whose silences have been counted on, even enforced (48).

Initially, it is difficult to follow who is speaking, much less whose story is being told, which further blurs the edges of separation between beings and between times. Such blurring, or perhaps more accurately, refusal of separation, invites the reader to intuit, through close attention, who they believe is speaking. What is clear is that the clerk (if not/and the author) has a powerful impulse to record, to enlighten, to witness in place: "here's where what we do is listen, lonely listen to the blood and the rowdy idioms of these cities jagging east, then west" (48). Active and wide-ranging attention flexes the intuition through the pain of loss, to arrive at the always-arriving scenes of memory whole, the newness of recognition made ancient by the acts of remembrance imagined, activated, and accessed by listening across geographic space.

One gets the sense that the lost archives of those cities and beyond are indeed accessible, even with the irreparable—incurable—ruptures of colonialism, displacement, enslavement, and racism. How? Through an imaginative self that remains open and willing to engage intuitively with questions that have lain dormant in the suppressed archive. In Verso 18.3

of the text, Brand offers this exchange between the clerk and the author: "Why did you visit these sites of terror? I went to visit the world. I went to visit the years of solidarity with the world I was in solidarity with" (105). The clerk asks and the author answers, both of them locating their phrases in terms of place, those places equanimous—sites of terror for the clerk and the world for the author, who then takes things a step further into time. How does one visit years, for example? The author explains:

> I had read thousands of newspapers, I had followed the arguments, I had chosen sides. I had lived through, like someone on the other side of a telephone line, all the events, all the events had shaped me though they had not happened to me in the same way as they had happened to the speaker on the other end of the telephone. (105)

Thus, one visits years by paying attention to both history and the present, by empathizing, standing in place alongside another via an imagining based upon feeling and research—a felt knowing. And what does one then do with that knowing, that newly created intimacy with the archive? For the author, communication follows: "I therefore visited to say to the air and the bodies, to the electrical wires—Here I am, I was on the other end of the telephone during all those years" (105). Communication was always possible, then, but the knowledge of that possibility couldn't be accessed without the intuited impulse to engage in it.

Ironically, I think the historical rupture imposed by slavery and colonization both necessitates intuitive communication and understanding at the same time it works to impede knowledge and communication of all kinds. Luckily, as Calvin Warren writes in "Black Time: Slavery, Metaphysics, and the Logic of Wellness," "Black time is without duration; it is a horizon of time that eludes objectification."[5] If that is true, then Brand's concretized and animated embodiment of archival existences holds an intuitive logic that needs no justification, but does benefit from elucidation. With *The Blue Clerk*, she provides a text that understands implicitly how slavery operates as an architecture in western systems of thinking, believing, and relating—"a violent metaphysical enterprise" we navigate. He asks, in parentheses: "(Can we envision modern civil society without slavery?)."[6] Brand answers Warren's question via the archive that the blue clerk shepherds, and that the author channels. If "thinking in Black time forces a reconsideration of the critical categories of analysis—history, linearity, progress, movement and ethics,"[7] then Brand's poems as archival engagement directly apply the tenets of Black time, not only forcing the reconsideration Warren posits, but bypassing the named categories altogether. Or, by integrating them into the prose poem form she operates in, absorbing those categories into the intuitive-imaginative space that the narrative invites.

Warren writes that for folks whose existence has been characterized by a continuous barrage of externally imposed definitions, controlling "the production and semiotics of meaning" is paramount.[8] However, instead of adopting the negative connotations of the "homelessness" and "disorientation" Warren mentions,[9] Brand uses movement to document the traces of stories in the archive alongside the present and possible future resonances of those stories and the ruptures. Brand's grammar in *The Blue Clerk* is profoundly human, not systemic in a synthetic or anthropogenic way, but in a natural way—instinctive, vibrant, simultaneous in attention. Such a grammar exists not in opposition except as its existence itself might be perceived as oppositional, even if not conceptualized that way.

Brand does not try to "get over" what Warren calls the event horizon[10] as much as she moves through it, using an intuitive structure of language—poetry. She creates anthropomorphic metaphors via the clerk's attention to letters which almost metamorphose into animals: "The clerk is noiseless, intent on the marsupial sighs of each letter of the alphabet" (221). The humanity of that metamorphosis is also linked to injury or injurious growth—not without violence. The clerk's description of the marsupial sigh follows: "A cyst in the floor of the mouth, a ruptured salivary gland. The marsupialization of the ranula, cutting a slit into an abscess. Allowing the sublingual gland to re-establish its connection with the oral cavity" (221). Thus, we have a repeated image system that returns to the notion of rupture situated within the body, but also shows the rupture's ability to cause healing, to re-create connection.

When I met Brand at the National Women's Studies Association conference in Atlanta on November 10, 2018, she said thank you for reading *through* the work, the word *through* emphasized by implied italics in sound and a hand gesture imitating a dive through air. If "we need a new grammar to describe black experience with the event-horizon as it fractures ethics and metaphysics" as Warren calls for,[11] perhaps that grammar also contains an ability to move through, a through-line not built necessarily of metaphysical or ethical arguments, but a dailiness which embodies those arguments intuitively. As Brand writes: "And it is not that our days and nights are not filled with the anxiety of finding a job, a place to live, things to eat, dangers of violence, domestic and public, but our lives are also filled with a comfort and certainty of the truly catastrophic happening at a distance" (64).

The catastrophic and the everyday exist simultaneously, and thus both are quotidian. Living with and moving through that kind of reality requires a sensate fortitude, and that fortitude is anything but ordinary. The narrator muses of the author: "She would like a nice life, the kind she hears about on the right-hand page . . . where the clerk does not exist. I would like to be plain, the author says. But the clerk rejoins . . . To be plain requires so much work, you have to sandpaper all the viscera, and every branchial cleft" (81).

Plainness is cast aside in favor of sensorial clarity, accuracy, and physical endurance. The clerk declares, in reference to natural disasters: "I have plans; I have no plans. They disappear in the Gulf of Mexico like brown pelicans and hermit crabs in an oil spill. Isn't it time we stopped saying spill? That wasn't a spill it was a deluge" (43). The precision of words serves as an intentional counterpoint to the notion of an accidental oil spill; the point here—that the destructive flood of oil that takes the lives of living things "has no mercy" (43) and the language should reflect that accurately. Indeed, the clerk similarly continues in alignment: "I have no mercy" (43)—i.e., the clerk maintains a merciless attention to the archive's integrity.

Katherine McKittrick, in her essay "Worn Out," explains: "black impossibilities are not new: so many of us are too real to be real."[12] Brand's acute awareness of that impossibility permeates *The Blue Clerk*, down to the imagined clerk, author, and narrator that as a trio perhaps stand in for facets of Brand herself—perhaps. But they are made to feel as real as blackness, and I have come to the conclusion that blackness and its concomitant realities feel impossible because, in large part, blackness is love. The love that blackness is has survived impossible circumstances, continuously transcending or moving through the egregious dailiness of oppression, and the concurrent catastrophes of colonization, climate disasters, and other endlessly-enforced inequalities. It is love that exists across and in defiance of time, and in spite of the re-wounding of time's passage. Passage of time—again we return to the Middle Passage, that seemingly inescapable site of trauma, as a thing imposed continuously. Love is also such a force, however. *The Blue Clerk* contends with that love via the very constraints that would obliterate that love, and in full use of all of the impossibilities blackness contains, even when blackness isn't explicitly claimed as a stance.

Significantly, Brand talks little of blackness directly, as identity or otherwise. Hortense Spillers, in "Mama's Baby Papa's Maybe: An American Grammar Book," writes that Black women in the white imagination are necessary for the continuance of white domination: "My country needs me, and if I were not here, I would have to be invented." But for Brand, the conversation with Spillers seems to focus on what the latter calls "confounded identities." She maintains that "they are markers so loaded with mythical prepossession that there is no easy way for the agents buried beneath them to come clean."[13] Brand's character or avatar of the blue clerk acts as such an invented agent, unburying an archive, tasked to deliver the left-hand pages, to produce and preserve the happenings across time despite persistent obstacles and systemic attempts at complete erasure. Too, the global legacy of slavery means that the common experience of familial and ancestral rupture applies widely.

The Blue Clerk thus is also in conversation with Michelle Wright's discussion of epiphenomenal time as opposed to the "linear progress narrative" in *Physics of Blackness,* in which "time predicates motion" rather than the reverse.[14] The relationship of time concepts to movement impelled by imperialism haunts the versos; repeatedly readers witness continuous movement through both time and space. Wright, quoting Dan Falk: "René Descartes [. . .] saw time as a measure of motion but considered the idea of duration as something subjective, 'a mode of thinking.'"[15] Brand does the same kind of thinking-writing with time, and additionally, feeling—not that that feeling seems to do anyone any kind of good. The author reflects: "I used to think that poetry had the force of action and still, sometimes, in sentimental moments you may find me waxing on that subject. But it does not have the force of action, as can easily be proven. Poetry is not even information" (177). That seems to dislodge my argument for poetics of intuition on the surface, yet as this verso continues, and in subsequent poems, Brand slyly offers up proofs of what that quote denies. First, though, the author continues: "I know I've said over the years that poetry in its most profound meaning tries to perform the job of saying that which needs to be said or thought, to apprehend the slippery quality of being human. Now, that all sounds childish and sloppy to me" (177). Then the clerk interjects, disrupting the denial with a single short question: "Now, as opposed to when?" (177). Brand thus presents us with the feeling that the repeated *now* is what exists—in the past, present, and future. Wright articulates her theory of epiphenomenal time with that kind of *now*, "always in process—that is, the present and future are not discrete moments but rather are conflated into the one moment that is the now."[16]

After the clerk's challenge question, on the subway the author comes to "meet my early self, my young and tender self" (192). Instead of warning that young self not to rely on love—"I depend on something so thin, says the author, so thin" (178)—she allows her to continue her journey, *naiveté* intact: "so the author leaves her tender self on the train" (193). Rather than cause a rupture in her past self's thinking, she (perhaps lovingly) protects it, and arguably retains it even in her present cynicism.

Given that sense of protection, it is significant that Brand leans into the color blue for the clerk. The clerk who reconstructs, outside colonial constraints and outside the limits of place and time, the archives of memory and history and indeed living itself, is not black, but a phantom-like being made of blue ink, recalling both ocean depths and the vastness of the night sky—mysterious presences, unfathomable. Throughout *The Blue Clerk*, Brand's poems offer us color: blue, yellow, violet as painterly presences that invite us to imagine and create futures in which beauty remains steadfast under the world's (and time's) violent onslaught. The poems' existential concerns embody visually the same evolution that we (can) undergo, perhaps using color the same way Brand uses time and space—to shake loose common assumptions, and to allow for an infusion of imagination into the real to make it more real—as real and affective as memory itself.

Further, perhaps, as Hartman writes, Brand in writing so imaginatively collapses time—the archive as a conversation with those past, future, and living now—collective memory within that imagining and vice versa.[17] While Hartman's essay focuses on writing about slavery, and Brand's narrative expands beyond it into the future, *The Blue Clerk* does contend/cannot help contending with that historical rupture upon an encounter with Ghana's notorious Elmina castle:

> In December, any December, standing in Elmina, the dirt floor, the damp room of the women's cells, nation loses all vocabulary. Loses its whole alphabet. I have no debts. I have no loves. [. . .] Of course the earth is beneath your feet and so there must be place or the feeling of place or gravity. But which nation ever said of a woman she is human? (40)

There is defiance in those lines, a defiant affirmation of humanity externally denied. And by the end of the book, we return to an Elmina populated by gods—presumably, the ghosts of the people who passed through, though I doubt Brand would approve of my describing them in such a pedestrian way. The clerk arrives at the sacred-haunted site accompanied by the author. Their interaction with the gods unfolds in a way that releases them to the past, it seems:

> We awakened our gods, and we left them there, since we never needed gods again. We did not have wicked gods so they understood. They lay in their corners, on their disintegrated floors, they lay on their walls of skin dust. They stood when we entered, happy to see us. (223)

Their survival meant remembrance, devotion: "We were pilgrims, they were gods. They said with wonder and admiration, you are still alive, like hydrogen, like oxygen. We all stood there for some infinite time. We did weep but that is nothing in comparison" (223). Warren writes, "black grief is untemporizable,"[18] and Brand offers Verso 55 as proof.

The poems in *The Blue Clerk* take refuge in the imagination, releasing geographically-based constraints in favor of imaginative freedom, which feels more in alignment with a self in conversation with the world she traverses. McKittrick notes further: "I think that Brand argues that the cosmogonies of black geographies are not about geography, as we know it." Instead, "black is in the break, it is fantastic . . . a mirror, it is water, air; black is flying and underground; it is time-traveling, supernatural, interplanetary."[19] If that is true, if blackness is a liminal kind of totality,[20] then Brand uses blackness as a site of possibility, of infinite creative options, even when colliding with the troublesome archive. Brand finds time a descriptor for place, and place stands in for time—again, a reversal, creating an opportunity to think differently about nearly everything. That circularity asks the reader to surrender to a kind of knowing related more to interior feeling than to externalized or learned/delivered information. Poem-like, via the mechanism of repetition, we are invited to meaning(s) that intend to be understood through that feeling.

In other words, finding the repetitions embedded in the book rewards the reader with an imaginative critical argument based on feeling, with the body as a site of sense and sensing, rather than externally imposed restrictions. By using the uncontainable elements of time, space, and the imagination to frame her journeying through the world and the archive and memory, Brand fashions an intuitive compass that reaches a kind of transcendence which manages to be earth-bound and boundless at once. Roland Barthes writes of such texts as "[texts] of bliss: the text that . . . unsettles the reader's historical, cultural, psychological assumptions . . . brings to a crisis [their] relation with language."²¹ It is appropriate to use philosophy and the notion of bliss as a touchstone for reading *The Blue Clerk*, as the study of thought connects to Brand's textual approach across genres and fields, and the act of reading is just as important to the book as its material quality as a created thing.

Verso 31, for example, makes the case that the jazz album *Pithecanthropus Erectus* by Charles Mingus "is not music, let us say, it is sound; it is a text of philosophical charge" (165). What Brand writes after, or aims for, via intuition and feeling, is a way of understanding and communicating without the burden or violence of hierarchic categories. She maintains: "as I read it there is no way of translating this text yet. Its language rejects a conventional translation; that is, once you attempt to translate it into the sense of a language with vowels and consonants say, that is the sort of language that directs sound" (165). It seems that, in directing sound, a listener is invited to follow, to participate, to become part of the experience of the text. Said another way, to experience the text is to understand it—as one would a poem—but not to "direct sound in a particular direction . . . let us say into the direction of known conventional languages that we use to 'communicate' with." (165). Try to force or concretize the understanding, and "you are lost. Or the meaning is lost to you. But why talk of translation. That is not really the point" (165).

Indeed, intuition and surrender relate to one another in the form of knowing—a confident knowing that is felt rather than articulated. "Mingus suggests another territory," one that a listener can traverse and absorb, witness and feel; she repeats much of Verso 31 in Verso 32 on the next page, deepening her conviction: "No, it is not music," she insists; "its ineffability demands another larynx" (166), again making physical the mode of comprehension.

Listening repeatedly to all twenty-five minutes and five seconds of the album[22] on a new release of the 1973 recording, one gets the feeling that its capaciousness and variety led Brand to devote those several versos to it, but further, perhaps, its engagement with the musical archive. In a 2018 review, *Rolling Stone* called it "a niche document"[23] (Shteamer para.7), and credits the less famous musicians who backed Mingus for the album's success overall: "what looks marginal on paper turns out to be sheer joy coming out of the speakers, thanks in large part to Mingus' lesser-known yet enormously gifted sidemen."[24] The reviewer's choice of description—"what looks marginal on paper turns out to be sheer joy"— sidles up to Brand's discussion of the piece as "a text of philosophical charge" (166). What does joy have to do with philosophy? Perhaps the answer resides in repetition.[25] If "the persistent connection of physical and territorial suppression, attachment and extermination with cultural inadequacy" has hounded Hegelian definitions of black culture, as James Snead maintains in his essay "On Repetition in Black Culture,"[26] then the Charlie Mingus Jazz Workshop disconnects from that narrative. Indeed, "Mingus suggests another territory" (166) as does *The Blue Clerk*—a territory that perhaps cannot be translated, but it can be felt—intuited and loved for itself, as itself, in its philosophical charge and sonic beauty.

Snead writes that "The African . . . overturns all European categories of logic . . . [and] allows 'accidents and surprises' to take hold of his fate."[27] The improvisation and indefinable flow of jazz compositions stands in for such "accidents and surprises" which favor the joy of creating, especially in the midst of difficulty caused by racial oppression. Thus, the act of improvisation *itself* becomes the repetition rather than the recordable compositional elements themselves. If indeed, as Snead argues, repetition in Black culture is "often in homage to an original generative instance or act,"[28] then perhaps further, repeated listenings allow us to participate in the creativity we celebrate. Completion in its traditional sense then seems less important than completion through participation, and recompletions upon return can vary or disappear, depending on the reader and their mood or intention. The poems in *The Blue Clerk* at times function with that cut; after a repetition, the unexpected enters; sometimes hard, sometimes soft; sometimes insistent, sometimes playful; dense, or laden with white space serving as quiet or silence—in conversation with the compositional range of the song she devotes repetitive attention to in the book. Snead maintains that "repetition takes place on . . . the purest tonal and timbric level."[29] Brand is trying to get at that tonal accuracy at the deepest level of language—and chooses the intuitive integrity of poetry to deliver it.

Brand's ruminations via the author, the blue clerk, and the poems themselves explore an identity defined by its feeling—internally derived, not externally imposed. If, as Snead points out, there has been an enforced separation of European culture from Black culture,[30] Brand's poems discard the notion that the veil of force is inevitable. They easily expose the nature of humanity as whole, living, and translate efforts to the contrary—however legislated or monumental—as unnatural, fragmentary. In *A Map to the Door of No Return*, Brand says that "To write is to be involved in this act of translation, of succumbing or leaning into another body's idiom" (193). With *The Blue Clerk*, she goes further, creating an inky body through which to do that writing, to write the author's thoughts down only to lose them without regret, secure in knowing that archival spaces exist regardless of documentation, open remembrance, or legibility.

Dionne Brand's engagement with the fullness of Black existence is virtuosic and specific, painfully aware of the world's chaos and the impossible blackness McKittrick works to define. But the book is highly attuned to beauty, capable of attentive stillness even as it is anti-static. In that way, it employs intuition as a source of strength and intelligence, not taken for granted or ignored, but useful and actively incorporated into the author's and the clerk's dynamic ways of knowing. *The Blue Clerk* documents Brand's concern with culture, using recursiveness and repetition as light scaffolding for very heavy subject matter, the content providing a fleshly covering. As they compositionally approach the human, the poems in *The Blue Clerk* radically foreground the integrity and temporospatial expansiveness of poetic investigation, limned by intuition and, interchangeably with love, impossible blackness.

Poetics of Intuition and Feeling

Intuition holds ancient importance as a way of knowing, despite the mystery of its workings.[1] Intuition is the gut feeling, the felt understanding, the physical energy of what we know, translated into language. It provides an integral scaffolding to the construction of language into a text—what disappears when the text is complete, the insulation we don't see, but feel.

Scholar Akasha Hull connects intuition with our very aliveness. In the chapter "Bringing Beauty from Above" in her book *Soul Talk: The New Spirituality of African-American Women,* she describes aliveness in terms of wholeness, linking the body to feeling and intellect as part of consciousness.[2] That the discussion of intuition occurs in a chapter on beauty highlights its relevance to the making of beauty, to include art, which includes literature—acknowledging writing as artmaking, an active process that often engages intuitive methods.

As a writer and visual artist (however interiorized my visual practice), I am absolutely working in concert with intuition as I compose a poem or play, or draw or make a collage or a painting. I have not necessarily tried to define that creative process, but I feel the engine of intuition driving the act of making. When we drive or ride in a car, the engine isn't visible to us—the car's construction, its safety, requires the engine's enclosure. Nevertheless, we'd not move forward without that fundamental machinery. Too, most of us don't know *how* an engine works, just that it *does.* A mechanic, of course, is the exception; but even they must learn the finicky particularities of different types of engines, in all kinds of moving objects, and formal education can sometimes be irrelevant to the employment of that knowledge in fixing or maintaining them.[3] For the purposes of approaching a poetics of intuition, I'm less concerned with that specific how; rather, I find it vital to articulate *how to recognize its pres-*

ence in the experience of both reading and writing—and to respect that intuitive data, without furtive layers of secrecy or apology.

One identifying word for intuition in writing and other kinds of artmaking: channeling. A useful Merriam-Webster definition for channeling, the verb: to convey or direct.[4] Hull, in interviewing poet, novelist, and activist Alice Walker, clarifies the difference between passive channeling and a more unified or complete approach to making. This approach neither minimizes the unseen (consciousness) or the power of technical know-how gained through sustained practice; rather, it suggests using the mind to intentionally connect with "the larger realm of soul-spirit"—unifying "intelligence-training-skill-knowledge-discipline" and discernment as a means of reaching toward completely free expression.[5] If we know that such unification is effective, why does intuition hold such a diminished or hushed role in discussions of creativity and literary analysis? Why must measures of the creative process rely on a version of the scientific method to be considered intellectually valid or valuable?[6]

The prominence of so-called intellectually-based approaches to explicating literature has meant that intuition's value has been much overlooked—if even considered at all. Typical Western approaches to analyzing literature separate feeling from intellect, authorial intention from objectified product, and creative impulse from structural result.[7] Such pseudoscientific approaches to what is essentially an art, one that elicits both feeling and thinking, leaves unexamined one-half of the human response in terms of both creation and reaction. That ignorance sets up an analytical hierarchy that privileges the intellect over emotional and physical responses. Further, by focusing more on comparing differences than similarities, it can create a destructive—rather than *constructive*—system of thought. That kind of system foments homogeneity, not the diversity we claim to value in the present moment. The entire system of analysis must make room for a more elastic analytical system.

The late intellectual, activist, and literary critic Edward Said, in his collection of lectures *Humanism and Democratic Criticism*, goes after establishment literary critics like Harold Bloom as they opposed non-white entrants into the literary canon.[8] Said excoriates them for divisive discrimination rooted in racism, and goes on to note that guarding such exclusion advocates for homogenization.[9] His sarcastic tone points out the absurdity and hypocrisy embedded in such homogenization—especially when considered against the backdrop of America itself as a site of genocide—and Said maintains that such rigid stasis is unoriginal, stagnant, and hostile ground for new voices.[10]

University students have rebelled against such stasis in recent years, pressuring English departments to diversify their curriculum and causing many departments to remake their offerings or risk continued falling enrollment.[11] By contrast, much literature by indigenous writers, for example, cannot possibly be described as unimaginative or stagnant. Even depictions of the past in stories and histories and memories, both traditional and new, make room for cyclical movement and transformation. Indeed, in her essay "Imagining Indigenous Futurisms," editor Grace L. Dillon writes that "all forms of Indigenous futurisms are narratives of *biskaabiiyang*, an Anishinaabemowin word connoting the process of 'returning to ourselves,' which involves discovering how personally one is affected by colonization . . . and recovering ancestral traditions . . . [I]t requires changing rather than imitating Eurowestern concepts."[12] A person-centered approach to narrative makes liberal use of intuition as an awareness rooted within knowledge of both the self and an individual's culture as much as possible. Such works give primacy to *how* one feels and what one knows *by* feeling—delivering that knowing through story based on cyclicality. Intuition has thus held an unspoken foreground in much native literature and the writings of other so-called marginalized peoples—the global majority.

Said posits that more inclusive ways of thinking about literature, particularly canonical literature, in an overall humanist discourse lie in the etymology of the word *canon* itself, which has an Arabic root with two meanings that seem like opposites: a restrictive one that relates to law, and one that is freer and associated with music—multivocal, inventive, fluid.[13] Thus, a canon can be unified by innovation and discovery alongside strict formal concerns, while still allowing for deep complexity of craft, content, and context. That simultaneity particularly suits many examples of native literature with its generative narrative impulse fueled by motion, and tradition infused with orality. This unification, in practice, feels inclusive and open to those with the capacity to tell the stories with integrity, and further, avoids restricting the literary canon to only those with access to the kinds of knowledge touted as most valuable by and delivered through Western institutions according to their perceived authority.

In "The Ruins of Representation: Shadow Survivance and the Literature of Dominance," Anishinaabe writer and critic Gerald Vizenor writes that "representations of the tribal past are more than human mimesis and more than the aesthetic remains of reason in the literature of dominance."[14] Episodic structures throughout the novels, stories, and poems to be discussed in this chapter, alongside a fragmented temporality, ask the reader to rely more on feeling than logical progression. Surrendering to the author's pace and style of storytelling then rewards the reader with deeper understanding.

For example, we can return to Mahkatêwe-meshi-kêhkêhkwa's nonfiction narrative *Life of Black Hawk, or Ma-ka-tai-me-she-kia-kiak: Dictated by Himself,* which uses the same unified and continuous narrative style we find in Leslie Marmon Silko's *Ceremony,* published more than a century later. Neither book has chapters, section breaks, or transitional markers. Mahkatêwe-meshi-kêhkêhkwa's life story doesn't even have space between paragraphs. Though we cannot possibly know for sure if that was the translator's or publisher's decision or the author's, the singularity of the narrative structure feels very intentional. And while Silko relates Laguna stories and what Western readers might call mythologies that on the page resemble poems, Mahkatêwe-meshi-kêhkêhkwa's true-life story gives us an impassioned, of-the-moment record of one person's cogent understanding of and resistance to infectious settler philosophies of trickery and pretense:

> If the Great and Good Spirit wished us to believe and do as the whites, he could easily change our opinions, so that we would see, and think, and act as they do. We are *nothing* compared to His power, and we feel and know it. We have men among us, like the whites, who pretend to know the right path, but will not consent to show it without *pay!* I have no faith in their paths—but believe that every man must make his own path![15]

His reasoning here to me looks very much like a unification of thinking and feeling, or intuition ("we feel and know it"). The notion that knowledge comes from a spiritual source from within, and further, integrity, gives the logic of his conclusions an unassailable quality. He even structures his sentences through image-driven action set in a place and/or a time with aliveness and feeling suffused throughout, humanizing the mythology white settlers seemed intent on casting into more controllable realms of death and the past.[16]

The book's structure serves as one of our earliest examples of how feeling functions structurally in translated indigenous literature. There is an impulse toward non-interruption, structure-as-stream mirroring the way memory functions as changeable and living, demonstrating a unification of feeling and thought. Mahkatêwe-meshi-kêhkêhkwa's sentence work[17] holds that unity, just as his circumstances hold the contradictory desires to protect and preserve his family, and remain on his land: "I would rather have laid my bones with my forefathers, than remove for any consideration. Yet if a friendly offer had been made, as I expected, I would, for the sake of my women and children, have removed peaceably" (63). There is a fluidity to the sentences in this narrative, with an awareness of shifts in thought that flow naturally, gathering and returning. Mahkatêwe-meshi-kêhkêhkwa's stated intentions, however, did not matter to the settlers, and even though General Gaines's "people were permitted to pass and [. . .] treated with friendship by our people," his tribe was starved out, crops destroyed, attacked, and denied recourse, until ultimately forced out (63–64). Now a prisoner, he deeply lamented the loss of his country, and his anger remains an undercurrent in the language.[18]

Indeed, Mahkatêwe-meshi-kêhkêhkwa focuses on exposing the hypocrisy of white settlers rather than divulging any anthropological information about his former life aside from the ordinary—planting, harvesting, playing, working, being in community—the life settlers encroached upon and violently disrupted. His intuition and experience having told him that settlers cannot be trusted, he clearly offers readers a prescient warning steeped in intuition honed by experience: "I am very much afraid, that in a few years, they will begin to drive and abuse our people, as they have formerly done. I may not live to see it, but I feel certain that the day is not distant" (94).

He closes his narrative with a wish for peace, and clarifications regarding rumors that mean to clear his name. Both are tinged with the knowledge of the duplicity of settler media, military, and politicians—but also, as throughout, a sly doubling-down on the importance of honesty and keeping one's word. He knows the danger his people face, and in speaking to white readers, tries one last time to appeal to their sense of decency, praising those he encountered in his travels. Unfortunately, he even offers a dubious opinion on how the institution of slavery should be handled, outlining a plan which would help his people participate in the new economic system by buying, selling, and ultimately helping to "remove the black-skins."[19] While it is quite understandable that to remove white settlers would be an impossible task—as arguably would be any advocacy for freedom or equality for formerly enslaved Black people in 1833—Mahkatêwe-meshi-kêhkêhkwa still seems to be engaging in the very same self-serving double-speak he accused some of his own people of using as they began to deal with white settlers. Has there ever been an escape, historically, from transactional relationships between violent and violated entities when negotiating access to rights and resources, from risking association with a state entity in the name of protection and ally-ship regardless of past duplicity? *Life of Black Hawk* would tell us no, and amid the systematization and false reward of that mode of hustling for survival, we may not even be aware that we have succumbed to it.

In Silko's *Ceremony*, the main character Tayo similarly deals with the legacy of broken treaties, stolen land, a self that had been fractured by war trauma, but for him, that is done largely via his "crossblood" status—the physical representation and living consequences of colonization. Silko generously gives the reader several Laguna stories to frame his journey in a way that connects him to both parts of his heritage. Here, such stories again depict actions one must take in order to restore balance to the world, and to the self, because they—the world and the self—are not separate. In one story early in *Ceremony*, as Tayo's post-traumatic stress from Vietnam threatens to claim him, "warriors / who killed / or touched / dead enemies" could take action to prevent similar mental torment. If they engaged in preventive measures and ritual actions, like playing "flute and dancing / blue cornmeal and / hair washing," they might avoid a haunting spirit. They might be able to avoid a situation where "everything would be endangered . . . / the rain wouldn't come / or the deer would go away" (34).

Later in the novel, as Tayo continues to try to heal via Laguna knowledge, he goes on a vision quest that is finally fruitful, centering him in his intuition, which he could finally trust because of what he had already experienced: "Suddenly Betonie's vision was a story he could feel happening—

from the stars and the woman, the mountain and the cattle would come" (173). A sense of faith and wellbeing, a promise of future abundance arrive through the senses—sight ("vision"), sound ("story," accounting for the orality of the narrative), and touch ("feel happening"). Further, in that one sentence, we see the inextricability of present spiritual and physical well-being from land and story, from dream and so-called reality. And after the destruction wrought by broken treaties, wars overseas and socioeconomic oppression, neither the Laguna nor Tayo could trust words, so they/he trusted feelings engendered by Laguna knowledge.

Returning to the structural aspects of the two books, those versed in English-language literature will recognize the absence of distinctions alongside continuous narrative in John Milton's epic 17th-century poem *Paradise Lost*, which Toni Morrison echoes in her 2008 novel *A Mercy*. Morrison's novel, an allegorical rendering of the 17th-century origins of racial, sexual, and gender-based conflicts in the US, relies on the reader's intuition and intellect equally. We could call that unification discernment. In the introduction to *Dear Science and Other Stories (Errantries)*, scholar Katherine McKittrick nods to groundbreaking theorist Sylvia Wynter, who "theorizes race outside raciology and positions blackness and black studies as an analytics of invention."[20] As a book about "black livingness and ways of knowing," *Dear Science* maintains that the current systems of analysis work insufficiently with regard to Black literature.

Many scholars already reckon with death—genocide, environmental disaster, police killings, and medical neglect among them—an inescapable topic, and extremely important to understand; I will not repeat their work here. With regard to intuition, I believe life is the driving force to reckon with, even if that drive for life exists in opposition to death-dealing forces and their ever-present aftermath. Tiffany Lethabo King writes: "To perceive this distinct yet edgeless violence and its haunting requires a way of sensing that allows moving in and out of blurred and sharpened vision, acute and dulled senses of smell . . . Edgeless distinction is a haptic moment, shared, and a ceremonial Black and Indigenous ritual."[21] This "way of sensing" sounds to me like intuition, and the kind of self-trust that can disappear under sustained duress, of course. But if it survives or recovers, nurturing intuitive knowing can at least lay the foundation for strength of character and a fight for life.

"I'm interested in ways of seeing and imagining," writes Christina

Sharpe, in discussing an element of wake work, "the varied and various ways that our Black lives are lived under occupation; ways that attest to the modalities of Black life lived in, as, under, and despite Black death."[22] The Black and indigenous female characters in Morrison's *A Mercy* often use intuition to help them survive unimaginable horrors—plague, colonialization, enslavement, witch trials, threat of sexual misuse, and starvation. Set in early 17th-century America, a time and place in which they have no legal or social agency, no real support system, and not even the right to their own humanness feels primordial. The novel portrays an origin story for the United States we now inhabit—a story that demonstrates just how multicultural it was from the start, and how faulty the romanticization of North American settler colonialism is.

Lina, an indigenous woman and one of the main characters, reflects on their vulnerability in that world, both lonely and unprotected without a male guardian.[23] The white landowner/enslaver/patriarch in *A Mercy*, Jakob Vaark, starts as a poor farmer, and Lina is his first worker. They toiled together in "an unrewarding life" until he marries Rebekka, a life in which Lina fractured and buried many of her memories but savored select knowledge, a kind of "self-invention" made of a measured observation of past and present.[24]

As he begins to prosper, we find that Vaark does not quite value Lina's kind of knowledge, and neither does his wife after her husband's death—as much from fever, as from outsized ambition. Lina's presaging of their collective ruin comes from both observation and awareness, but no one listened to Lina, least of all Florens, the young enslaved girl who fell totally in love with the free blacksmith and chased after him as a cascade of deaths befell the farm, heedless of what Lina foretold as "the shattering a free black man would cause."[25]

Morrison chooses to use Florens's love as a flashpoint, showing how the complexities of colonialism divide oppressed people through feeling; intuition can be skewed by fear, and further by fantasy, as the blacksmith doesn't fully share the intensity of Florens's feelings. Lethabo King points out that characters like Lina and Florens had to make "horrific choices that often had to be (and have to be) made to survive under relations of conquest."[26] Lina's intuition remains highly accurate, and yet, she is powerless to transform her knowledge into action that could stay the impending calamity.

Morrison, however, still portrays her as highly aware of her own value and intelligence.[27] For her part, Rebekka's experience with anabaptists who "trusted their own imagination" held Satanist connotation, her Baptist fear-based beliefs only shaken in the midst of her own proximity to fever death, because unlike her, they boldly "dared death . . . to erase them."[28] Lina's indigeneity and related subjectivity places her outside of understanding or relevance beyond the function assigned by the settler-colonial system at its formation. As a reader, you might almost feel sorry for the narrow-minded oppressors in the novel if their ignorance wasn't so deadly to everyone involved. This schism, the futile intuition Lina holds, and the ignorance of force, holds nothing but death for most of the characters in A Mercy—outsiders, mostly, even the patriarch, the promised dream of the New World ending in death for each striver.

It is significant, too, that Lina is a storyteller, which helps her to bond early with young Florens,[29] and Morrison's delivery of Lina's backstory has a fairy tale quality, beginning "Once, long ago."[30] Lina's sense of self survives partly due to intuition, which enables her to refuse inculcation even in her orphanhood and semi-exilic status—exiled from her home community after their deaths from Europe-originated plague, but unlike the characters of African descent, at least still on the same home continent.

Abandoned by the Presbyterians who initially adopted her as a child, and newly in the employ of Sir, her name for Vaark, "she decided to fortify herself by piecing together scraps of what her mother had taught her before dying in agony." She combined that knowledge with what she learned in the years since from the Europeans, and "recalled or invented the hidden meaning of things. Found, in other words, a way to be in the world."[31] Morrison writes of Lina's inner self-knowing as cognizant of her own humanity, a knowledge no oppression can truly erase.

While there is no singular way to define the work of more than five hundred distinct Native[32] nations in North America, "Peoplehood: A Model for the Extension of Sovereignty in American Indian Studies" by Tom Holm, Ben Chavis, and J. Diane Pearson offers an approach to the explication of works by Native authors that centers what they see as common integral elements of indigenous ways of thinking, living, making, and more. They assert that "the four factors of peoplehood—language, sacred history, religion, and land—were interwoven and dependent on one another,"[33] describing Native literature as cyclical, nonhierarchical, people-centered and land-based. Those four aspects are intertwined and in conversation, rather than competition. The authors also compare civilization and non-civilization in terms of feeling and intuition to discuss the ways Native peoples who place value on truth and feeling (versus deception and so-called intellect) become negatively characterized, pointing out how protagonists in native literature must "eventually return to their Native roots for renewal and healing."[34] The protagonist's healing is often tied to the healing or restoration of the land as well, alongside native-specific knowledge: "The land, the ceremonies, the language, and the stories drawn from the Native group's sacred history make the protagonist whole and resolve his or her conflicts."[35] In contrast to conflict scenarios in which indigenous characters must choose between native and non-native existence, focusing on the above aspects helps strike down erroneous and stereotypical views of native characters, as well as help the characters to clarify and rebuild their own self-perception.[36]

Ceremony becomes more and more overt in presenting the contrast inherent in the protagonist's internal and external conflicts as the novel progresses, as Tayo goes to great lengths to try to retrieve his uncle's cattle and finds himself constantly thwarted by white ranchers. Those encounters contain more than his present situation; they hold history and possible futures, depending on his reactions and theirs, and they contain lessons of Laguna stories threaded throughout the novel. But vitally, it also exposes "The lie. [. . .] The liars had fooled everyone, white people and Indians alike; as long as people believed the lies, they would never be able to see what had been done to them or what they were doing to each other."[37] As Tayo realizes the truth about the ranchers and his own feelings about them, he understands the larger implications: "If the white people never looked beyond the lie, to see that theirs was a nation built on stolen land, then they would never be able to understand how they had been used by the witchery [. . .] white thievery and injustice boiling up the anger that would finally destroy the world" (177–78).

Silko binds time and memory in *Ceremony* in a way that makes past, present, and future feel simultaneous. A year, a hundred years, a minute, an hour, a millennium can exist in a few sentences as concurrent presences; a simultaneity of time which informs an intuitive knowing that later informs actions—actions which become warped if the truth is denied and replaced by falsehoods: "[T]he lies devoured white hearts, and for more than two hundred years white people had worked to fill their emptiness; they tried to glut the hollowness with patriotic wars and with great technology and the wealth it brought. And always they had been fooling themselves, and they knew it" (178).

Tayo recalls the land's history, one inextricable from Laguna history, and embedded in story: "The white ranchers called this place North Top, but he remembered it by the story Josiah had told him about a hunter who walked into a grassy meadow up here and found a mountain-lion cub chasing butterflies [. . .] The Laguna people had always hunted up there" (172). When Silko relates what was left of Laguna-occupied land near the mountain, just a small reservation after the National Forest Service, the state, and Texas ranchers took what they wanted, the tone turns mournful. The simultaneous matter-of-fact simplicity of the language, alongside the complexity of Tayo's past(s) and present, and alongside the Laguna stories interspersed throughout, offers the reader an opportunity to surrender to the same physical and philosophical journey the main protagonist takes. His loss feels soul deep, and he remains swallowed by it—until finally arriving at a more integrated sense of self through many trials that vitally lead him to both acceptance of the truth and self-acceptance. To arrive there, Tayo has to surrender, however difficult that might be, to all of it. To accept the process of intuited understanding and the wisdom it presents is to accept himself, and to trust in the eventual return of "Sunrise, / accept this offering, Sunrise" (244).

The omniscient narrator in Simon Ortiz's long poem *From Sand Creek* also represents a kind of intuitive knowing delivered through story.[38] Although the narrative is imbued with factual information about the titular place and the brutal massacre with which it is forever associated, memory is the driver, and intuition the richer inheritance—upending the notion of victimry. Further, by filling the interstitial spaces between Sand Creek remembrances with Veterans Administration (VA) hospital scenes, he invites the reader to arrive at an understanding of time as simultaneous, demonstrating how stories and remembrances reach toward aliveness and survivance in the face of war and genocide. Indeed, *From Sand Creek* holds history as a living presence. History is alive in the consciousness and in the bodies of people bearing the weight of colonial occupation's multivalent aggression, and it is alive in the spaces and places and communities they occupy. Using a combination of horizontal prose sentences on the left-facing pages and vertically oriented, lineated poems on the right, Ortiz offers an elegiac telling of a horrific event and its legacy in a way that highlights the intersection of history and story, past and present, survival and survivance.

Vizenor maintains in "Aesthetics of Survivance" that such stories are "a narrative estate of native survivance" (1), and Ortiz's work demonstrates that victimry neither defines people or their stories. Instead, native remembrances relate a more accurate and human history, enabling the retention and reinforcement of a comprehensive understanding based on the truth of those who witnessed and experienced the brutality of the event, as well as those who have inherited its lasting effects—aligning intuitive, storied ways of knowing with fact, institutionalized or not. In his essay "Towards a National Indian Literature: Cultural Authenticity in Nationalism," Ortiz writes: "Story is to engender life," driving home the point that story is exactly what "Indian people have depended upon in their most critical times."[39] By placing the narrative of the Sand Creek massacre alongside the narrative of Billy and his comrades, Vietnam-era veterans hospitalized at the VA,[40] "where stricken men and broken boys / are mortared and sealed / into its defensive walls,"[41] Ortiz highlights the practice of sequestering certain parts of the truth from sight, sealing off human evidence of the cost of war—the devastating results of the violence perpetrated by the American government and military hidden away, repressed, and subject to undignified institutional conditions, to say the least.

In discussing the field of native studies in "The Peoplehood Matrix," Holm, Chavis, and Pearson further point out the importance of noting who decides which stories get told, and how, given the multidisciplinary, relational nature without a single theoretical base.[42] Rather than seeing that interdisciplinarity made of "loose connections" as a fault, however, they describe the absence of centrality as a source of richness and complexity (8). The Peoplehood Matrix provides an encompassing means of analysis through a native-centered intersection of language, sacred history, place territory, and ceremonial cycle—a visual diagram that uses those four factors as a theoretical framework for analysis (13).

Using this framework to analyze one representative passage in *From Sand Creek,* we can see that Ortiz turns bloodshed into vibrant, active, powerful elements of nature, and in doing so creates a cycle, a ceremony featuring all the permutations of water, in which he imagines the people might "drink to replenish / their own vivid loss."[43] Sacred history is tied into those images, as is place, and though he uses the English language, the style of that language and the content within is decidedly native-derived and focused. In terms of intuition, the book provides remembrance itself as a way of knowing, a knowing that is not separate from the present, incorporating a tangential discussion of time as it relates to intuited understanding.

Toward the end of *From Sand Creek*, Ortiz writes of the VA soldiers' anger as infused into the hospital's architecture as a destructive force—and in the process of the anger's release, frees the veterans (84). That anger is righteous, justified, alive, and reflects Vizenor's argument that Indigenous peoples in North America and beyond have resisted empires, negotiated treacherous treaties, and, as strategies of survivance, by stealth and cultural irony participated in the simulations of absence to secure the chance of a decisive presence in national literature, history, and canonry. Native resistance of dominance, however serious, evasive, and ironic, undeniably traces presence and survivance over absence, nihility, and victimry (Vizenor 17).

Indeed, even as we find Oklahoma Boy so stricken on the penultimate page that Ortiz almost transforms him into a piece of furniture, then further, disdainfully becomes "American, / vengeful and a wasteland / of fortunes," Ortiz still makes clear that transformation is only "for now" (Ortiz 93). Ortiz makes it seem as though Oklahoma Boy need only wake up from the dream/nightmare, or more accurately perhaps, find a way to clarify "the swirl of his mind" (93). In that clarification lies intuition, a vital component of healing and the protagonist's impulse to go back to his home and homeland—the return mentioned in Holm, Chavis, and Pearson (18).

And in the swirl of language and story, importantly, and finally, *From Sand Creek* makes significant use of space on the page. But that space does not denote absence. In poetry, space is a breath, a place of rest, and a source for thinking, imagining, and understanding. Creating room on the page and between words and lines allows the reader to integrate the images and stories more fully, to feel more deeply the power and emotion driving the narrative. *From Sand Creek* ends with further transformation, a dream named and painted as truth, with a strong proclamation and reclamation of presence, a clear survivance rich with intuitive knowing (99).

In terms of a poetics of intuition, this practice can often fold into a continuance that holds memory and the present moment, futures and histories, as felt experiences capable of presenting through story a holistic human existence. Said further sees the fluidity and openness of the unresolved elements of shared history with regard to marginalized stories particularly, and urges further and deeper excavation.[44] A thorough poetics of intuition uses varied sources not to create a falsely multicultural patchwork of understanding, but considers intuition as a primary or major source of the kinds of knowing that literature offers through its characters, its structure, its thematic elements, and/or meaning as delivered/presented to the reader. It can also serve to situate indigenous literatures in a larger discourse about poetics—e.g., how literature is made—making more room for feeling and intuition as valid, even necessary, components in analyzing literary meaning, structure, intention, and emotional impact.

Paying attention to feeling and intuition as tools for both analysis and creation of literature seems simply more complete. In *The Life of Poetry*, her 1949 book of essays on poetry, politics, and culture, Muriel Rukeyser puts forward the idea that poetry is emotional and that that is a kind of knowledge; that emotion has value; that intuited feeling is truth—as distinguished from fact, but no less worthy of examination. Her life-based approach to analyzing poetry and thinking about its creation supports the characterization of intuition as a way of understanding literature's meanings and makings. Rukeyser believed that "However confused the scene of our life appears, [. . .] it can be faced, and we can go on to be whole. If we use the resources we now have, we and the world itself may move in one fullness."[45] And as Betonie says in *Ceremony*, "This night is a single night; and there has never been any other."[46] Such intuitive ways of knowing and perceiving, feeling and intuition, are valuable resources—valuable to our mental and physical wellbeing. They help us, as conscious, thinking beings, to practice closing the gap between intellect and emotion, and in literature can guide the reader toward more accurate truths that lead to more complete kinds of understanding.

Muriel Rukeyser

A Study in Imaginative Poetics as Praxis

Poetry and imagination are inseparable, not just at the level of the poem but in the practice of writing as well. But where and how else might we apply imagination as a critical practice? What might an imaginative poetics look like in practice beyond writing—in other fields of knowledge and in everyday life? In this chapter, I examine a representative array of Muriel Rukeyser's works across several genres: her book of literary and cultural analysis, *The Life of Poetry*; the "lost" Spanish Civil War novel, *Savage Coast*; the biographical play, *Houdini: A Musical*; *The Gates,* a book of poems; *More Night*, an illustrated children's book; and a late poetry chapbook, *The Outer Banks*. Treating her diverse oeuvre as a case study, I will read them for her use of imagination as a common thread connecting genres and fields of knowledge. I'll touch on her interest in the image (poetic, cinematic, and photographic); relationships between people and landscapes; interior feelings of fear, failure, and alienation; and, importantly, her attempts to move beyond social constructions such as race, class, and gender. I'll discuss the ways she did not always move beyond those constraints herself, despite a lifetime of activist work, and make note of the mixed critical reception she received over the course of her nearly fifty-year writing career—mixed, and often biased against her sex and the queerness of her writing style.

I'll start with *The Life of Poetry.* First published in 1949, reprinted in 1974 and again in 1996—sixteen years after her death in 1980—this collection of essays shows poetics as an imaginative intellectual practice. The gorgeous sentence constructions and the potent personal observations are woven with literary analysis and cultural criticism, showing us evidence of a creative mind that insists on as complete an expansiveness as possible. Jan Freeman, in the foreword to the latest printing, calls it "a book that breaks boundaries and assumptions about the place of literature and the arts in American life."[1] Rukeyser presents poetry as integral to a full human experience, decrying the invasion of fear and exactitude into the study and teaching of poetry. As Freeman puts it, she "suggests that by living with the senses and the imagination open, living with poetry, human beings can prosper and attain peace" (ix).

The book spends a lot of time defining poetry and its place in the world, its power and potential, with those ideas in mind. Beginning by laying out resistances to poetry and admonishments against fear, Rukeyser argues that poetry's value is on par with that of the sciences, and further, that poetry and science are not as far apart as it may seem on the surface, citing the inquiry, imagination, and feeling involved in both (80).

Indeed, imagination threads through all thirteen chapters, operating as not just theoretical exercise, but living praxis. Instead of taking divisions between fields of knowledge as givens, or as fixed categories, she makes myriad connections with fluidity—firmly placing poetry at the center, as the beating heart, the organic engine driving those connections. She links subject areas like poetry and science, claiming that connection as vital for a human future that favors curiosity over closedmindedness, holistic thought over hierarchal fragmentation, cooperation over competition, and emotional articulation over enforced silence and shame-based repression. Idealistically, perhaps, Rukeyser's poetics recognizes that when imagination leads us, bold innovation and greater human understanding becomes possible: "Art and science have instigated each other from the beginning [. . .] their roots spread through our tissue, their deepest meanings fertilize us, and reaching our consciousness, they reach each other" (162). *The Life of Poetry* offers proof of that proposition, as she goes on to methodically compare science and poetry, pointing out similarities between the two and demonstrating that a unity between them strengthens meaning and deepens the effectiveness of knowledge.[2]

We write poetry and create meaning through a system of associations made in language. When Rukeyser writes that "Science is a system of relations" (165) she aligns the two, and further, adopts the language of science in describing form in poetry: "The form and music of fine poems are organic, they are not frames. They follow the laws of organic growth"

(30). For Rukeyser, creative freedom and imagination are connected, and that connection comes alive in both science and poetry. She invites the reader to think of the two fields as sites of human advancement *because* they are rooted in an imagination allowed to develop freely: "The security of the imagination lies in calling, all our lives, for more liberty, more rebellion, more belief. As far as we do that, our culture is alive" (30). *The Life of Poetry* guides us to live with poetry, to use it as we do science—and to think of both as vehicles for evolution that make us more fully ourselves as humans.

Poet Adrienne Rich writes in the foreword to *A Muriel Rukeyser Reader* that Rukeyser "was beyond her time—and seems, at the edge of the twenty-first century, to have grasped resources we are only now beginning to reach for: connections between history and the body, memory and politics, sexuality and public space, poetry and physical science, and much else."[3] Like Rukeyser's preferred biographical and poetic subjects— the unknown and unsung among people and events—a canonic status on par with her more well-known contemporaries seems to have eluded her.[4] At a time when, globally, nations and populations clash at the fissure between violent intolerance and radical inclusivity, her work is ripe for a heightened attention that positions her work for greater appreciation and influence. As well, the mistakes she makes in discussing race can offer lessons in how *not* to portray people of races other than one's own, while at the same time interrogating the whiteness of imagination that kept her from completely dismantling racial hierarchies in her work—a tendency that contradicts her future-forward approach to writing and analyzing literature.

Rukeyser wrote fervently about human possibility, coupling intellectual exuberance with an unusually tight focus on the image (poetic, cinematic, and photographic). She pays special attention to the unity of nature, humanity, and the cosmos; love and friendship; the rejection of fear; overcoming failure; and attempting to address the enforced social constraints around race, class, and gender. Though she did not always move beyond those constraints herself, Rukeyser's insistence on even addressing such thorny issues make her a trailblazer in twentieth-century poetry and poetics. As Rich further observes: "[S]he spoke also as a thinking activist, biographer, traveler, explorer of her country's psychic geography [. . . and] understood herself as living in history—not as static pattern but as a confluence of dynamic currents, [. . .] a fluid process which is constantly shaping us and which we have the possibility of shaping."[5]

Rukeyser's passion for delivering craft and content which embody such possibility led her to develop a unique lyric yet documentary style. She wrote in nearly every genre and blended them in compelling ways. Scholar Dara Barnat notes that "Rukeyser is one of the most pioneering, prolific poets of the twentieth century [. . .] The extent of her influence is embodied by [poet Anne] Sexton's oft-mentioned claim that Rukeyser is the 'mother of everyone.'"[6] Indeed, she received numerous prestigious writing awards during her career, which spanned nearly five decades—starting at age twenty-one with the Yale Younger Poets Prize for her first book in 1935, and later a Guggenheim fellowship, the Shelley Memorial Award, and many others. Her spirited biographies of obscure 16th-century scientist-traveler Thomas Hariot, maverick politician and Roosevelt rival/partner Wendell Willkie, and theoretical scientist Willard Gibbs received positive critical attention if not wide readership. And her books of poetry were often reviewed, if not always favorably, particularly during her midcentury activism: "Rukeyser's work attracted slashing hostility and scorn (of a kind that suggests just how unsettling her work and her example could be) but also honor and praise."[7]

How critics and the public perceived her work is important to note, because she never quite settles into the kind of literary career that her record might signify. Instead, she took risks—continuing to investigate and write about controversial topics, attend antiwar protests, teach at labor schools, and speak out against social injustice. Critics at times perceived her passion as sentimentality and naiveté, her style as either too simple or too convoluted and uneven, her content as strange and didactic. Prioritizing imagination rather than conformity to popular expectation, she created a formidable body of work that is unafraid of mirroring the world's roiling mess of internal and external conflicts. Her work is earnest, in a cynical field and world; it is also hopeful, and *The Life of Poetry* in particular is bold enough in that hopefulness to believe that, if compelling and urgent enough to influence readers' thought, poetry can lead to concrete action.

The book opens with an unmistakable call: "In time of crisis, we summon up our strength. Then, if we are lucky, we are able to call every resource, every forgotten image than can leap to our quickening, every memory that can make us know our power. And this luck is more than it seems to be: it depends on long preparation of the self to be used" (1). Rather than a self-aggrandizing impulse, hers approaches a tone of recruitment into public service. However, for Rukeyser, that service also extends to the continuous act of self-knowing, a vital prerequisite to building a system of cultural belief that refuses future consignment to the trauma and destruction of "open warfare" (1). Publisher Jane Cooper closes her introduction to *The Life of Poetry* by saying, unequivocally: "Reader, she will want to change your life. No, she wants you to change it."[8]

Rukeyser's sustained belief in change meant that activism made up as much of her life as writing—in fact, the two seemed inseparable. Entering the public record in 1932 with an arrest while reporting on the Scottsboro Boys trial as a young journalist for a Vassar College student publication,[9] her involvement in liberal causes and organizations eventually led the infamous House Un-American Activities Committee to target her as a communist agitator, and J. Edgar Hoover's FBI began investigating her starting in 1942.[10] Her FBI file, now declassified, is 121 pages long (including front matter), and her case doesn't close until 1974—six years before her death at age 66.[11] Her dedication to social change lasted until her death, and even if she failed to succeed in tangible ways like policy shifts, she wrote in the tradition of poets who spoke out about social justice issues in their writing, and worked in political and nonprofit arenas in addition to or instead of teaching.

Despite her convictions and front-line activities, however, a careful reading of her work reveals that her approach to race, like Whitman and Melville, still often operates from a baseline position of ingrained white supremacy. Whether the assumption of that position is intentional/conscious or not, an examination of her work cannot ignore that disconnect. But, rather than dismiss her contributions because of such perceived (and actual) failures and failings—failure being another subject she addresses from the perspective of its value—we can study that rift in logic and rhetorically obliterate its source argument. We can unravel the tired argument of writers' biases as reflecting the limits of their times, eliding writers' responsibilities to do the same kind of evolutionary self-examination and education they advocate—she was alive at the same time as writer and cultural critic James Baldwin, for example[12]—and present methods of reading, analysis, and teaching that can leave such apparent oversights undetected or unexamined.

An early work provides a good case study, showing both Rukeyser's good intentions and where she falters in this regard. *Savage Coast,* a novel based on Rukeyser's travels to Spain[13] to cover the People's Olympiad[14] in 1936, spotlights people who might otherwise serve as silent background. Their voluminous dialogue and myriad portraits demonstrate the aliveness of many cultures, and helps create a tableau of the human richness of the time. Set almost entirely on a moving train on the eve of the Spanish Civil War, the novel speeds—literally, on a train—the reader through a turbulent political landscape to show a character evolution for the protagonist, Helen. Helen's curious, open perspective serves as a counterforce to the ambient violence—an inquiry steeped in humanity and imagination that feels ongoing, active. Rukeyser provides a nonfictional note as an afterword to the novel. In it, she expresses her admiration of the strong spirit of participation which characterized the people she met who were left without an Olympiad to attend, and with fascism to fight however they could, in their home countries or elsewhere. The afterword ends with the sentence: "Going on now. Running, running, today."[15] Thus the work keeps moving in line with Rukeyser's obsessions—continuity, presence, flow, focusing energy forward with conviction despite fraught circumstances.

Savage Coast blends realism, manifesto,[16] and the avant-garde in undulant prose that journeys quite widely, yet stays grounded in the insistent link between personal and public turmoil. Helen, as Kennedy-Epstein notes, gets swept up in the energy of revolutionary activities on the train despite her initial outcast feelings, finding both love and camaraderie among the breathtakingly diverse group of people traveling to the Olympiad: "The more Helen participates in the resistance, the more she becomes herself."[17] Recovered, the novel widens the narrative field, pushing the boundaries of both form and content in imaginative ways that incorporate her sense of social change alchemizing within the individual.

And yet, that same impulse to incorporate an array of stories into one's own for the purposes of forging connections can become appropriative, traffic in white saviorism, risk misunderstanding, or create problematic conflations of experience. Helen spends a lot of time observing, and our view of the landscape, portraits of other people, and events gets sandwiched between her actions and dialogue. Her movements retain interiority: "she had crossed the Channel, gone down to Paris on the fast train, whipped across the city, and come on this one, all in a daze of excitement, carried away with the excitement of it, but still locked into herself, traveling alone" (11–12). Although there's an omniscient narrator, everything feels united with Helen's perspective, and she's "so painfully" self-aware: "conscious of herself years ago as the white, awkward child, and later as the big angry woman" (12). In her observations, we get a sense of her desire to connect, her fear of rejection or exclusion, her use of observation to escape all that painful self-reflection. Early in the novel we see how intimidated she seems, how much of an outsider—a status often explicitly related to her body, rendered disabled by a leg injury. Her disability is not subtle, but visibly meaningful to her lived experience and sense of self: "She felt self-conscious because she was not athletic," with her usual role in public settings relegated to "watching, always; the nerve in the leg pulled with a memory of past games, past sidelines, answers" (18). Her vulnerability, suffering, and outsider status allow her to connect with peoples similarly afflicted by society's insistence on conformity; Helen finds beauty in the very aspects that society rejects.

Unpublished until 2013 and considered unfinished, the novel's editor Rowena Kennedy-Epstein notes in the introduction that the work "was brutally panned [. . .] rejected by her editor [. . .] for being, among other things, 'BAD' and 'a waste of time,' with a protagonist who is 'too abnormal for us to respect'" (x). Indeed, the novel languished for decades, "misfiled in an unmarked and undated folder in the Library of Congress" (x). In her essay "'Her Symbol Was Civil War': Recovering Muriel Rukeyser's Lost Spanish Civil War Novel," Kennedy-Epstein notes that its belated publication adds significantly to literary sources related to that historical moment[18] and further writes: "The rejection of the novel highlights the constraints and expectations of women's writing in the 1930s and 1940s, under which women were often lauded for their smallness and modesty."[19] The audacious sweep of *Savage Coast* stood in direct contrast to such narrow expectations, and its challenging prose met with distaste and confusion: "the contemporary reader found the hybridity of such a work illegible, and particularly the gender transgression implicit in its experimental intertwining of the quest narrative, the romantic plot, radical politics, and the epic impulse."[20]

While the novel's apparent difficulty is rooted in the poetic style that drives *The Life of Poetry*, such formal complexity doesn't fall far from the riddle-like density and self-examination characteristic of other modernist novels.[21] The main character's perspective, however, reads more expansively than the usual Bildungsroman, as Helen's personal conflicts become intertwined in the lives and struggles of those around her: "her symbol was civil war [. . .] endless, ragged conflict which tore her open, in her relations with her family, her friends, the people she loved" (12). The novel therefore reaches for self-knowing through observation of how fellow humans live, relate, love, travel, fight, and all the rest—doing so under the cloud of war and fascism quickly taking over the world.

There are many moments of languages not spoken by one or another passenger interfering with exact understanding, and yet result in a good-enough exchange; in many moments, a conglomerate of nationalities encounters each other in a kinship of enthusiasm for the *Olimpiada*. Many moments of confusion and laughter and danger crash together in a speeding blur of color and bodies and cacophonies of sound. Fascinated by the proximity of such human multiplicity, a tone of admiration infuses stark descriptions, perhaps a study in articulated envy of other people's perceived ease and freedom to *be*: "the old woman with the wicker basket, all in careful rusty black, pulled out some almonds and handed them to the young boy [. . .] his iodine-colored eyes startling behind the clear-oil yellow of his skin" (24). And the pair are traveling together, not alone as she is; a disparate family group, performing acts of care and connection: "He kept looking for approval to the dark, stout man sitting between them, whose fleshy, deep grooved face could not have been farther removed from his own. The furrows ran vertically and double between his eyebrows and from his fleshy nostrils around the full, kind mouth" (24). Rukeyser seems to avoid the pastoral by being sure to note the roughness of the train's population, and this approach has the effect of idealizing the ordinary. In her hands, the third-class car holds international glamour based on love and solidarity.[22]

Kennedy-Epstein maintains that in *Savage Coast*, Muriel Rukeyser "challeng[ed] the kinds of histories that privileged certain narratives over others, and saw the need to archive, document, and secure in text the stories of those who had been left out of master narrative—particularly the exiled, women, and refugees" (xi). As a Jewish person, one could argue that Rukeyser very much identified with such populations, however gently her intermediary gaze's layer of whiteness—albeit well-intentioned—seems to romanticize them. At the same time, her admiration comes through without illusion. She manages to both escape flattening by the sheer volume and richness of description, and offer a complex generalization that gives readers a uniquely international time capsule.

Despite her prevailing interest in casting light on the lives of oppressed groups and the social obstacles they faced, Rukeyser did not shy away from writing about white men; indeed, she highlighted those men who—like she did—bucked convention. Beyond the novel, the subjects of the three biographies she wrote chronicle the lives of men whose overlooked significance made them rather unsung heroes in her eyes. She takes care in chronicling how their steadfast work ethic alongside powerful innovation and imagination was either treated with hostility or ignored in their time. In those highly researched yet fabulously poetic biographies, Rukeyser champions their failed efforts alongside their accomplishments, their imaginative intentions alongside the tangible impact of their work. I won't address them at length here, but one last note worth mentioning is how 16th-century scientist Thomas Hariot's career trajectory seems to mirror Rukeyser's somewhat, with his "traces" in science akin to her status in poetry, of being "read and admired in pieces" (xiii). She finds points of connection everywhere.

Indeed, science and the imagination figure as prominently in Rukeyser's poetry as social justice issues; one could even argue that Rukeyser connects the two. All of her books address social issues and systems of thought, reflecting how Rich describes Rukeyser in citing her arrests as a journalist in Spain, Alabama and West Virginia, in Vietnam and South Korea, covering unjust treatment of African-Americans, workers, and other oppressed people: "she was by nature a participant, as well as an inspired observer, and the risk-taking of one who trusted the unexpected, the fortuitous without relinquishing choice or sense of direction."[23] But the work was not only content-driven. Rich again points out Rukeyser's imagination extended to form and genre: "we are trapped in ideas of genre that Rukeyser was untroubled by [. . .] We call her prose 'poetic' without referring to her own definitions of what poetry actually is—an *exchange of energy*, a *system of relationships*" (emphasis Rich's).[24]

Even in minor works, Rukeyser maintains the same message of openness and relational energy. Like the full-length and better-known 1948 collection *The Green Wave*, her indie chapbook *The Outer Banks* uses island and sea metaphors to present the notion of an open self—an open way of being that shifts, through a litany of elemental images and approaching actions, the notion that time and creation have set definitions. The images in *The Outer Banks* embody a relational (not one-way) exchange of energy through movement, a constant flow of defiance and questioning, not just mere existence. Once again she uses motifs of skin color to depict the relational:

He walks toward me. A black man in the sun,
He is now a black man speaking to my heart
crisis of darkness in this century
of moments of speech[25]

Importantly, Rukeyser uses language of vocalization ("speaking," "moments of speech,") to describe her listening, just as "the dark young living people" use song—an art form that is both physical and emotional. However, we don't know what exactly they say, and even though the black man transforms as he moves, his movement is in relation to the poem's speaker. His speaking seems relevant only in the fact that it is directed "to my heart." The black man's voice, the young people's voices are active, but still, they are anonymized; and as presences in the poems, they only exist to illuminate or educate the speaker, not as liberated and complex people within or outside the poem's world. Sadly, that means they turn into flat representations, in service to or made procedural within the speaker's awakening. By contrast, following those lines: "Women, ships, lost voices," as if what was lost (voice) must be recovered, can and will be recovered by the living who defy the guardians (xii). Those "lost voices" are "moving, calling you / on the edge of the moment that is now the center. / From the open sea" (xvii).

The vastness of the sea at times turns violent, and yet remembrance calls back through light: "Sea-light flame on my voice / burn in me" (i). One might call this a utopian poem in the vein of Walt Whitman, with his exuberant praise—at least message-wise—and his similar habit of turning nonwhite people into flat emblems. But Rukeyser holds a Melvillian darkness as well, not ignoring the landscape's destructiveness: "to the depth turbulence / lifts up its wavelike cities / the ocean in the air / spills down the world" (v). Rukeyser synthesizes the tendencies of both writers, repeating images of origins within moments in time, writing new beginnings in ways that feel infinite—as in, she can keep going infinitely. That act carries with it the potential to change modes of thinking and behaving which do not respect the living (human, animal, ecosphere) if the reader is open to it. Her poetics captures aliveness in a body relationally depicted: "They are in me, in my speechless life / of barrier beach" (xi). Rukeyser rejects separation: "There is no out there. All is open. Open water. Open I" (xi). She ascribes to the humanist imperative for writers and global citizens to understand the varying experiences of our fellow living creatures, however naïve it may seem, and however self-relational her habits of describing nonwhite people. Her earnestness invites us to abandon cynicism, to embrace imagination and the conversation it creates, to deepen our relationship with the world around us, and be willing to risk mistakes, rejection, and failure.

Too, her work occasionally holds a note of reproach and a tone of lambast. *The Gates*, her last book of poetry before releasing *The Collected Poems*, perhaps characterizes her as too prickly for canonization, too problematic to widely promote. She refuses to shy away from messy and difficult topics, especially what she witnesses outside of whiteness. In the poem "Burnishing, Oakland," she describes a man at work in a shipyard, "holding a heavy weight / on the end of a weighted boom / counterbalanced"[26]—a clear metaphor for the balancing weight of justice. She uses the act of burnishing—"high scream of burnishing / a path of brightness" as a scene of building, making, maintaining—while presumably police surveillance of and perhaps impending violence toward black people occurs nearby, "outside," the tension kept from exploding because "Panther cars" surveil the police right back (71). The following stanza holds some mystery:

Statement of light
I see as we drive past
act of light
among sleeping houses
in our need
the dark people (72)

The pronominal separation in "we drive" and "our need" contrasting with "the dark people" marks a clear separation between them and the speaker, with the speaker's witnessing contrasting with the Black Panthers witnessing from their cars. Using machine/animal mediators such as "Panther cars," however, rather than fully identifying them as revolutionaries or even citizens, for example, alienates and dehumanizes—i.e., the speaker's witnessing from a point of privilege does little to humanize the people involved. Rather than speculating further about their lives or motivations, Rukeyser returns instead to the act of burnishing as a way of describing "the shine, the scene," the central action of the poem holding apparent opposites or extremes—"statement of light," "act of light," "dark people," "dark houses"—and connecting them via the burnishing work of "one masked man / working alone" (72).

In some ways the poem fails; the premise borders on triteness and the depiction of tension between Panthers and police rather subtle given the history of police brutality and murder toward the group, particularly in Oakland, that Rukeyser certainly would have known about. The figure with which she seems most obsessed—the builder, the working man, the person moving forward into the future by the act of making, perhaps akin to her father—seems to mediate her social concerns and place them in the background.[27] Reading generously, however, reveals that she wrote to engage the issue at a time when few white writers did so with any kind of self-reflexive depth. The invisibility of black struggle is blatantly portrayed, and we can discern an intent to illuminate, even if the use of "the dark people" as emblematic accessory feels typical of people who write from white-centered perspectives. She witnesses, does not turn away or engage in empathic exercises which might ring hollow, and doesn't attempt to relate directly; the absence of comparison of woes is notable.

However, the poem that opens *The Gates*, "St. Roach," can, four decades after its publication, be read as condescending if we infer comparisons to skin color in the use of light (distinction from "the others") and dark (a presumed mark of difference from the speaker). Personifying a pest by addressing it, but using the basest language of insult in an apologetic tone that feels like less apology than excuse-making, can cause further injury. Rukeyser couples a litany of harms done to the roach alongside another litany of taught divisions between the poem's "I" and "you": "I could not tell one from another / Only that you were dark, fast on your feet, and slender. / Not like me" (3). By the second stanza, the poem turns—from another litany of what the speaker feared, avoided, misunderstood, remained actively ignorant of—and Rukeyser chronicles the wonder of the moment of discovery. But again, the language is condescending and presumptuous: "Yesterday I looked at one of you for the first time. / You were lighter than the others in color, that was / neither good nor bad" (3).

The roach metaphor thus becomes even more offensive if we take the roach to mean Black people, or people of color. Indeed, the speaker's desire for connection mixes with past learned repulsion, making it appear that the desire/wonder is somehow admirable, noble, or full of hope for a connection by the end—an authentic relationship would be a stretch. The repeated phrase "One of you" underscores separation and difference between human (speaker) and insect (roach/subject). The closing lines seem tender: "You were startled, you ran, you fled away, / Fast as a dancer, light, strange and lovely to the touch. / I reach, I touch. I begin to know you" (4). But, is that ending-as-beginning enough? Is it begun in the right spirit? That is, does the result match the intention, and if so, how effective is the poem on a craft level?

The use of repetition ("the first time" repeated three times in the last nine lines, for example) doesn't really transform in meaning, although it does emphasize the shift from not knowing in the first 22-line stanza. "You" is used in an almost accusatory manner 24 times in that stanza, compared with 14 "I" or "me" statements, and three active "they" statements: "they told me you are filth," "they showed me by every action to despise your kind," "they poured boiling/ water on you, they flushed you down" (3). The poem's "We" also appears active: "we say you are filthing our food / But we know not at all"—alongside the negative-oriented "I," the refrain "never" an absolute, almost a claim of innocence, a refrain of ignorance: "For that I never knew you, I only learned to dread you, / for that I never touched you" (3). In many ways, this poem effectively shows bias as insidious and ingrained, that even in reaching out for connection, such reaching out using a dehumanizing metaphor of vermin while proclaiming innocence another type of violence. With such a precarious extended metaphor, how much could Rukeyser or the speaker ultimately know, even with earnest inquiry?

Another reading of the poem, however, could reject that interpretation, and say the roach in the poem has nothing to do with skin color; instead, perhaps "St. Roach" references the Holocaust, since Rukeyser is Jewish, and remembering that, under Hitler's reign, Germans often referred to Jewish people as vermin leading up to and during the World War II genocide. Perhaps the ending desire to "begin to know you" means Rukeyser is reckoning with a history suppressed by a metaphor used to justify the systematic extermination of a people. But even if we do not conflate Rukeyser and the speaker in terms of a possible shared Jewish identity, one could view the poem's I as the voice of embodied ignorance trying to free itself, aspiring to be universal and genderless, cross-historical and inherently political. That simultaneity may give Rukeyser more credit than deserved, but perhaps not. Either way, questioning the poem allows the reader to grapple with serious questions of how we address each other, how we think about and articulate the positions we assume in discourse.

In the case of "St. Roach," centering the "I" prioritizes the witness's feelings over the observed "other," creating a tone of pity and presumptiveness in what Saidiya Hartman (in discussing a white slaveowner—Rankin—giving testimony about the horrors of the slave trade) calls the "slipperiness of empathy."[28] Rukeyser's characterization of the roach through a rather generic set of presumptive sentences flattens the possibility of an equitable connection or a full understanding. While the speaker in Rukeyser's poem doesn't pull Rankin's move and imagine herself inside the roach's body, the lines create a sense of pity rather than empathy, slippery or not—though one could infer that the speaker mourns the chasm between their experiences. Her poem does, however, use the roach to serve as a vehicle for the speaker's epiphanies, and the personification of the roach doesn't quite humanize them—too much focus has already been placed on their difference. If we can only feel empathy for a person or group of people in relation to ourselves, and not because of their inherent humanity, we miss the opportunity to respect and acknowledge their personhood outside the realm of our perception.[29] And, if the roach is meant to represent Black people, Hartman's question—as to whether the white person who sees and comments on the suffering Other can empathize without placing themselves in the narrative—echoes.[30]

Rukeyser relies on empathy heavily in the vast majority of her work; her care feels authentic, but her language choices and internalized white supremacy keeps it slipping into the same kind of problematic territory Rankin inhabits. Later in *The Gates* comes "The Wards," a poem set in a hospital, where "a man burns in fever; he is here, he is there, / Five thousand years ago in the cave country" (39). The speaker also travels— "wandering in Macao, / I run all night the black alleys" (39). But instead of despairing, feeling frightened or complaining, Rukeyser's speaker retreats into existential reflection: "Time rounds over the edge and all that exists in all. We hold / all human history all geography" (39). Her use of empathy here feels less slippery because she takes a wider perspective on it across time and place, holding both the lightness and darkness of human experience inside of her own—though she still exoticizes that experience via the assumed mystique of Macao and danger of black alleys.

Yet, she earnestly persists. Throughout *The Gates*, Rukeyser aims to shed light—a word thematic in this book and others of hers—on ignored or maligned individuals or populations, attempting to depict a fuller sense of humanity's connectedness: "Give us ourselves and we risk everything" (39). The fifteen-part title poem closes the book. Stage direction from the outset lets us know the action occurs on a "Scaffolding," and "The Gates" imagines the speaker as advocate for a poet in solitary confinement on one level, and as advocate for humanity on another: "the marvelous / hard-gripped people silent among their rulers, looking / at me" (87). Again, the "me" here drives her empathy and resultant social justice action. Going back to *The Life of Poetry*, we see that Rukeyser doesn't separate the poem and the poet; in talking about Whitman, another I-centerer, she says "Out of his own body, and its relation to itself and the sea, he drew his basic rhythms" (77), depicting the poetic imagination as in physical and intellectual relationship with the world. We can learn from both Rukeyser and Whitman that we can complicate our poetics further; maybe we begin with our earnest I-centered exuberance and empathy, but we can use deeper attention and greater imagination in moving language toward a greater encompassing that may invite further changes in thought and speech.

But is real change even possible in a world obsessed with proofs, with propriety and conformity and domination? Harry Houdini provides a stellar example of Rukeyser's continued attempts to invite readers into that conversation. In *Houdini: A Musical*, we find her at the height of her imaginative powers, building on her views about fear's dangers and linking social concerns to her fascination with possibility and science and imagination. Houdini is the perfect vehicle, as he demystifies his magic physically and intellectually while retaining the wonder of the spectacle. In the very first act and scene, in an exchange between Houdini and Beatrice, who would later become his wife and stage partner, Rukeyser portrays control of fear as the key to Houdini's ability to perform his tricks—and his ability to escape locks in particular. Houdini, in response to Beatrice's initial fear of those tricks: "I have to control my fear, and every muscle in my body."[31]

Houdini asks questions like: are magic and illusion the same? And ancient mistakes—is it our job now to keep living with the consequences, or do we redefine the legacies, advance them forward? An exchange between Houdini and Volonty (a fellow performer and fortune-teller who Rukeyser takes pains to describe as a Black woman) occurs after a bluesy song about hard times makes excellent use of humor in attempting to answer:

VOLONTY

A real escape artist. Tell your fortune, good looking?

HOUDINI

No, thanks. Against my religion.

VOLONTY

What religion would that be?

HOUDINI

What I live by. Pompous as ever. And, of course, born Jewish. My father said we're not magicians because of what Moses did.

VOLONTY

Kill the Egyptian?

HOUDINI

There's that, but you know when they were in the desert? No water, but there was the cloud by day. And God told Moses to strike the rock with his staff. Water gushed forth. Moses let them believe it was all his doing; he didn't give credit. That's why he wasn't allowed to go into the Promised Land. And we're not to *be magicians*.

VOLONTY

And whose credit? Oh, I see. But you're a magician.

HOUDINI

Come on. You know better. I'm an illusionist.

VOLONTY

Same difference. (52)

Houdini's hype man, Marco Bone, further describes him: "This is a man who breaks all constraints" (82), and Rukeyser clearly does the same in her writing. *Houdini* moves through time masterfully, with shifts often signaled by Marco Bone's narration, at other times seamlessly blending the transitions of Houdini's life through dialogue or song. Somehow, drama feels like a more natural container for such shifts, characteristic of Rukeyser's other work, particularly *Savage Coast*, in which temporal shifts feel much more unsettling—as jolting as train travel. In the play, they feel sweeping in a more magical way, though both feel just as intentional. The reader becomes swept up in the action of *Houdini* because of the explicit performative aspect, whereas with a novel the natural reader response is to follow a narrative thread. Rukeyser is concerned with the reader, to be sure, but in a way that challenges us to evolve as we participate.

Indeed, while her relationship with the reader is invitational, she remains acutely aware of resistance to change, and dramatizes it in Houdini. Rukeyser uses the Greek chorus, an Ensemble, throughout the play to represent the voice of society as enforcer of norms—often violent in speech, then in physical threat. The Ensemble insults and berates Houdini toward the end, after the Washington, DC, hearing about whether to ban fortune-telling and in which he tries to explain the difference between that and his illusions, and in so explaining, finding himself branded as a nonbeliever. The Ensemble's wall of ignorance is tough to breach, particularly when Sir Arthur Conan Doyle proclaims to all that Houdini "has powers greater than human powers" (133). Houdini balks, and later in response to the Ensemble's question "Do you attack faith?" he insists humorously otherwise, reiterating that self-knowledge and unified existence enables him to perform his illusions:

HOUDINI
Our emotions are part of our bodies and ourselves.

ENSEMBLE
How do you juggle? How do you escape?

HOUDINI
I don't call it religion. (141)

By the end of the play, after Houdini is caught off-guard and punched by a medical student, leading to his death (the irony of him being killed by institutional healers is not lost on Rukeyser), and with the Ensemble "*Singing, crowing, laughing, a chaos of noise,*" he emerges "*out of the blackness to the point closest to the audience*" to deliver a closing monologue that invites them to embrace what he lived life in service of:

I believe the incredible,
Swallow anything, eat the inedible, [. . .]
And I make, I make by touch, by touch.
Great touch by which we do all things,
Even our imaginings.
Even numbers, even words—
[. . .] Open yourself, for we are locks,
Open each other, we are keys. [. . .]
(Gently claps his hands together and stretches them out) (150)

Her dramatic biography of Houdini thus becomes another way Rukeyser connects science and poetry, intellect and feeling—unifying them, proclaiming that they have a relationship that matters, that they exchange an energy that infuses our culture with aliveness. Using drama makes that aliveness more immediate when performed, and invitational to multiple voices in a more public way than poetry with its tendency toward intimacy. Worth saying explicitly: she did not experiment with genre, in the sense of theorizing or testing out methods of making. Rather, she chose the most fitting container for what she wanted the work to do.

Given that deep-seated concern with life and with genre, it makes sense, then, that she also wrote for children. Rukeyser seeks to depict the fullness of the human experience—and possibilities for evolution—through personal relationships and tender moments. In *More Night*, its pages unnumbered and illustrated with watercolor drawings, the grandmother of a young boy, Jacob, tells him a story about what happens in and who occupies the night. Her storytelling begins with Jacob asking her "What's night?" and he uses a pet name for his grandmother—Damma, and repeatedly asks her to add more to the story ("More night!"). The text's dream-like rhythm and enjambed appearance on the page makes it a long poem-story, perhaps blurring genres there to mirror the spellcasting qualities of bedtime stories and night itself. Rukeyser describes the people who work at night (nurses, fishermen, firemen), names animals who come out ("whippoorwills, nighthawks. / The black-crowned night heron"), lists plants, planes, elements of the universe. The images are dream-like as well, and indeed after the story ends, Jacob dreams about a diver who gives him an undersea neighborhood tour before returning him to his parents. He stirs in a rather liminal state by morning, half-awake and halfway still in the dream. His grandmother says he'd been dreaming, and he wants to know what a dream is. She answers beautifully: "A dream is a story / you tell yourself."

By the end, it's clear that the grandmother wants to instill a sense of wonder and respect for what happens at night, what comes alive after dark, and doesn't want the child to fear the night. Notably, the illustrations depict people of many races and classes, and the images of Jacob and his family hold great tenderness—lots of hand-holding, hugs, eye contact, cuddling with animals. The penultimate image is of a smiling Jacob with his hands raised high, the sun on the left on a yellow page and moon on the right on a deep blue page. The text reads:

The moon says, "The
sun is shining." It
reflects the light
of the sun.

Such unity and mirroring, typical of Rukeyser, demonstrates the absence of separation of the elements—a wholeness, a full understanding of the world, both lightness and darkness together not in polarity but harmony, as two halves of a whole, but also marked by the spectrum of seeming opposites within that whole—multiplicity.

Rukeyser's intellectual curiosity leapt across genre limitations to produce a body of work that could be characterized as a philosophy of the imagination—an ambitious, powerful and valuable undertaking. Indeed, her work's thematic consistency over dozens of books of poetry, prose, and even juvenile literature, but perhaps most of all "how early she embraced the realm of the technological and scientific imagination"[32] could classify her as more of a philosopher than a poet, demonstrating both the meagerness of labels and the expansiveness of her gifts.

Muriel Rukeyser believed that poetry had the power to effect personal and cultural change if people overcame their fear of poetry, allowed its transformative emotional power to filter into their daily lives, beliefs, behaviors—making a crucial habit of reading deeply and seeking understanding of themselves and of other people in the world. By approaching genre openly, intentional yet fluid, not only did she embrace a creative practice based on freedom, but she offered her readers a clear demonstration of poetry as an undercurrent in and partner to prose, making poetry thus more familiar in its blended form. Her writing style mirrored the complexity and expansiveness of her content—considering the poem, the sentence, the paragraph, the page, and the book as permeable containers, allowing the reader to move through them as the world does, depicting and inviting that movement as a process of evolution and unfolding—not unlike a poem. Rukeyser's brilliance lies in this encompassing, at its best, and in the case of more opaque or difficult works, still presents a notion of the possible that holds value in the study of how a work is made in general, and her way of making specifically. Even though she qualifies as a trailblazer, she still struggled to truly represent equality across racial and national lines in her work; yet her persistent attention to social justice issues—even when she fails—gives us excellent source material for examining subconscious bias in literature, and by extension, biases that continue to poison human relationships.

In literature, as in other fields where personality often determines popularity, we can take a page from Rukeyser and go out of our way to pay attention to writers whose names we don't find resting at ease, oft repeated and canonically ensconced. We can search for those whose books stack up in shadowy corners, awaiting a brighter, more intrepid future light to find them, and in so doing, invite readers to discover more about themselves, to imagine beyond received expectations or definitions. "My one reader, you reading this book," Rukeyser asks in *The Life of Poetry*, "who are you?" (189). Rukeyser's agility in moving between literary modes while retaining thematic integrity means, as Rich says, that "her work repays full reading"[33]—a full reading worthy of such a vital and dynamic writer.

Poetics of Disability

The Mess of Insistence

Mess, chaos, and disorganization can create anxiety, barriers to understanding, outright rejection. Allowing for those things in a book? Certainly unconventional, and not easy to retain. However, I'd like to try composing something that demonstrates the way my mind works, and I'd like you, reader, to surrender any expectation of orderliness. Not much about this chapter follows the usual essay format or academic protocols. It is not created to incite proof competitions or tone-policing in the form of any claim to objectivity. It is also not a legal argument. It is based on my educated opinion and lived experience. I digress, I sidestep, I talk around, I repeat myself, I rant, I contradict, I skim surfaces, I say too much about the wrong things, I don't return to some topics that get introduced at random, I refuse to arrive at a single point.[1]

Instead, a little spiral of a story unfolds.

I had an epiphany on the morning of April 30, 2022. The realization brewed wordlessly, as an undefined knowing, for as long as I resisted becoming a professor, having witnessed the physical, creative, intellectual, and emotional toll I saw university work take on so many other people who looked like me.[2] Exclusion and ostracism, jealousy and sabotage, outright racism and pernicious sexism. In academia, a veneer of pretense and at least a partial reliance on secrecy and silent suffering seemed required. I know that I am a whole person, and when it comes to my creative work, I need total freedom. I had a hard enough time fragmenting myself in other institutional settings like the military, my PhD program, and even art school—I'm an art school dropout.[3] I didn't want to be a professor if it meant flattening my writing, teaching, and service to the field into something dispassionate—line items on acronymic forms subject to measures and proofs processed by strangers, or worse, colleagues who didn't understand me or respect my work. Far too often, the fear academia stokes in the name of hierarchy and prestige—evaluations, publications, committees—precludes that freedom.

To sidestep the fear, I waited many years to even apply for a tenure-track position. Rather than adjunct teaching, I worked at a more reliable corporate job with health benefits to support myself and my son, writing my books early in the morning and sometimes late at night, determined to do something I loved and keep a roof over our heads at the same time, on my own terms; to keep us fed and housed—to raise him in some semblance of comfort. Comfort is something I didn't have growing up. We got evicted more times than I could count, my sisters and I coming home from school to find our things packed and our bicycles sold, leaving behind friends and teachers before we could even truly connect. We lived in people's basements, back houses, attics, and spare rooms; we lived in motels and shelters. I refused to subject my son to that awful uncertainty. So, I waited until I'd published five books before becoming a professor, with the fifth gaining more attention and acclaim than any of the others,[4] which led to an invitation to apply for an assistant professor position that I then accepted.

But let me switch timelines again. In October of 2021, at the age of 46, I found out that I am neurodivergent.[5] Some people classify neurodivergence as mild, moderate, or severe, but I don't. I don't even like the way non-disabled people have named what I have: *attention deficit hyperactivity disorder*. Like many other people assigned the female gender at birth, the hyperactivity I have is mostly interior, thought-based, my inattention reflected in speech and social interactions rather than physical, stereotypical childhood behaviors like jumping around or fidgeting—one reason why AFAB folks tend to be underdiagnosed.[6] My research tells me that a better name would acknowledge the involuntary component, a genetic deficiency of a chemical in the brain—dopamine[7]—that is incurable, and affects every aspect of a person's life.

Among many other realizations that I will still be processing for years to come, having an official diagnosis of ADHD means I know the reason why I've always felt things very deeply and didn't understand the logic of trickery—called "too sensitive" and "too literal" all my life. Perhaps that is why I felt such deep moral injury during the transition out of global emergency to accepting the horror of the pandemic as a part of life. Even if I wasn't personally affected, we're just willing to endanger millions of our most vulnerable in order to—what? Appear normal? What a despicable word, normal; what a diabolical ruse; what a sin-covering scrim.

Do I sound angry? I hope so. I think anger is an appropriate response. Bitter? No. I won't swallow that poison. But I will use the space I take up to say that the kind of fear and denial that leads people to discard their fellow humans, and even risk their own health for such low stakes as normalcy, is a failed logic. Our institutions have also failed us, and we have broadly failed each other.

Alongside the devastation of grieving my mother's dementia and navigating her daily hallucinations during that time, I saw the abject lack of care for disabled people during the second year of the pandemic writ large beyond the university. The institution where I taught removed its mask mandate when the government did. Masks and vaccination requirements, along with any political will for public health funding—gone, with one stroke of a Trump judge's gavel.[8] Then, just a few months later, President Biden declared the entire pandemic over,[9] while hospitals filled past capacity,[10] care workers burned out,[11] and cases of long Covid continued to grow.[12] As of the time of this writing, near the end of 2023, our denial-based approach to public health means that the COVID-19 virus remains largely free to invade the endothelial cells in our bodies,[13] sixty thousand miles of blood vessels undergoing a slow and constant assault[14] that has the power to permanently dysregulate our immune systems[15] and damage vital organs.[16]

Disabled people's disabilities didn't go away just because the mandate did. The pressure to "unmask," the celebration of a "return to normalcy," struck me as deeply sinister. The realization that no institutional, community, or familial protection existed beyond platitudes—nearly broke me. I started to wonder if I belonged in a place that seemed to physically exclude me, by virtue of bypassing health and safety measures related to the ongoing pandemic. I started to wonder if I wanted to teach anymore if it meant endangering myself and my son.

Public health policy's tendency to blend media misinformation, minimization, and politicized gossip is actually as old as human civilization.[17] Resistance to mitigation measures like masking and quarantining did not start with this pandemic. Even safety measures like seat belts were, at first, vehemently resisted by "a small but vocal minority of people," including some car manufacturers, resulting in the passage of laws requiring the universal installation and wearing of seat belts.[18] But, as we've all seen, the public is also personal. Actions of other people affect us, and our actions affect other people.

Because I am disabled, I could die—yes, even with vaccines and booster shots, and yes, from the beginning, the CDC has maintained that both physical *and* intellectual disabilities (like ADHD) are considered higher risk conditions[19]—from COVID-19, or, to give it its full name, SARS-CoV-2—severe acute respiratory syndrome coronavirus 2. Severe, acute: its very name refutes the "mild" label that has swept aside any possibility of widespread awareness of its dangers. Instead of relying on community measures of protection, I am expected to protect myself against the erroneous beliefs of hundreds of millions of people—on top of everything else I deal with, I'm to research and fund the correct measures to keep death, hospitalization, and long Covid at bay. Meanwhile, I'm also meant to forge a high-pressure career in a world that revels in a violent pretense of normalcy rather than the more humane light of truth.

I'm supposed to write poems and essays and books in the midst of that pretense, and, in order to get tenure or be deemed a satisfactory employee, when I finish something that institutional forms calculate as relevant, add them to a tedious, labyrinthine form. Slap on the labels *productivity, value, accomplishment*. In a further exercise in absurdity, I'm to rank them according to a hierarchical system that, in poetry, remains somewhat informal and goes vastly unarticulated because—I feel—to hierarchize poetry is too subjective an exercise to be useful. But I'm supposed to participate in that evaluative pretense every year, and go to work every day. I'm to be available by phone and text and email during working hours, as well as outside of them. I'm to appear in front of a group of young people my son's age and speak and listen—brilliantly, unprotected—in the poorly ventilated, crowded, often dilapidated classrooms devoted to humanities studies. Of course, I will be thanked along with colleagues for the sacrifice with a seemingly-generous salary that hasn't really kept up with inflation, and with word-salad platitudes about our fortitude from overpaid administrators in generic mass emails. And if I don't accept that pretense, I'm reminded that I'm lucky to hold my privileged position in the first place, and therefore, I should be grateful for the job—even as it puts my and my son's health and lives at risk.

And yet, to be valued in my work, and by extension, in general, I'm supposed to suck all that up and carry on, just like our Navy chiefs told us to while I was serving. I'm supposed to fragment myself—wear one face in public, another in private—and work, *like normal.* But I can't. The gap between institutional expectation and my reality is too wide for me to traverse. So, I don't traverse it, or fragment myself, or pretend. I decline almost all opportunities to socialize and network because I know I'll likely be the only person in the room who wants to acknowledge the risks of SARS-CoV-2. All the way through 2023, I taught online when I could. I still use safety equipment and wear it shamelessly, despite the risk of stares and sneers and snide comments, however odd my HEPA filter mask from Korea looks, or how out of place my portable purifier and CO_2 monitor look. I brought all that to class, carting them until I couldn't, until my limbs started to float out of their sockets, because, post-surgery, I wasn't supposed to be carrying anything. But I am getting ahead of myself.

If I was expected to become my own system of support at work, I reasoned in 2023, then I needed my own equipment—and, further, my own system of thought to power that system.

I know it seems like I'm talking around this poetics of disability when I should just get to the point.

But what is the point? Do I even want to write this book? Does my little outrage even matter? Am I just type-screaming into the heartless void?

I do have a point. The point is that a poetics of disability acknowledges the paradox of participating in public existence when that engagement risks a person's wellbeing at best, and their lives at worst. Not only is it a system of thought when it comes to literary analysis, or the creation of literary works, it applies to life. It is a philosophy of orneriness and intransigence, and it involves demolishing pretense and making a mess of that thin façade.

Because I've published so many books and always have several more in the works, the people who hired me said that tenure would be a slam-dunk, that I shouldn't worry; and yet, the hoops of proof continued to spin before me as I waited in the shadow of possible denial.[20] Already a year late, being met with administrative requests for further proofs and the minutiae of dossier corrections—with urges to complete it right *now*! Even if you literally *just* had major surgery!—reminded me of my ongoing physical risk in public spaces, of forced compliance with policies meant to end me, and I balked—I almost didn't finish. Demand avoidance, another characteristic of ADHD, transformed finicky .docx templates in my mind. The form's electronic rectangles in which to alphanumerically repeat myself felt like the death of creative impulse; straight shapes transformed into hamster wheels, replicating in my mind and my email inbox like so many routine forms of performance, the cage of bureaucracy smelling of hay and scat and stale water to be licked from a plastic tube.

Toxic.

A friend came to my rescue, recommended hiring an executive assistant to do the most egregious tedium. I paid this assistant with some of the money from my Disability Futures[21] grant; and with another chunk of it, I paid for temporary housing in Denver, where I went to have that surgery in October 2022—two weeks spent in an Airbnb to recover, because my doctor said I should be fine by then, that some of his patients were back to work in three days. My doctor, who didn't wear a mask in the office because the CDC basically said meh, who cares about disabled people?—let them go into hiding or try to protect themselves; it's not anyone else's problem.[22] Four *months* later, in February of 2023, I was still recovering, having had to fight for the right medication to get through the postsurgical pain—even while I was in pain and was being "gently nudged" about tenure paperwork, a year delayed because administrators believed I needed to wait for student evaluations: to prove myself worthy.

I am still not fully recovered. In fact, at the beginning of 2024, going back to work after a beautifully healing sabbatical in the fall of 2023, carrying books back and forth to a building half a mile from my office and parking garages several times a day three times a week set me back. More hoop-jumping to get a disabled parking tag to get some relief, to get accommodations—another word I dislike—more forms, more barriers to maintaining health, more institutional doubt. I am lucky to have had access to three rounds of therapy in the past four years, including cognitive behavioral therapy or CBT (which isn't perfect, but it did help). Without that treatment, the extra time, energy and emotional weight that process takes would have—and has in the past—kept me from seeking those needed protections.

Disability poetics means recognizing you can't make art or teach or [insert anything beyond basic survival, and indeed survival itself] if your health gets trapped in legally enforced precarity. Sometimes you get dehumanized and monitored because the medicine that works for you— Adderall, in low therapeutic doses in my case—gets abused by a minority of people, even if you have no interest in or history or risk of drug use. A term called "the ADHD tax"[23] means neurodivergent folks often spend money to the point of hardship in order to help our brains function in a neurotypically-oriented world. Disability poetics acknowledges how much disability costs, in time and in money and in fractured relationships and lost opportunities—despite the common myth that disabled folks' supposed neediness drains public resources, or that people with underlying conditions should expect to die of SARS-CoV-2, since they were already vulnerable.[24] Self-sacrifice becomes an enforced inevitability, imposed in both language and cultural practice. Public health doesn't mean protection, only the appearance of it. Sometimes. For a while, anyway. Until it doesn't.

But I digress. I had an epiphany on April 30, 2022. It wasn't at all unique to me, but that day was the first time I felt the sharp, severing implications: academia wants my mind without regard for my body, aside from its service to labor and pretense—to pressure myself into the working façade of diversity. Academia wants me to adapt backward into silence. Academia doesn't want *me*. Academia wants me to fragment until I don't recognize my own feelings, until I identify more with the simulation of personhood and professionalism they promote than reality. Of course, that could apply to any institutional or corporate job. Even marriage, in some cases. But, in another twist of neurodivergence, my mind naturally defaults to the baseline notion that others think like I do. Logic informed by feeling tells me that we ought to behave like and build systems that show we care about other people, and not just say we do.

This epiphany has a related precedent. Some years ago, I realized men wanted the inverse: to use my body without the fullness of my mind; but, as with academia, their desire also came without real regard for either my physical or emotional wellbeing. I realized that without the outer shell of beauty, I did not even have the power to command the pretense

of men's care or attention, unless that care was a step toward possession or domination. And if I refused that sinister attention, the interactions often turned violent—verbally, if not physically. I avoided men as
much as I could and didn't date much for most of my life. I grew up in
Los Angeles, often in sketchy neighborhoods, and the streets were com-
monly patrolled by parasitic men. My parents taught me as a young girl
to walk down public streets quickly, with my eyes trained straight ahead,
to eschew speaking to strange men with more than a head nod if their
verbal demands for my time seemed insistent enough to turn physical or
dangerous, to keep walking, speed up. In our training for careers in academia, our doctoral professors tell us much the same: to keep our heads
down, to follow procedures, to be strict and impersonal with students
and colleagues alike. At least, mine did. It feels, almost, protective—if you
don't realize how adversarial it is.

And yet, students often come to us—us, Black teachers, teachers of
color, mostly female or femme-presenting or otherwise queer—as they
are suffering, weeping, dealing with incredibly real real-life situations in
which there had been a breakdown in support for harms, ill health, recovery from addiction, homelessness, and family illness. Many of the students I've worked with, many more than I expected to encounter, shoul-
dered caregiving responsibilities for parents, grandparents, and other
family members in the absence of the spare $100,000 per annum needed
to place a loved one in a reputable elder care facility.[25] I regret that I listened to my professors during the first semester I taught, in 2017. I found
myself referring to institutional policies and protocols instead of my own
humanity, even when my heart knew better. That horrid feeling led me
to counter institutional expectations placed on me so I could make room
for what students actually needed—a freer and safer and more flexible
space in which to learn, through the study of poetry and other literature,
that critical thought and compassion are not separate.

The mind and body are connected, and both must be cared for.

What if the ideals that colleges and universities profess to impart in
their marketing slogans—illusions of inclusion, community, collegiality—
were incorporated in practice? What if, culturally, we acted in ways that
showed how much we value human life over profits?

In my relationships with men, I learned continuance meant obedience; keeping the peace meant pretense, an uncomplaining demeanor,

a smiling surrender to harm, descent under threat into a grateful self-abnegation. To possess: to have or own something, or someone; or, that they identify with, or belong to or with you/your organization; twin patriarchies, using promises of love or respect to seduce us into compliance with a parasitic and insidious illusion of belonging as protection, or camaraderie, or care, or—even more laughably—true acceptance, you *just as you are.* An expected agreement: to maintain the illusion in a contract of mutual but not equal exchange, one not stated explicitly—implicitly known. Or so they think.

My brain doesn't work like that. I require literality and honesty, two things neurotypicals seem to despise in practice, even if they say they find such "bluntness" refreshing. I don't think I'm blunt. My words are not meant as weapons, but as directness that speeds up communication—gets right to the point, rather than layering language with airy softnesses that can inflict harm, like viruses, invisibly. And I know the practice of intellectual and cultural appropriation, and universities using "diverse candidates" as a front to appear inclusive, to quiet claims of bias, to attract students who believe, with the same hope I held when young and awakening, that those appearances of inclusion are real. I knew all that and charged into an academic career anyway, thinking my books might protect me from the hoop-jumping and pretense. And maybe, had we not experienced the utter disaster of the pandemic, I might have remained in that enticing bubble of idealism. Naively, I thought I could do my work and make a difference for students and the field. And I know I have, to a degree—but I didn't truly calculate what that would cost me in terms of my health and wellbeing. A poetics of disability asks that we remember; asks that we gauge the physical, emotional, and financial costs, up front, of any analysis or action we undertake. And if we don't remember, try to forgive ourselves. And if we can't forgive ourselves, to at least have patience with ourselves through the trauma.

My neurodivergence also made me believe information would protect me; I thought logic would be convincing on its own. Instead, I have often felt consumed by practices of exclusion and appropriation, while I also feel separated from them and harassed by their pernicious insistence. I feel like a product of academic training, yes; and I also suspect I have simply become a name/face of scholarly and creative success within a corrupt system so I can have a semblance of autonomy, to have a safe place to live in order for my disabled son to have healthcare, to fund my writing projects where I get to rant about Things That Matter that I can do very little to change.

More than once, in the military, in school, people in authority asked me: *What are you doing here?* According to their sociocultural calculations, I didn't belong; my very existence didn't compute.

Simply by showing up to teach in a classroom full of unmasked students and unclean air that my $249 Aranet4 CO_2 monitor measures at 3,254 parts per million of CO_2 (1,000 ppm higher than subways or crowded restaurants)[26] risks my life, as well as my son's. The institutions that employ me and the country where I was born and the strangers I encounter all demand that I act pleasant and thankful while I hotbox a deadly virus, preferring that I ignore its severity, and perhaps even allow it to replicate in my bloodstream. A poetics of disability means I cannot—and will not—pretend my way out of that reality, even if my insistence on informed awareness costs me friendships, collegiality, opportunities, points on evaluations, publication, or tenure.

During 2023, to teach, I arrived to my classroom carrying a slate blue train case I bought in Paris in 2019. It holds portable air purifiers, air sanitizing spray, a UV sanitizing wand, Clorox wipes, and plenty of N95 masks. I arrived early to go through my cleaning routine, wearing my trusty $299 LG PuriCare electronic mask with two small 99.97% HEPA filters that last 30 eight-hour days, cost $30 each to replace, and $60 to ship from Korea. I love that it has a microphone. I love that it lasts eight hours per charge. I often joke that I don't spend money on designer bags—I spend money on designer safety gear. In 2024, I still use a portable purifier and wear an N95, but now have access to and use a virus-killing nose spray, eye drops, throat spray, and mouthwash. When I travel, I still use the electronic mask and portable purifier. Extreme? Maybe. But so is debility and death.

Before the pandemic, I thought of teaching as a calling. Now that I have been treated as disposable, it's a job. I take pay, and I offer knowledge and, yes, I still care. I still love to teach poetry and theory and literature, and I love having a part in helping students learn to think critically and communicate clearly, to express themselves freely, to treat themselves gently, and to become more deeply familiar with their particular gifts. At the start of every semester, I lay my tired body down on that old hamster wheel—right on top of that bright stitch of wires engineered to move in place, and I spin at a pace I can't control but try my best to slow. I recognize the cognitive dissonance as I consume the smells and sights of school, as I'm consumed in both simulation and reality—my half-covered face, my labor, my mind, my words, my time.

But consumerism and commodification can't be the only answer. That feels too easy, too convenient, too basic—especially when what I share of my mind at work runs counter to how the academic system operates.[27] Stuck in this destructive routine of fragmentation, out of dependence and habit, necessity and sparks of exuberance, out of foolishness and hope, how can anyone escape?

One answer: don't even try to escape, because you probably can't. One answer: write and think through the futility. The multiple and related stigmas of disability, of housing and financial precarity, and gender-based violence enter the classroom and influence our teaching, our social lives and activities, and the creative work we make—whether we address that fact or not. But we must address it. A poetics of disability is anything but a settled routine. It embraces dynamism, evolution, correction, and contradiction. Disability as poetics—in both theory and practice—recognizes that the veneer of normalcy obscures the messy perils that our social systems are designed to perpetuate.[28] We get fooled into thinking we're the messy ones, we're the problem, when the system itself is chaos, is functioning as intended, and, as one headline read in 2018, cruelty is the point.[29] Thinking, writing, teaching, and working through a lens of disability asks us to go around those systems, to figure things in the muck, to fight despite the obstacles, even if that fight just looks like sleeping, or reading Tricia Hersey's *Rest is Resistance*; such a poetics also asks us to recognize when things are intolerable. And, especially when we can't do a damn thing to repair harms we didn't cause, disability poetics asks that we recognize this apparent futility and messiness as the heart of the work of complete understanding. It's also important to note that you don't have to be disabled to act with the integrity disability poetics impels. You can recognize and act with integrity regardless of your health status.

In the 1963 film *Stolen Hours*, main character Laura Pember, a wealthy white American divorcée with a racing driver ex-boyfriend-turned-close-friend navigates sudden illness and several heterosexual relationships. She tries in vain to hide her physical pains, to continue throwing parties and playing carefree hostess while secretly dealing with blurred vision, migraine-type headaches, fatigue, and tremors. Worried, the racing driver, Mike Bannerman, tricks her into being examined by a team doctor at one of her parties. Dr. Carmody flirts with her, having been told that she wouldn't submit voluntarily to an exam, but is then himself semi-platonically seduced by her charm, determining her worthy of his medical *and* personal attention after initially dismissing her as an airheaded heiress.

A few days after his surreptitious examination, she's brought to hospital for tests that require her to shave her head. Our benevolent and handsome Dr. Carmody, affectionately called John by now, partners with the best brain surgeon in the country to treat her. The surgeon parrots John's original gender bias while encouraging him to withhold disclosure of her diagnosis—the tumor would recur, and she only has a year to live at most. The brain surgeon mentions gruffly to John that Laura ought to be grateful for the time she has left, when he's operated on many more "worthy" patients—a mother of four, a brilliant medical resident—whose lives were cut brutally short, doubting that Laura Pember has done anything of note or respect.[30] John delivers the news to Mike outside Laura's recovery room and says to Mike that he can't tell him what to do, as far as notifying her about the outcome, but shares that *he* wouldn't want to know.

How many medical professionals allow their biases and misperceptions to interfere with how they address, treat, and discuss patients? Where is Laura's consent in this morass? John discloses her prognosis to Mike Bannerman and Laura's sister Ellen halfway through the film, giving them the news while Laura rides a horse around her estate on a beautifully sunny day, oblivious of her condition, her post-surgical bald head hidden under a safety helmet, celebrating—performing?—good health. John tells Ellen he waited to say something to avoid causing her undue distress, but Ellen cries anyway (44:05–15). Bannerman still doesn't want the doctor to tell Laura, but John goes to find her anyway. He feels it unethical to hold back the information any longer. But something changes when the moment arrives. Her gratitude to him, for saving her life with that initial surreptitious flirtation-exam, comes before his disclosure, and he loses his nerve—basking, instead, in her deep affection. They start to spend even more time together, with Bannerman and Ellen tenderly approving of the deception. An interesting turn, since Ellen tells a contrite John, apologizing for sharing the devastating news, that she wouldn't have forgiven him for withholding information if that were her.

When Laura shares her beloved private cottage in Cornwall with him, something she hadn't done with anyone, John impulsively asks Laura to marry him. Surprised and pleased, she agrees, they embrace, and in the next scene we get a bit of foreshadowing. Laura visits his office, and the receptionist leaves a patient file cabinet open, giving Laura the notion to snoop. She dismisses the receptionist and finds her own medical file. As she woodenly processes what she reads in her file, we see Dr. Carmody in a new way. His rush to get married starts to feel a bit creepy. His actions don't seem loving, but patronizing; he babies her, takes her to the market for fruit and flowers, says "I'll make the decisions" when she doesn't want to pick which fruit. Right there on the street, she drops the bouquet of chrysanthemums he bought, and confronts him about why he didn't tell her the truth, making her doubt not only their relationship, but that he ever knew her at all. "Didn't you know I wanted what was between us to be real?" Her intense emotion contrasts with his flattish, clinical first response: "I believe in telling patients." Before driving off in her convertible Mercedes, Laura responds: "That's what a *doctor* says, not a human being!" So, the woman he wanted to marry is now a patient again—or, she never stopped being one to him (59:15–1:00:07). The very word, *patient,* reduces her to the subject in the brain surgeon Dr. McKenzie's handwritten note on the last page (the only one colored pink, instead of white) in her medical file: "Recurrence will occur within one year with a rapid onset of symptoms—blindness—and death" (56:31).

Laura doesn't explicitly call off the engagement, but her dramatic exit allows us to infer. In the next scene, we see her in the same periwinkle coat, checking into a hotel. Later that night, she's wearing a strapless, knee-length black cocktail dress with a diamond brooch. She tries to make a move on her friend and ex, Mike Bannerman, but in gently rejecting her advances, he slowly reveals he knew about her diagnosis as well. His rejection stings, but not as much as his betrayal; she vows to live to the fullest.

A woman after my own defiant heart, as I wrote about this film on May 15, 2022, in a room that smelled like the pink roses my younger sister sent me for Mother's Day—a younger sister who'd later demand that I surrender to the idea that "everyone will get it, just stop with the COVID already," even though I've likely had it twice[31] and am still dealing with the havoc it's wreaked on several of my vital organs, even though she and her family get it so often their "new normal" is accompanied by a continuous coughing soundtrack and recurring visits to the ER, a younger sister with whom I am not, needless to say, still in touch. The open window I looked through showed gorgeous white clouds and a sky with infinite gradients of blue. I hadn't taken my ADHD medicine that day, but I'd slept and felt mostly free of the low-grade chaos usually buzzing through my mind. Instead, I'm learning to feel at peace with the anger I used to use as fuel. I'm learning that that drive can come from respecting my revolving fascinations, that I can notice my emotions and identify them before I let them pass by, in a light blur, like so much scenery.

Side note: When I started watching the film, I didn't know *Stolen Hours* had a racing driver and depicted actual racing, but that's part of what kept me engaged when I happened upon it during my recovery, because I love Formula One.[32] After their fight, Laura waits for Mike in the pit at his urgent request, and she overhears his team saying they don't want to give him his lap times. They want to avoid sharing anything worrisome about his performance in the name of preserving his confidence and his focus on the race (1:05:45–46). This parallel withholding causes her to step away to reflect, and on her walk, she witnesses an accident off the track in which a spectator has been struck and is nearly dead. Laura tries to preserve his dignity until his last breath (1:06:20–1:08:24). Our friend Dr. John Carmody shows up and draws her right back in at that dramatic and pivotal moment.

By the next scene, they're married. He takes her to his hometown, where his father cared for a community populated by folks he calls "these people" while deriding city patients as "some silly Harley Street affair with a list full of hypochondriacs" (1:12:45–50). Struck by the beauty of the landscape and friendly population, Laura has fallen right back in step with him, making herself at home in his family property on a bluff overlooking the Atlantic, a beatific smile on her face as she basks in its ordinariness, and later hoists a British flag, saying cheerfully, casually, and colonially, "I'm taking possession" (1:14:25). She serves tea in a pleated white skirt, orange twinset, and pearls, becomes a surrogate parent for a young boy, Peter, who takes care of his alcoholic mother and seeks Dr. Carmody's care (1:16:24–45; 1:15:19). She hosts parties for the neighborhood children—dutifully performing what was expected of a woman, wife, and well person at the time. At the end of the film, she makes a show of turning on bright lights, the same ones she couldn't stand at the start of her illness, trying to prove that she's not sick.

Almost immediately, however, the tremors return. Her sister Ellen, visiting her, sees, and the devastation on her face presages Laura's death. For her part, Laura calmly asks Ellen not to tell John, who's preparing to attend a high-risk pregnancy for a patient named Mrs. Hewitt. She wants some agency over that information, wants to keep her own secrets—mirroring their past withholding—and insists that her husband's patients need him more than she does (1:30:59). This makes for good drama—competing wants, patterns of parallel behavior, seemingly well-intentioned secrets kept about tragedy, and emotions manipulated into silence and stoicism.

Laura moves robotically through her last hours, faking health, performing ease and happiness. In real life, such role-playing can lead us away from ourselves, away from care: a kind of self-death, a light-hearted veneer meant to flatten the messy emotional experience of the dying process before physical death occurs—a flattening that seems like more of a performance or comfort for the living. *Stolen Hours* glazes over the layers of complexity within the processes of living and dying, treating illness and maintaining health, self-love and loving relationships. As she approaches the moment of her death, certainly actress Susan Hayward gives the character Laura impeccable dignity—gliding upstairs, asking Peter to describe the view from the window that she can't see, quietly bidding him goodnight. She'd already said a lighthearted goodbye to John as he left. But the tragedy isn't her death; it's the problematic journey she underwent, and the way the film romanticizes secrecy and role-playing.

If we are meant to believe this kind of problematic romance between doctors and patients is acceptable, romantic enough for a film even, dramatizing the balancing act between knowing and not-knowing, worthiness and unworthiness in terms of disability, then we are meant to believe that an *illusion* of care takes precedence over *actual* care. We are meant to believe in and preserve the *illusion* of ethics and morality, rather than promote *actual* ethics and morality in practice. And indeed, we are meant to believe in an illusion about disability—that it is an individualized character trait and personal responsibility, that one's lot is to suffer alone and preferably in silence, even if you are lucky enough to be rich. Rather than understanding disability as a common human event, one that is not meant to operate in the realm of secrecy and stigma, but must be addressed openly, with awareness-based public solutions and informed care, if real solutions are to be systematized long-term.

The melodramatic rendering of a duplicitous doctor-patient love story in *Stolen Hours* tells us much, even sixty years on, about Western culture's illusions regarding healthcare, the roles we play in the façade's mainte-nance, and the emotions we try to corral into control at the expense of honesty. Another tragedy: Peter, the child, is the person who witnesses Laura's last living moments, helping her up to her room as she's lost her sight, tucking her into bed after describing the view from the window (1:33:50–end). He's used to caregiving, after all, as a poor young lad with an alcoholic mother, so what's another trauma? As Laura dies in a soft bed in her husband's childhood home, having insisted on being left alone while John took her sister with him to deliver a baby that a miscarriage-plagued mother planned to name after him in a gesture of gratitude for the gift of his obstetric care, I couldn't help thinking: what will happen to Laura's money? Perhaps a callous question, but I couldn't help but ask it. And, not surprisingly, it goes unanswered. The film seems to take as implicit our acceptance of the romantic notion that John doesn't need her money, but really, clarity tells us that an unethical doctor married a rich woman he knew was going to die soon.

Perhaps he didn't actually need her money, perhaps he did fall in love with her, but as her husband, he likely stands to inherit her wealth—money, to go with the stolen hours. Meanwhile Laura dies far from her home, alone in an attic bedroom, having experienced the supposed hap-piness of stereotypically unselfish, wifely pursuits. Viewers are meant to believe, in the end, that her death is noble, accomplished on her own terms. What more could a woman ask for, right? Her silent surrender to traditional role-playing seems to be what the film celebrates, not her actual life, before or after diagnosis. She's no longer bold, clever, dynamic, sparkling; she's subdued, sweet, doting—throwing herself into the life of a doctor's wife as if that had been the dream she never knew she wanted to come true. She's a shell of her former socialite self, almost as if her ter-minal illness means penance for a formerly decadent life—and that we, the viewers, ought to see the performance of that penance as desirable, fitting, and noble.

So, what is the source of blame, then, for the truth of my earlier epiphany? That academia wants my mind without my body, and I should consider myself lucky they even want that? What illusion obscures such parasitism, slides the satin oxblood lipstick—let's call it NARS Opulent Red—onto the sheer piggery of it? Is it, like Debord said, the spectacle of consumption, or the spectacle of role-playing heterosexual happiness? Is blame even useful or productive?

How to shatter the illusion that living with integrity among evil's banality in refined and smiling disguise, or living in a disabled body and asked to fake wellness, rallying an insistence on *fineness* as stoic spectacle, embracing suffering is noble? Are we, like the character Laura, doomed? At our end, is our sole or most aspirational option to grasp at the last perception of love-as-life with someone who has lied to us but gets to keep whatever is ours when we die?

Once the sociocultural commitment to maintain harmful illusions about disability at all costs becomes clear, especially with reference to gender or race or class, the pattern of pretense no longer exists as a viable response to such a system. To have that knowledge and operate otherwise creates harmful dissociation, disillusionment, and burnout. My ADHD brain now calls the illusion-addiction background noise, and I can ignore the mental clutter until the toxic buildup gets in the way of my functioning in the simulacrum, but even that takes a continuing toll on my mental and physical health.

Disability has so often been portrayed by humans as a negative existence, one eliciting pity at best, derision and harm at worst,[33] but hardly ever actual care. Why is that? Is it that we truly believe only vulnerable people ask for care, that vulnerability is somehow a fault or a disease itself, and that no one deserves care unless they can pay for it? That reminds me of the terrible advice to let babies cry without comfort, dysregulating their nervous systems in some kind of twisted discipline that teaches them their needs will only be half-met when they learn to suppress the very human requirement of loving attention. Yuck. A poetics of disability maintains that an absence of the *pretense* of health disrupts carefully tended illusions of normalcy. Culturally, we're told to show good health, to answer *fine* if asked how we're feeling, and to add nothing further, to don a smiling veneer of non-complaint and quiet compliance. This pretense is portrayed as admirable, as if appearing to strive for perfection is better than actually feeling well; as if perfection is in any way an attainable outcome, whatever outsized effort a person might produce, even in illusion, instead of a harmful farce, even at times the source or cause of disability itself.

Disability reminds humans that we are inherently vulnerable—requires us to face that reality in our daily lives. Vulnerability is in fact inseparable from the nature of our existence—perfection in human beings, to state the obvious, is impossible—so, why not embrace and accommodate that aspect of our humanness, especially at the level of language? If, as Toni Morrison posits, we use "a critical geography" that offers "much space for discovery, intellectual adventure, and close exploration as did the original charting of the new world—without the mandate for conquest,"[34] then we must also mark a place on that map for disabled ways of being that can exist free of derision, fear, and cultural habits of exclusion.

Disability poetics notices and articulates—despite the violent denial built into the systems underlying our society—the belief that more need means more care, but that care doesn't have to be earned, whether by character or currency, or any other form of hierarchal worth-centered categorization.[35] We could recognize that giving is admirable and valuable on an immeasurable human level instead of restricting it to the quantifiable measures administrators and statisticians are so fond of translating into charts and graphs. Active inclusion of disabled folks in society as the default means perceiving the use of resources toward care, even for a single person, as worthy of dignity, respect, and support—and, further, that everyone benefits from that care and allocation of resources. That means removing the notion of *uselessness* from our perceptions of disabled people.[36] That means a radical opening of our minds to real, privileging care over the pretense of it, and to our eschewing the dangerous fantasy of normalcy that erases entire populations and millions of individual lives.

If the fallacy of normalcy can truly enact such erasure, rendering anyone outside its extremely narrow and ill-defined parameters invisible, *disposable* even, then let's say so out loud and not even pretend to care. Let's go back to the time of barbarism—if we ever moved beyond it, that is, given that Rome wrote the histories, not the peoples who resisted their violent imperial expansion.[37] Reality for disabled people bears little resemblance to the pretense their healthy peers, families, and neighbors often cling to. Depending on the situation, ableist reality is either just a break from the brutality of disabled life or functions as its incitement—the thousand cuts of forced smiles and daily microaggressions or the torrent of outright hostility, isolation, and exclusion. If a disabled person doesn't perform expected happiness, like Laura does in *Stolen Hours*, they risk losing relationships with people they often depend on. When you are disabled, other people think they know what you need better than you do. They might ask you what you want, sometimes pretend to listen, and do what they want anyway—especially if you, the disabled person, can't stop them.

I now live in a small, mostly white college town in the south. No more laid-back and smiling Colorado cool, but real-deal redneck country. My son tried to work in retail the summer we moved here, in 2021. He's a young adult and wanted his own money. He has disabilities that the manager said she could accommodate—*accommodate*, that problematic term again, for something a person requires in order to live—but his coworkers were a different story. Even during the nationwide mask mandate, they hardly complied with proper masking, and several of them ate raw peanuts in the break room despite the sign saying someone on staff had an anaphylactic allergy and my son having also explicitly asked them not to. They didn't care. Why would they when some of their favorite comedians joke that life-threatening food allergies are hilarious, sometimes equating them with a weakness deserving of derision and exclusion from society in the name of their personal convenience?[38]

Lacking a safe work environment, my son had to confine himself to home in order to avoid the racism and ableism he was facing along with the coronavirus. He wanted to go back to school, but didn't feel safe—again, very few masks in sight, not to mention worries about mass shootings.[39] I saw him retreat further into himself. I fought doctor after doctor for him to get more effective treatment for his chronic migraine diagnosis than a shrug and a psychiatric referral, especially after his migraines veered terrifyingly into hemiplegic territory. At the same time, I saw my vibrant, dynamic, fierce, talkative, and outgoing diva of a mother slide into a depressed, near-catatonic state, when her closest sister—my favorite aunt Valerie—died of SARS-CoV-2 in April 2022. The only thing that brought mom back from the brink: daily visits from one of my sisters, my driving to New York to visit her after the funeral, and all of her daughters calling and talking to her almost every day. Once the government lifted the mask mandate, my mother also got SARS-CoV-2—twice in the span of three months, and her health declined further. The workers in her care facility not wearing masks anymore meant that for months, she lost her ability to speak. She was also diagnosed with Parkinson's, and she would have been completely bedridden if my sister and I hadn't purchased a wheelchair for her.

As caregivers, we do so much, but our care is no replacement for professional support. Between surgery in October 2022 and summer 2023, I knew my mother needed me, and I couldn't be there. Not only was I physically unable to travel post-surgery, I still had to work. I still have a job, a contract with the institution that hired me, and, despite everything, I continue to fulfill my obligations. I teach, I write, I grade, I attend many, many meetings. I can't deny, though, that the toxicity and petty infighting that seems to characterize so much of academia causes me to tune out. *Way* out. I have zero interest in institutional combat.

After my aunt died and I helped my cousin get through the funeral, after I found out I needed surgery, after my mother's health declined even further, I had no energy for the petty interpersonal finagling my job seemed to require. None of that mattered. The fibroids I knew I had for years, smallish before the pandemic, grew so large that I became dangerously anemic, unable to do much more than sleep for one-third of every month due to extreme fatigue and blood loss. The doctor wanted to slice open my abdomen and cut out all my reproductive organs, a procedure requiring a six-month recovery at minimum for a healthy woman—two years for me. I refused to believe that was the only solution. I wanted to travel, to finish my books, and the last time I'd had surgery—a laparoscopic appendectomy, not even the intense slice-and-dice of fibroid removal—I didn't fully recover at all and had medical trauma because of the dismissive way doctors treated me. That surgery reduced my vitality, aged me, stole my time and muscle tone, and I had no illusions that any other kind of surgery would be different. My doctor, however kind, couldn't hide her frustration and impatience with my questions. That made my anxiety worse, and I kept researching procedures.

Meanwhile, the pandemic raged on. The year before, my sense of self started crumbling, and I was fighting to stay sane. I was the strong one—

the soldier; the mother; the paladin, as I was sometimes called by my Gen Z niece—and I just couldn't cope anymore. Plague and fascism—those deadly external forces and their implications—weighed on me, stealing my future plans and my autonomy, and in August of 2021, my usual intrusive thoughts took over the space my shattered illusion once occupied. They teamed up with grief to reason that choosing my own kind of death would be preferable to a slow and painful one, or one from SARS-CoV-2 against my will. I'd run out of drive, care, hustle. Not for the first time in my life, I felt like a failure. But this was the first time since I'd quit art school more than a decade earlier—and even then, I still had a sense of determination. Ominously, nothing replaced my customary optimism but emptiness.

I don't remember what stopped me, what called me to ask for help in time to save myself. I got lucky; the person I reached knew what to say and how to help me. She listened, a fellow Black woman, and that one layer of understanding meant I could rest after disclosure, be understood in a deeper way than I could've hoped for from a veterans' suicide hotline. Eventually, I learned to recognize my apparent failure as an illusion as well. In asking for help, I subverted the impossible task of serving as a solo system of care and support for myself and others, while pretending *to be fine*. In therapy, I learned to articulate what I needed for support. I slept more. I found alternate treatments for fibroids after searching outside my local area and looking out of state. I kept a detailed log of my son's symptoms, compelling enough for the neurologist to prescribe the medication he needed in order to finally get relief for his debilitating daily pain. I lightened my grading load, performance schedule, and service work, and decided to just do *less*. For the first time in my career, I risked censure and recused myself from some of my responsibilities instead of adding to them.

Indeed, after I emerged from the acute phase of that health crisis, with varying levels of resentment and appreciation on my part, I engaged in a refusal so deep I found myself incapable of caring about the consequences of that refusal. I entered what I call a Bartleby phase. "I prefer not to" became a mantra of freedom from external pressures that threatened to destroy me—and countered the internal dialogue that harangued me to destroy myself because I couldn't possibly overcome those pressures, that even if I made the effort, I wouldn't succeed. No way out but death, right, if everything was conspiring to kill me—or, at least, didn't care if I lived or not?

So, why don't I do what I want? I asked myself, loudly. And I began to answer, *I will.*

Disability poetics is not an exercise in blame or excuse-making, then, but rather a more complete recognition. In the 1993 film *Tombstone*, the Doc Holliday character says of Wyatt Earp, who gathered a small crew to pursue a violent gang that killed his younger brother, "Make no mistake. It's not revenge he's after. It's a reckoning."[40] Reading and thinking about and analyzing films, books, music, society and its systems—anything public, really—through a lens of disability helps us to approach that reckoning fiercely and directly, dismantling our own veneers, sublimating how people and social systems perceive us in favor of elucidating how they *treat* us. Such a poetics allows a literary or cultural analyst to approach that articulation with clarity rather than obscuring the complete view in the name of surface appearances or propriety. Sacrificing one's public and relational sense of self—as the character Laura does in *Stolen Hours*— according to persistent cultural biases painting disability as shameful, as a thing to hide or suffer through humbly, holds no honor. Instead, that sacrifice indicts any society that denies sick and/or disabled people dignity and respect when it comes to their health, their care choices, or their death.

While the world clings to its destructive simulation of comfort, instead of dealing with the perceived discomfort of reality, writers continue to cut open the scrim. Who do we think we are, we writers, trying to put our minds in the way of erroneous thinking? Is that arrogance? Or is it deep care? We *know* we know; we have seen, and we want you to see. We implore you with all the talent and beauty and urgency we can muster. We are "Rowdy" Roddy Piper's character in the 1988 film *They Live*, trying to get people to put on the X-ray sunglasses and understand the disingenuous messages fed to us beneath the simulation's luxe gloss. A poetics of disability uses rhetorical invention as well as tradition, gentle cajoling as well as dirty fighting tactics and sucker punches, mimicking and masking, whispering and yelling, weeping and engaging in the longest fight scene in human history to facilitate understanding.

Sometimes, though, I think about the chaos eternal as depicted in

Lucretius's *The Nature of Things* and lose hope that humanity will ever change. We think we've advanced, but no—those speaking for disability-centered care continue to work and speak out despite being ignored, suppressed, harassed, dismissed, even harmed. I think about consumption—tuberculosis—a contagious disease that started to spread unchecked among communities of all classes and ages with unpredictable severity and which, according to the PBS documentary *The Forgotten Plague*, was allowed to kill one of every seven people who'd ever lived up to that point.[41] Did folks change their behavior in the 19th century in order to control this rampaging disease, to ease human suffering? History makes clear they didn't. And now, as we face our own ongoing plague? Little seems changed. History will show that, too—provided we're wise enough to ensure posterity, that is.

Lydia X. Z. Brown has already done the work of offering salient alternatives to ableist terms that, whether read literally or symbolically, perpetuate harm and harmful perceptions.[42] Will people bother to pay attention, and change their language and behavior, if there's no law or rule or academic policy to make them? If we go back to the years-long seatbelt debate in the US in the 1980s, that answer is no.[43] Will humanity ever willingly evolve, learn self-trust, and trust vulnerable people to know what they need? The pandemic has squashed most of that hope in me. Nevertheless, I persist in bringing what I imagine for myself and the people I love—trust, care, ease, and even delight in relationship with other people while navigating public spaces—into practice as often as possible. Disability poetics insists on that reimagining regardless of legalities, insists on new rhetorical, behavioral, and cultural habits in as gentle or as stringent a way as needed in the moment of awareness and beyond, flexing as time passes and circumstances shift—just as disabilities involve deep noticing, and periodic shifts in modes of awareness and action, to include fighting.

And we don't need violence in that fight. I am okay with being a secret force, quietly energetic, foundationally sound, instigating shifts that seem imperceptible until real change happens.

"The only lasting truth / is Change,"[44] wrote Octavia E. Butler in *Parable of the Sower*, and disability poetics understands the harshness of that truth, as well as the infinite possibilities of its seeded application.

A Sea of Troubles

Questions, Choices, and Actions
Toward Redefining Literary Culture

Follow-up on *The Report from the Field: Statements Against Silence*

NOTE: When I presented an excerpt of this essay at the Association of Writers and Writing Programs (AWP) Conference in Portland, Oregon on March 31, 2019, I wore a purple Song of Solomon T-shirt for strength. Why? At the end of that novel, Toni Morrison writes: "Wanna fly? You got to give up the shit that weighs you down."[1] It was time to release my anonymity. I did not cry until I got to the part about other women's stories, the ones I listened to and cannot repeat, the ones that sometimes flash up in my memory and make me have to sit still and breathe.

In July of 2018, I hosted a Q&A with author Roxane Gay in honor of the publication of her memoir *Hunger*. When I asked a question about how she chose what to disclose and what to keep private, she said she didn't describe the details of the gang rape she endured at age 14 because she didn't want a troll on Twitter repeating those details back to her. I feel similarly about details regarding traumas I have endured. I share what I feel like I could endure in the air I have surrendered to, and not what might weigh me down. I do also fall under and rely on the tradition of trauma narratives, notably the Harriet Jacobs text discussed earlier in this book. Like Jacobs, I disclose my experience in order to present my analysis of the general state of affairs with regard to sexual assault and harassment in literary spaces, and I intend it to lead to action-driven possible solutions to the overall problem. Choice is of paramount importance to survivors, and what I disclose or keep to myself, as part of "proceedings too terrible to relate"—to use Frederick Douglass's oft-quoted phrase[2]—is my choice. I choose not to split hairs of incidence and circumstance, as happens often with survivor stories, but rather to focus on the broader picture in an effort to shift our cultural practices—and our colleagues and students by extension—away from harm, and toward more humane and professional behavior.

When he told me in so many words that I might as well jump out of the window if I couldn't succeed in a relationship with him, I seriously considered it. I sat in front of him in my own home and stared out the window as he talked at me. He was about to head back to Brooklyn, but first sat in my used office chair with his leather bag at his feet and the afternoon sun behind him and told me what was wrong with everything I did/said/thought/remembered. Anytime I responded, he became crueler, so I stopped speaking at all. Instead, I pictured the length of flight, or fall—brief, I imagined—and I wondered how many bones might break, who would find me, and whether I should leave a note. I had never been spoken to with such low meanness by someone who claimed to love me, to worship me even. It didn't sound like love, and ultimately whatever he said or did to make me feel supported was countered with something casually or even overtly destructive. Whenever I was writing, for example, not paying attention to him and refusing his many attempts at distraction, he would say that I wrote too much.

I considered the chances of failure if I jumped from my three-story walk-up—and by failure, of course, I mean living. At the time I had little money. I was working part time while dealing with chronic health and mobility issues and was the author of two books with small presses, the second of which had just been published a few months before. My family and I were somewhat on the outs because of our relationship. The same was true with my friendships. The other people in my life didn't understand what I saw in him, and one friend said it was like I had disappeared. As I contemplated literally doing just that, however, I decided that killing myself because a man found me worthless ultimately failed to feel like a satisfactory resolution.

I ended the relationship shortly thereafter. He kept in contact—wrote emails, sent text messages, called. He would blame my dumping him for his subsequent bad behavior professionally and toward other women. I never blamed myself, but I kept remembering the charming attention from the start of the relationship, and even missed it. I was his KQ and he often reminded me of that possession. Had I not broken up with him, he said, he wouldn't have to be "messing around" with anyone else. I could not have imagined that the coercion I experienced on a regular basis throughout the relationship—off and on for a few years—might be extrapolated to everything from unprofessional comments to violent encounters. When I was with him, he talked so much that my own thoughts didn't have room to take root anyway, and if they did, he proceeded to tell me ceaselessly how wrong they were, having the effect of making me doubt my own sanity.[3]

Although I have begun this essay with a dramatic instance of my experience with a then-well-known poet, musician, and former professor, this will not be a justification for why we dated in the first place, nor will I detail the abuses I endured. Like Akasha Gloria Hull states in "Working to Redeem the Planet," I believe in addressing abuse in a way that "shifts the balance of power from abuse and victimization to the inexorable movement toward wholeness," and while I do not consider myself heroic or anything beyond plainly human, I do want to be a part of a group of change-makers who "consciously participate [. . . as] *not victims but redeemers*, not even survivors but redeemers, turning what has been done to us and what we are doing to evolutionary account" (*Soul Talk* 178, emphasis hers).

Accordingly, this essay is also not a defense or examination of the Collective—Dr. Bettina Judd, Dr. Ashaki Jackson, and myself—which was founded specifically in order to address the abuse my ex perpetrated in the literary community. It is not a recounting of the confidential stories of the 32 incredibly brave and powerful women who spoke with the Collective, only a handful of whom were willing to go on the record even anonymously—as published by VIDA, the women's literary organization, as part of their March 7, 2016, *Statements from the Field* series.[4] This essay is not about his vitriol, which he spewed constantly about nearly every other major poet, including MacArthur and Pulitzer Prize winners—including his so-called friends, some of whom have communicated to me that they think he got ostracized unfairly—to say nothing of the "minor" poets he often ridiculed unless or even if he could control them or make them feel indebted to him, aggressively using his influence in literary power circles to elevate some poets and suppress others. But perhaps those friends are afraid of the implications—perhaps they, too, have used their power or position in the poetry workplace to violate bodies and minds, disturbed their colleagues' and students' peace and progress, and used them as objects or unwitting pieces in a perverse game of literary chess. One can hope that in the wake of revelations about my ex and others that they've changed their behavior and/or made steps toward amends, whether of their own volition or as a result of outside pressure.

This essay is not about them, however, nor is it even about me. It is instead intended to be a catalyst for a larger conversation about what we tolerate, condone, and cover up in the name of love and poetry. It is preposterous to think that any abuser's perceived talent is a reason to allow them back into the workplace to abuse again, that the "work" of one institutionally lauded person is worth more than the safety and well-being of countless others. I don't even want to write this essay. I would rather be doing my other work. But the house of poetry is a mess, and I can't work in a dirty house. So once again, it's up to Black women to clean it up,[5] whether or not we get the credit, whether or not we can expect even to be acknowledged,[6] whether institutions support us or not. When institutions and laws could not or would not take action, the Collective worked behind the scenes to get this man to stop his cruel behavior and to implement preventive measures. Our efforts were met with some success, but it feels precarious. Several times since the VIDA statement appeared, he has been hired by writing retreats, his band is still active, and folks continue to grumble about the "ethics" of public call-outs;[7] even more sinister, there are several other known abusers who remain high-profile and still go unnamed publicly. While most venues removed my ex from the roster when made aware of the 2016 statement due to pressure from the poetry community, more needs to be done. We need something formally in place to prevent a culture of complicity and silence around abuse. We need systems of support for survivors.

It is time to insist that poetry is a workplace, not a hunting ground. It's time for professionalization, and not in an institution-protecting, lackluster, repressive, surface, or placatory way. It's time to start radically protecting people, to create an environment of integrity and respect, to say no to bullies, narcissists, predators, handlers, and enablers. As I told a reporter at *Jezebel*, for whom I served as an anonymous source for a 2016 article I will not name because it lacks integrity and compassion,[8] their time is up.

In the wake of my book *I'm So Fine: A List of Famous Men & What I Had On*— which uses celebrity and fashion to illuminate issues of trauma, self-empowerment, and resilience in the midst of rape culture—people keep telling me their stories. How they were sexually violated by someone they trusted, by strangers, by lovers, by relatives, by employers, by colleagues, by professors, even by their own students.[9] Women and femme-presenting individuals are not safe anywhere. Younger, less experienced poets are especially vulnerable, because they are often dealing with deep trauma. Many poets arrive at poetry to deal with that trauma and emotional difficulty, as their work often details explicitly—particularly in regard to sexual abuse. I don't want to name any poets specifically, but a simple web search and perusal of the work of queer and female poets attests to this.

The famous poet I mention but do not name in *I'm So Fine* often mocked the attempts other poets made to create safe learning spaces and seemed to seek out the most wounded of us on purpose, using what he saw in our poems against us. If survivors told anyone about what he did to us, he could point to that trauma, saying we weren't credible because we were already talking about those things in our poetry and had already been victimized—or, to use his frequent term, were "crazy." He didn't have to do much to make us appear unreliable or to intimidate us into silence. He just had to pay attention. He certainly wanted to know about all of *my* traumas, of which there are indeed many. But something told me not to share everything with him. I think I survived that day, up until that day and forward, because I managed to keep some small part of myself to myself—even if he wanted that part, too. I just wouldn't let him have it.

Before we went public with the anonymous testimony through VIDA in 2016, I was urged to put my name on my account, to be the face of the outing of a poet who had been terrorizing other writers for nearly three decades. I had nothing to lose, presumably, in making my position public—at least not my livelihood, because I wasn't working in academia at the time. In the aftermath, however, I got incredibly sick. I threw up. I couldn't digest my food properly. I lost weight. It was like my body could not hold all I had heard, could not even hold the truth I had to admit to myself. I was grieving. I wept. I screamed. I experienced a constant fluctuation of emotions: fear, anxiety, rage, and sadness. I wrote this essay with bile in my throat. But I have to keep going.[10]

When I was first approached about helping to publish a startling number of accounts of abuses this poet had committed, I had just made peace with the fact that he had, indeed, been abusive and coercive toward me.[11] But he and I were still on speaking terms. In fact, I had just recommended his work about conspiracy theories to a student, albeit with the qualification that he was problematic. He had even asked me just a few weeks before the first private revelation that was shared with me to visit him in Iowa, where he taught. He wanted me to drive there and visit for a few days. Later, I found out that he had asked a number of other women to do the same, to visit him to authenticate his presence there, because his inappropriate behavior at Iowa toward both students and colleagues was garnering negative attention. I'd said no since I was scheduled to speak at another university that same week. I also couldn't take any more time off from my job, and, because I have disabilities, couldn't justify the physical toll the long drive would take. He started calling and texting and emailing constantly again, berating me if I didn't answer quickly enough or write superlatively enough, so I said no. I told him I couldn't do it again and wished him well. He didn't seem too phased. He called the director of the program at the university where I was speaking to tell her to "take care of me"—after telling me by phone that he'd gotten me the gig (a claim, the director was quick to tell me, that was false).

Yet, I wished him well. Why would I do that for a man who made me feel so worthless I had considered ending my own life? Please hear me when I say this: that isn't the right question. I will interrogate issues of internalized misogyny elsewhere. The questions most pressing, for my purposes here, are: what kind of world do we live in that *my* choices are interrogated, and not *his*? Why are those he abused excoriated and not the institutions that looked the other way when confronted with the truth of his actions, along with the actions of many others, whose names also cropped up in this process—some of whom did go on to accept restorative justice measures, some of whom still fear revelation of their awful acts? Their fear, though, pales in comparison to the fear experienced by those who have been and remain vulnerable to predatory behavior.

I do not presume to speak for anyone else when I say that, for me, the word *victim* holds little empowerment. I do not presume to speak for anyone else when I say I'm not interested in recycling shame-based narratives or socially-enforced fear or negativized vulnerability. I *am* interested in bodily autonomy. I say I am not a victim because *I* say so, because *I* get to choose how to characterize my own experience. The world we live in often labels those of us who speak up as disgruntled, disempowered, and dismissible as common complainers. There is little care in public discourse about sexual harassment and violence, and legislative recourse routinely fails people who experience sexual assault. It's not hard to recognize that the two forms of neglect-in-the-name-of-objectivity are related.[12] So, why speak up at all? It's easier to keep things quiet, to preserve the status quo, right?

I believe that's a deeply flawed and unproductive line of reasoning. Instead, I wonder (rhetorically, and yes, sarcastically):

How is enduring violence easier than ending it?[13]

How does pretense preserve anything but eventual destruction?

I challenge us all to ask ourselves: What kind of community—a word that gets thrown around a lot in poetry circles—do we want to create? An even better question: What kind of workplace do we want, now and in the future? What kind of workplace do we want for our children, many creative in their own right? Do we want to reward and elevate despotic and violent narcissists just because we think their poems are good? Or do we want to make sure that our institutions, the ones we insist deserve veneration, indeed venerate us back—venerate meaning to exalt and celebrate the humanity we purport to value in creative work? There are models for a mode of relationship-building based on treasuring human beings rather than the pernicious mythologies created by an elite few. I urge you to seek out tools and resources through the Time's Up organization, news articles, and American Training Resources—as well as to do your own research—and to insist upon positive change.[14]

As a workplace, it behooves us to ask ourselves: What do we value? Is it only money and the veneer (and the apparent protections) of "success," and if so, why profess to value the humanities? Don't pretend the world of poetry is a safe "community" for those who know how to live and love from the heart. This is indeed a workplace, and in a workplace, we expect certain standards. Some people exploit those expectations, using their power and position to bully others into silence. When it comes to enforced silence like that, though, time truly is up.

It should be noted that before the VIDA report came out, several partners of the Collective offered my abuser the opportunity to admit his wrongs, to make restitution, to apologize for and stop his abusive behavior. He declined.

Why am I going public now, then, in print, when it would appear I have a lot to lose? I'm a tenured professor at an R1 university, and my creative work is well known and well regarded. I could keep my head down and my mouth shut, focus on the future, and risk nothing. But I can't choose accomplishments or income over integrity. I can't be silent and simply allow myself to be carried by this momentous tide. I take the risk of being seen as a troublemaker because I refuse that label: my actions protest and attempt to protect my colleagues and students from professional and personal harm. That is not making trouble for anyone but those who cause such harm, whether individuals or institutions, and if we are indeed a profession to be respected, a culture of harm *cannot* be an option or an aspiration.

I have lost everything more than once in my life. Elizabeth Bishop said the art of losing isn't hard to master.[15] I think I could do it again. The conclusion I came to during this process was that if poetry continues to value abusers over budding writers, women, and femme-presenting writers, elevating the powerful few over the masses of strivers, then *I don't want it*. I will have learned that, like so much else in this world, the fields of poetry and academia are not for me—the two are entangled in my mind because I came to poetry through academia, prefer to work on the page, and do not have the physical stamina required to excel at performance poetry. Public space is generally not for me anyway. My presence is often considered disruptive, my Blackness, womanness, and disabledness barely tolerated when it isn't a surprise, or I'm dismissed when I choose not to be used for my beauty or my labor. Where could I, and people like me, exist, if not in the spaces we claim as our own? Was my earlier question the wrong one? Is it instead a case of my being thrown out the window, not of jumping through it of my own accord?

I can't predict that. I don't have a plan. What I know is how to fight to be my full self even in a hostile environment, to state, as Audre Lorde did as she faced cancer: "I am not only a casualty, I am also a warrior."[16] I may end up defeated, but that will be on my terms, in the full light of truth and the kind of integrity I believe we cannot live without.

A word on justice, on public call-outs, on authority and power. We—survivors—do not need to consult any authority before saying no to violence, to silence, to shame, to oppression, to harassment, to offensive comments, to dismissal, to being told we should have done things differently, to existing in an openly hostile workplace. The only authority we need over our own wellbeing, our bodies, our minds, our healing, our creativity, our work, is OURS. Our authority over ourselves is enough. If we are claiming it for survival, no one—no institution, no celebrity, no journalist, no famous writer, no professor, no colleague, no lover, no friend, no relative, no stranger, NOBODY[17] has the right to tell us we can't.

We are our own authority.

The power is OURS. No one else has the right to weigh in on our feelings and expect their opinion to matter more than ours. As Dr. Bettina Judd has said, "Those who question that authority should question their own motivations and ask themselves why they would choose to repeat the impulse to question a survivor's autonomy."[18]

Maltreatment, bullying, and harassment, especially in workplaces where the line between the personal and professional are blurred, has been normalized for far too long. Traditional approaches have criticized victims rather than perpetrators for far too long.[19] Law and policy is used to sustain silence over abuse, rather than prevent it, when non-enforcement takes place.[20] That non-enforcement protects institutions, not people, especially not women and femme-presenting individuals, and especially not those who are writers with limited resources and little or no name recognition. But—and I can't say this emphatically enough—*survivors don't lie about abuse.* According to RAINN (Rape, Abuse & Incest National Network), an estimated 98% of rape allegations are truthful. Yet, RAINN also notes that only 0.6% of rapists are convicted in court, and only a fraction of rapes are even reported in the first place.[21]

Educate yourself with further facts about LGBTQIA and nonbinary individuals, rape of men, military members, and more at RAINN's website.[22]

When the allegations against my abuser came out in 2016, I wanted to sequester myself. AWP was coming up, and instead of enjoying that annual event in my hometown of Los Angeles, I had panic attacks because he was threatening to show up. I skipped every panel except mine, and my jumpiness, paranoia, and irritability during that trip affected my personal and professional interactions—some irreparably. I stuck with close friends, went to the beach, dined out, got my nails done, and slept, though I did host the last event in my own reading series surrounded by friends, and I performed at a spectacular offsite event with the Black Took Collective.[23] After leaving that revolutionarily welcoming creative space, I thought about more than one older poet rolling their eyes a decade ago at baby poet me, at my enthusiasm, my joy at being considered a writer among the ranks of those whose work I admired. Already jaded, they knew I'd learn. For that I do not thank them. But when I see younger poets and some of my generation saying no, using their imaginations and love of self to create new discourses and new possibilities of kinship over competition, I thank them for their lessons and reminders. It is my privilege to listen and speak and imagine alongside you.

I especially want to thank the queer poetry community and younger poets for being an integral part of assisting the Collective in the gathering and confirmation of stories, for the eloquent statement of public support from male-presenting poets, for their courageous heart-work and matching actions.[24] It is time to consider such support invaluable; it is not disposable service work, a waste of time, nor futile effort. It is time to accurately name it an active shaping of the kind of workplace culture we want now and in the future.[25]

Fear is more than an emotional state. It is also processed in the body.[26] It takes time to learn how to reverse its damage, for shame to be transformed into self-acceptance and self-love. It can take a lifetime. Some never arrive at that transmutative state, and if you're fortunate enough to have been able to do that sustained, deep work, it can still be threatened at any time. When it comes to poetry, we need a workplace that allows for positive transformation, not accumulation of more fear, whether subtle or overt.

Now is the time to make room for many modes of survival and resilience. Instead of judging or worrying or condemning or questioning how a survivor of abuse, harassment, rape, etc., chooses to go about their revelations and recovery, instead of doubting the undeniable volume and severity of the allegations, worry about how you can change your behavior, your workplace, and the culture at large in such a way that no other individual has to wait in the shadows suffering under the weight of mistreatment, wanting to say *me too* but having no one in their corner to hear them with compassion and respect. Comment on colleagues' and students' work and thoughts, rather than on their appearance. Create an environment of listening, integrity, restitution. Read *The Revolution Starts at Home*.[27] Create an environment that compels abusers to admit to and stop the behavior instead of hiding behind institutional endorsement, respectability politics, and commonly-held (but outmoded and destructive) assumptions or beliefs. Instead of accepting the way things are, question why and offer positive alternatives that work for you, your organization, community, or institution.

A few years ago, I dreamed that Lucille Clifton sat on the chair next to my bed and told me I had to fight. I have been fighting since then, win or lose. I do it in my own way, in my own time, in all kinds of circumstances, not always of my own choosing. But when I can choose, when I am able to, I do. To paraphrase what a RAINN counselor told me when I called the hotline the night after I was first assaulted at age eighteen: Whatever that fight looks like for you, whatever you had/have to do to survive, was/is the right thing. And, in the immortal words of June Jordan, in "Poem About My Rights":

I am not wrong: Wrong is not my name
My name is my own my own my own
and I can't tell you who the hell set things up like this
but I can tell you that from now on my resistance
my simple and daily and nightly self-determination
may very well cost you your life[28]

The metaphorical life Jordan mentions is the life of silence and complicity, of lies and denial. The price of that life is the temporary pain of recognition, and the hard work of questioning and rebuilding on a more equitable foundation. What kind of literary life do we want for ourselves, our friends, our colleagues, our students, and our elders? We are creative people. Our field is the humanities. What if we created a more humane literary life in place of the current toxic one? What if we prized character over connections, generosity instead of exclusivity, honesty instead of hustling fast-talk? What if we refused to surrender to manipulation? What if we stopped genuflecting to bullies? What if we created a culture of respect, honor, love, and care? What if those ideals were not dismissed as theoretical niceties but made to underlie the choices we make in our interactions with one another? I would like to believe that that new life, that new literary world is already being created now. That is a world I want to live in, to work in, and to teach in. All it takes is practice.

Professional Practices: A Brief Guide for Creating Safer Academic and Literary Workplaces

This quick-reference guide is meant to serve as a resource for writers at all stages—those thinking of becoming a writer, student writers, and published writers at emerging, midcareer and established levels—so that we all may be in the practice of creating a professional environment with high standards that we all can benefit from. It is an outline of both problems and solutions, and is meant to be a call for leadership on the subject of professionalism in the humanities, in academic spaces and beyond, so that all segments of the writing population may focus more fully on their work.

Enclosed are guidelines specifically for the following urgent areas:

- Sexual predators in the overall literary community
- BFA, MA, MFA, and PhD Programs

The following spaces can also use clearer guidelines around how to foster a respectful environment free of abusive dynamics:

- Workshops
- Conferences
- Readings
- Publishing
- Judging Awards & Fellowships
- Mentorship
- Friendships and Romantic Relationships
- Creating Writing Groups and Organizations

Difficult and traumatic situations can stymie one's work and harm writers' physical, mental, and professional wellbeing. It is time to change the belief that writers are cutthroat lone wolves in competition for scarce resources, when in fact we are powerful creators of opportunity who often thrive in community—that includes academia, publishing, writing groups, friendships, and reading series. And luckily, we are capable of deciding what kind of literary community we want to create. This guide can be a resource not only in times of distress, but in affirming best practices and serving as a catalyst for creative innovation and empowerment when it comes to building communities that nurture writers—the makers of art we turn to now, and in the future.

Dealing with Sexual Predators in the Literary Community

Sexually inappropriate behavior in the literary community, as in other workplaces, has and continues to be rampant. Acknowledging and accepting that is step one. Perhaps the most egregious behavior is the predatory famous (usually male) writer abusing multiple other writers (usually female, often students). Some of those predators may have felt entitled to the bodies and labor of those they abused. Some may have gone unchecked in the workplace and in relationships for decades, with or without censure. However, we now have the opportunity, because of the momentum of activist Tarana Burke's #MeToo movement, to facilitate real change—to imagine a world wherein consent is valued over bragging rights and entitlement, where empowerment is valued over the exertion of power, where mentorship is based on mutual professional respect and generosity. Despite virulent backlash, we can remain steadfast in our efforts to implement solutions.

Burke came to the University of Colorado, Boulder on April 15, 2019 and I attended her talk. She described her work as considering sexual violence in the context of social justice: "Sexual violence doesn't discriminate. The response to it does."[29] In other words, it means changing the perception of sexual violence as a crime, or as a personal shame, to a more accurate characterization as a violent extension of discriminatory beliefs and practices. She advised us to lean into our differences to create allyship rather than continue the arguably unsuccessful American habit of melting-pot assimilation, which can be a denial or erasure of difference. I felt validated in my approach when she advised us to focus on leadership, accountability, and professionalization. Instead of letting the institutions we work and learn within—educational, criminal justice, etc.—influence or dictate the rules to us, she said we must influence the institutions.

Relationships traditionally occur between two people, but sometimes it takes an entire community to address systemic problems underlying those relationships. The media has been used because institutions have failed to protect vulnerable individuals from sexual predators and serial harassers, and it is a powerful way to attempt to shield potential victims and end the behavior. But we have the capacity to act differently, though admittedly some of the steps are easier said than done; however, it makes no sense not to try. Here are some steps all corners of the community can take to create a safer, more professional workplace.

1. Define and have mechanisms in place to facilitate a professional work environment, with clear and enforceable consequences for those who violate professional standards.
2. Believe accusers first. A thorough investigation will reveal rare falsehoods. But initial belief and support is crucial in discouraging abuse and inviting victims to speak up safely.
3. Have zero tolerance for predatory behavior. Do not make excuses for or cover up the behavior. Remove accused predators from the work environment immediately.
4. IMPORTANT: Change the way we think about the outing of predators. Make it a point of prestige to address accusations with integrity, and care for those abused. Make it respectable to honorably treat those who come forward.
5. Be complete in investigating the predator. Share resources with other employers of the individual, and identify and notify any other vulnerable persons or populations.
6. Attempt to reconcile. See if the predator will apologize, stop the behavior and agree to sustained treatment, and provide restitution as defined by the victims. If restorative justice cannot be agreed upon, the predator must not be allowed in literary circles to victimize others.
7. A more involved proposal: Create a committee for restorative justice measures as a rotating body. Volunteer service? Paid via grant

or Restorative Justice Fund? This option falls outside the scope of this document currently, but may be revisited in the future.

Please note that I have not mentioned the criminal justice/legal system. That system in the past has been used to further victimize those coming forward, and as a threat to institutions' pocketbooks, which enforces silence and enables more abuse. While accusers have every right to utilize those systems, they have not worked very well in terms of fostering cultural change. Many victims simply want the predator to stop the behavior, and they want to feel supported by their community. Most importantly, they want to be free to do their work and to thrive professionally. Creating a culture that makes true professionalism a common goal is the top priority. Burke urged us to "grow and promote empathy" in our classrooms and communities, to be consistent in calls for accountability, and to focus on survivors' wellbeing in implementing solutions. "Don't think you checked off a box just because you invited me to your school," she joked.[30] She called on institutions to put their money behind all the administrative language around sexual violence, and to talk about it openly as part of promoting campus safety. I would also like to see more leadership training in academic and literary spaces, perhaps facilitated through writer-led organizations, and funded by institutions for the good of all of us.

BFA, MA, MFA, and PhD Programs

As of this writing, there is no national oversight of MFA programs or workshops, no powerful union to put universities on notice when they violate the Title IX policies in place—and endangered by our current federal administration—to ostensibly protect students, faculty, and staff. However, we are not powerless as individuals or a population at large. We have the capacity to communicate and to act. These bulleted lists are by no means exhaustive, and will be expanded pending grant funding and time to do more research and interviews with human subjects.

Problems noted (not an exhaustive list)

- Disrespect in the classroom
- Patronizing tone, condescension

- Elitism
- Racism
- Sexism
- Homophobia/gender-based discrimination
- Refusing to use someone's correct pronouns
- Ableism
- Plagiarism
- Works targeting individuals in the workshop
- Lack of professional advice and mentorship support
- Retaliation for complaints
- Professional maligning
- Withheld opportunities
- Inaccessible opportunities

What to do when witnessing the creation of a hostile work environment

- Point out the issue in front of everyone
- Listen to the person being harmed and ask what he/she/they need to feel safe
- Do not make excuses for or apologize for another person's bad behavior
- Model professional behavior (integrity, honesty, focus on the work not the person during critique, productivity, collegiality, etc.)

If you are the one who harmed another person with words or actions

- Stop the behavior
- Apologize
- Seek help from friends, therapists, instructor, etc., to help you understand how to behave differently in the future
- Refrain from retaliation or backbiting
- Accept consequences with professionalism

Responsibility of authority figures

- Help create an environment that encourages confidence and self-sufficiency

- Train students to advocate for themselves
- Make room for different ways of knowing
- Give people speaking up the benefit of the doubt
- Err toward kindness
- Create an environment of generosity and collegiality
- Avoid fear-based language and aggressive behaviors
- Avoid making assumptions; listen and ask questions
- Provide accessible course materials (PDFs, audio books, electronic copies)
- Create an accessible classroom—speak to your department, if necessary, about lighting (for migraine sufferers, fluorescent lighting can be a barrier to learning); chairs (built-in desks can bar some folks from sitting comfortably); location (folks in wheelchairs, on crutches, or with other mobility issues need elevator access)

Student responsibilities

- Be assertive
- Do the work
- Avoid self-pity
- Seek help from friends, therapists, and outside of the program
- Trust your instincts
- Leave situations where you feel unsafe or uncomfortable, including situations in which sought-for help becomes problematic; keep trying until you find proper support for both acute and ongoing issues

Program responsibilities

- Listen to student complaints and keep students' wellbeing foremost in importance
- Address faculty and student concerns about accessibility, speaking up even if budget is a factor in making spaces accessible
- Act upon complaints about sexual harassment (and ableism, racism, etc.) with speed and integrity
- Follow and enforce institutional guidelines in place
- If guidelines do not work, create better guidelines

- Support students over institutional interests
- Be clear and transparent with information about opportunities
- Provide more teaching opportunities to encourage and foster professionalization
- Pair MA students with PhD students for mentorship
- Have clear guidelines for mentorship
- Career advice and implementable solutions for post-MA and post-PhD
- Go beyond simply using the language of inclusion; practice it
- Less cronyism—partner with folks across the program, not just friends

Community opportunities

- Self-advocacy training
- Emotional, professional, and physical distress: create guidelines for what to do in the moment and beyond
- Who do you go to if your program is not supportive? Create a list of sustainable resources for all members of the community
- Create a system of informing students and new writers of those resources

Readings

- If your organization doesn't already, invite disabled writers, Black writers, trans and nonbinary writers, writers of color and all permutations thereof
- Instruct readers to print their work for hearing impaired folks, and print out introductions as well (including large print, at least one but a number that is commensurate with the size of the event)
- Make sure there is a microphone available
- Make sure the venue is accessible to those with mobility concerns
- Make sure there is seating set aside for those with mobility concerns
- Read an access statement before the reading, and remind folks at least once during the event that they are free to access the space however they need to. Sample access statement, following the

example of The Ohio State University professor of disability studies Margaret Price, modified for literary events:

- We invite you to use this space in any way you like. The space is [describe it—i.e., a small room with carpet on the floors and no windows]. The door is [over here to the right]. The lighting appears to be fluorescent. If you need to move around the space, or sit on the floor, or stim, or knit, or text, or tweet, or leave the space and come back in later, or anything that makes this space accessible to you, then please feel free. We would also like to note the presence of the sign language interpreter, who is here [to the right/left of the speakers].[31]

Other areas that could use more behavioral guidelines:

- Funding
- Conferences
- Mentorship
- Creating Writing Groups and Organizations
- Friendships and Romantic Relationships
- Judging Awards & Fellowships

Appendix A

Astrological Chart & Report for *Invisible Man*

Go to https://www.astro.com/horoscope for a detailed natal chart if you'd like to see a visual of the chart. Input the following data: Male, born on 14 April 1952 at 8:00 am in New York, New York. This results in sun sign of Aries, an ascendant in Gemini, and Moon sign in Sagittarius. There are short passages explaining the significance of each major planetary and house placement. Brief excerpts quoted below.

Sun in Aries, Moon in Sagittarius

"You are disconcertingly direct in your opinions and convictions."

Saturn in the Fifth House

"You should make an effort to become involved with the various human experiences of love so that your communicative power is increased."

Venus in the Eleventh House

"You strive for peace and harmony and if it were left up to you the whole world would be more humane, kind, and considerate."

Notes

1. National Organization for Women, "Violence Against Women in the United States: Statistics." https://now.org/resource/violence-against-women -in-the-united-states-statistic/

2. Michelle A. Marzullo and Alyn J. Libman, "Hate Crimes and Violence Against Lesbian, Gay, Bisexual and Transgender People," Human Rights Campaign Foundation, 2009. https://assets2.hrc.org/files/assets/resources /Hatecrimesandviolenceagainstlgbtpeople_2009.pdf

3. "Violence Against Children: A Global Problem." https://www.sos-usa .org/our-impact/focus-areas/violence-against-children

4. "The Amazon Is on Fire. Here's Why You Should Care." https://www .cnn.com/videos/world/2019/08/24/amazon-rainforest-fires-orig-mg-lc-jk .cnn

5. On September 14, 2019, the *New York Times* reported that Bee Love Slater, age 23, became the eighteenth transgender person killed in 2019. More information at https://www.nytimes.com/2019/09/14/us/black-transgend er-woman-bee-love-slater.html and https://www.hrc.org/resources/violen ce-against-the-transgender-community-in-2019

6. Julie Bosman, Kate Taylor, and Tim Arango, "A Common Trait Among Mass Killers: Hatred Toward Women," *New York Times*, August 10, 2019. https://www.nytimes.com/2019/08/10/us/mass-shootings-misogyny-dayt on.html

7. "Attorney General Barr Gives Award to Lawyers for Backing Brett Kava-naugh," *Mother Jones*, September 14, 2019. https://www.motherjones.com/po litics/2019/09/barr-justice-department-award-brett-kavanaugh/

8. I use the term "we" here as Gwendolyn Brooks does in her poem "Paul Robeson," on p. 19 of her 1971 chapbook *Family Pictures*—an ode to Robeson as much as a call to and for Black people: "We are each other's business; we are each other's harvest; we are each other's magnitude and bond." In my hope for change, I would love to include writers and other culture-makers in that "we," not just poets, though I do not presume to speak for Brooks.

9. "We might see *Ion* as a first attempt to master poetry . . . *Ion* can be seen as the birthplace of the literary critic and of literary theory, in that it offers the outline of a first poetics, poetry mastered as a whole by the intellect, a pursuit of which Plato sees his contemporary poets, performers and audience as incapable." Pelagia Goulimari, "Mimēsis: Plato and the Poet," in Goulimari, *Literary Criticism and Theory: From Plato to Postcolonialism* (New York: Routledge, 2014), 6.

10. Paulo Freire, *Pedagogy of the Oppressed*, translated by Myra Bergman Ramos (London, New York: Continuum, 2006), 141.

11. See Goulimari, "Mimēsis," 7.

12. For more on the importance of feeling and social change, see Audre Lorde in *Black Women Writers at Work,* edited by Claudia Tate (New York: Continuum, 1985), 108.

13. For one political example, see Jessica Schrader's article "Trump Is Gaslighting America Again—Here's How to Fight It" in *Psychology Today*, August 31, 2018. https://www.psychologytoday.com/us/blog/mind-in-the-machine/201808/trump-is-gaslighting-america-again-here-s-how-fight-it

14. "Everywhere we are told that our human resources are all *to be used*, that our civilization itself means the uses of everything it has—the inventions, histories, every scrap of fact. But there is one *kind* of knowledge—infinitely precious, time-resistant more than monuments, here to be passed between the generations in any way it may be: never to be used. And that is poetry." From Muriel Rukeyser, "The Fear of Poetry," in *The Life of Poetry* (Middletown, CT: Wesleyan University Press, 1996), 7, emphasis in the original.

15. "However confused the scene of our life appears, however torn we may be who now do face that scene, it can be faced, and we can go on to be whole." Rukeyser, "The Fear of Poetry," 8.

16. "The American democratic experiment needed saving, he had implored in *Leaves*, was worth saving. For his effort, he'd been called 'preposterous,' 'nonsensical,' 'grotesque,' and 'scurvy.' A lesser man would have been shamed into silence. Walt Whitman determined to speak louder." Transcript of *Walt Whitman: American Experience*, PBS, para. 3 (aired April 14, 2008). https://www.pbs.org/wgbh/americanexperience/films/whitman/#transcript

17. "Song of Myself," lines 20–22, sec. 25. https://iwp.uiowa.edu/whitmanweb/en/writings/song-of-myself/section-25

18. See Ronald G. Shafer, "Whitman's 'Leaves of Grass' was banned—and cost him his federal job." *Washington Post*, April 30, 2022. https://www.washingtonpost.com/history/2022/04/30/walt-whitman-leaves-grass-interior-department/

19. For a comprehensive overview of texts criticizing Whitman, particularly poet June Jordan's reckoning with the "queer outsider" Whitman next to the one adopted late into the American canon, see Lavelle Porter's "Should

Walt Whitman be #Cancelled?" *JSTOR Daily*, April 17, 2019. https://daily.jstor
.org/should-walt-whitman-be-cancelled/

20. Rukeyser, *The Life of Poetry*, 160.

21. Thomas Lewis, Fari Amini, and Richard Lannon, *A General Theory of Love* (New York: Random House, 2000), 13, emphasis in the original.

22. Lewis, Amini, and Lannon, *A General Theory of Love*, 12.

23. Lewis, Amini, and Lannon, *A General Theory of Love*, 12.

24. Lewis, Amini, and Lannon, *A General Theory of Love*, 3.

25. Lewis, Amini, and Lannon, *A General Theory of Love*, 5.

26. Lewis, Amini, and Lannon, *A General Theory of Love*, 5.

27. For more on philosophies of artmaking in cultural and experiential contexts, see Audre Lorde, in *Black Women Writers at Work*, 112.

28. See OED, definition 1 for "poetics": https://www.oed.com/view/Entry/318383

29. See OED, definition 1 for "praxis": https://www.oed.com/view/Entry/149425

30. Muriel Rukeyser: "A poem does invite, it does require. What does it invite? A poem invites you to feel. More than that: it invites you to respond. And better than that: a poem invites a total response. This response is total, but it is reached through the emotions. A fine poem will seize your imagination intellectually . . . but the way is through emotion, through what we call feeling." *The Life of Poetry*, 11.

31. "[I]n the text of pleasure, the opposing forces are no longer repressed but in a state of becoming: nothing is really antagonistic, everything is plural." Roland Barthes, *The Pleasure of the Text* (New York: Hill & Wang, 1975), 31.

32. For more on feeling, language, precision, and meaning, see Toni Morrison, in *Black Women Writers at Work*, 126.

33. For more on thinking processes, language, and Blackness, see Toni Morrison, in *Black Women Writers at Work*, 123–24.

34. Ralph Ellison, *Invisible Man* (New York: Random House, 1952), 579.

35. Édouard Glissant elucidates further and calls for a solution in *Poetics of Relation*, translated by Betsy Wing (Ann Arbor: University of Michigan Press, 1990), 65.

36. "American poetry has been part of a culture in conflict. . . . I speak of the tearing that exists everywhere in western culture. We are a people tending toward democracy at the level of hope; on another level, the economy of the nation, the empire of business within the republic, both include in their basic premise the concept of perpetual warfare. It is the history of the idea of war that is beneath our other histories. . . . But around and under and above it is another reality; like desert-water kept from the surface and the seed, like the old desert-answer needing its channels, the blessing of much work before it arrives to act and make flower. This history is the history of possibility." Rukeyser, *The Life of Poetry*, 61.

37. Toni Morrison, *The Source of Self-Regard* (New York: Penguin Random House, 2019), 155.

38. See Hélène Cixous, "The Laugh of the Medusa," translated by Keith Cohen and Paula Cohen, *Signs* 1, no. 4 (Summer 1976): 883. https://www.jstor.org/stable/3173239

39. Glissant, *Poetics of Relation*, 9.

40. Lucille Clifton, *Collected Poems* (Port Townsend, WA: Copper Canyon Press, 2016), 323.

41. Glissant, *Poetics of Relation*, 1.

42. Lucille Clifton, "a dream of foxes," in *Collected Poems*, 486.

43. "It is impossible to *define* a feminine practice of writing, and . . . this practice can never be theorized, enclosed, coded—which doesn't mean that it doesn't exist. But it will always surpass the discourse that regulates the phallocentric system." Cixous, "Laugh of the Medusa," 883, emphasis in the original.

44. Jadakiss, "Blackout," on *Flesh of My Flesh, Blood of My Blood*, DMX featuring Jay-Z and The Lox (Ruff Ryders/Def Jam 1998), track 13.

45. "Everything good tends to clarify. By good I mean well written and well researched. There is nothing so strong as an idea whose time has come." Maya Angelou, in *Black Women Writers at Work*, 10–11.

46. Morrison, *Source of Self-Regard*, 132.

47. Morrison, *Source of Self-Regard*, 133.

48. Morrison, *Source of Self-Regard*, 137.

49. See OED, "peregrination," https://www.oed.com/view/Entry/140667

50. Cixous, "Laugh of the Medusa," 875.

51. For more on writers' responsibility, see Maya Angelou in *Black Women Writers at Work*, 5.

52. Barthes, *The Pleasure of the Text*, 50–51.

53. Angelou, in *Black Women Writers at Work*, 4.

54. "I believe talent is like electricity. We don't understand electricity. We use it." Angelou, in *Black Women Writers at Work*, 7.

55. Sara Ahmed, "Collective Feelings: Or, the Impressions Left by Others," *Theory, Culture & Society* 21, no. 2 (2004): 28.

56. Lorde, *Black Women Writers at Work*, 105, emphasis in the original.

57. Glissant, 18.

58. Edward Said, *Humanism and Democratic Criticism* (New York: Columbia University Press, 2004), 32.

59. Said, *Humanism and Democratic Criticism*, 37.

60. Of note: when Bloom died in October 2019, a 2004 *New York Magazine* article by Naomi Wolf resurfaced. "Sex and Silence at Yale" details a 1983 incident in which Bloom put his hand on the thigh of then-20-year-old Wolf, then his student. Yet Yale failed to exact any consequences with regard to her

(or many other) allegations of unwanted contact. More information at http://nymag.com/nymetro/news/features/n_9932/index.html

61. Said, *Humanism and Democratic Criticism*, 27.

62. Said, *Humanism and Democratic Criticism*, 27–28.

63. Naomi Goldenberg, "Archetypal Theory and the Separation of Mind and Body: Reason Enough to Turn to Freud?" *Journal of Feminist Studies in Religion* 1, no. 1 (1985): 55.

64. Goldenberg, "Archetypal Theory."

65. Lewis, Amini, and Lannon, *A General Theory of Love*, 6.

66. Here, it would also be useful to think of feeling, or "Feelin'" to cite the research of Dr. Bettina Judd. More information in Judd's book *Feelin: Creative Practice, Pleasure, and Black Feminist Thought* (Evanston, IL: Northwestern University Press, 2022).

67. Lewis, Amini, and Lannon, *A General Theory of Love*, 12.

68. For more on emotion as integral to both conscious and subconscious human awareness, see Ntozake Shange, in *Black Women Writers at Work*, 151.

69. Audre Lorde, *Sister Outsider* (Berkeley, CA: Crossing Press, 1984), 39.

70. Lewis, Amini, and Lannon, *A General Theory of Love*, 15.

71. Lewis, Amini, and Lannon, *A General Theory of Love*, 14.

72. For more on humanity and care: Shange in *Black Women Writers at Work*, 152.

73. "If there were no poetry on any day in the world, poetry would be invented that day. For there would be an intolerable hunger. And from that need, from the relationships within ourselves and among ourselves as we went on living, and from every other expression of man's nature, poetry would be—I cannot here say invented or discovered—poetry would be derived. As research science would be derived, if the energies we begin to know reduced us to a few people, rubbing into life a little fire." Rukeyser, *The Life of Poetry*, 160.

74. "Widening the Lens on a More Inclusive Science," *Science Friday*, September 6, 2019, NPR, 24:00–24:08. https://www.sciencefriday.com/segments/indigenous-science/

75. "Widening the Lens," 17:40–46.

76. "Widening the Lens," 23:45–48.

77. "Widening the Lens," 24:38–24:57.

78. Here, I mean intuition, not anything journalistic or related to political "fake news" debates. For an interesting article studying intuition and insight, see Thea Zander, Michael Öllinger, and Kirsten G. Volz, "Intuition and Insight: Two Processes That Build on Each Other or Fundamentally Differ?" *Frontiers in Psychology* 7: 2016. https://www.frontiersin.org/articles/10.3389/fpsyg.2016.01395/full

79. More discussion of this can be found in Laura Kutsch, "Can We Rely

On Our Intuition?" *Scientific American*, August 15, 2019. https://www.scientifi
camerican.com/article/can-we-rely-on-our-intuition/

80. Sara Ahmed: "Rolling eyes = feminist pedagogy." Ahmed, *Living a Feminist Life* (Durham, NC: Duke University Press, 2017), 99.

81. In this section, I am thinking of the supposedly honorable character Ned Stark, patriarch of the Stark family of Winterfell in *Game of Thrones*, the HBO series—but because the program was first a book by George R. R. Martin, I'm going to say it counts.

82. Here, too, I am thinking of a television series, one I couldn't finish watching, because the main character had so little integrity as to be unlikeable: *House of Cards*. Interestingly, Netflix later sacked lead actor Kevin Spacey when several sexual misconduct allegations against him became public. Find more information at https://www.bbc.co.uk/news/entertainment-arts-4188
4878

83. For a cogent set of guidelines for evolving language about disabled people toward more accuracy, find Lydia X. Z. Brown's blog on avoiding ableist terms in speech and in writing: https://www.autistichoya.com/p/ableist-wor
ds-and-terms-to-avoid.html

84. "It is apparent that one of the primary reasons we have not experienced a revolution of values is that a culture of domination necessarily promotes addiction to lying and denial." bell hooks, *Teaching to Transgress: Education as the Practice of Freedom* (New York: Routledge, 1994), 28.

85. Cixous, "Laugh of the Medusa," 887.

86. A note on intuition, trauma and neurodivergence: alexithymia—difficulty naming one's own or inferring others' emotions—can interfere with feeling-based intuition. In these cases, it can be helpful to track choices logically, to find patterns that make rational sense in a text, in your own work. This awareness becomes part of logical feeling—another kind of intuition. Not much research has been done on this topic, but for an interesting study on sentimentalism and rationalism, see Rodrigo Díaz and Jesse Prinz, "The role of emotional awareness in evaluative judgment: evidence from alexithymia," *Scientific Reports* 13, 5183 (2023). https://doi.org/10.1038/s41598-023
-32242-y

87. For a discussion of motherhood as a tone, see my interview with poet Ariana Reines in *The Believer,* November 2020. https://culture.org/logger/an
-interview-with-khadijah-queen/

88. Alexis Pauline Gumbs, "Introduction," in *Revolutionary Mothering: Love on the Front Lines,* edited by Alexis Pauline Gumbs, China Martens, and Mai'a Williams (Binghamton, NY: PM Press, 2016), 9.

89. One issue, school shootings, has been perniciously persistent in America in the face of legislative failure to regulate automatic weapons. For a resource on the problem and possible solutions, see the Center for Violence

Prevention at the Children's Hospital of Philadelphia. https://violence.chop
.edu/school-shootings

90. Rukeyser, *The Life of Poetry*, 31.

91. One example here: https://www.indigenouspeoples-sdg.org/index
.php/english/all-global-news/992-greta-thunberg-schoolgirl-climate-chan
ge-warrior-some-people-can-let-things-go-i-can-t

92. More information at https://blacklivesmatter.com

93. In an interview with George Yancy for the *New York Times* (December 10, 2015), hooks states emphatically: "We can't begin to understand the nature of domination if we don't understand how these systems connect with one another." https://opinionator.blogs.nytimes.com/author/bell-ho
oks/

94. Said, *Humanism and Democratic Criticism*, 11.

95. Said, *Humanism and Democratic Criticism*, 11.

96. Said, *Humanism and Democratic Criticism*, 11.

Chapter 1

1. Poet and educator June Jordan: "Love is life force." "The Creative Spirit: Children's Literature," in *Revolutionary Mothering: Love on the Front Lines*, edited by Alexis Pauline Gumbs, China Martens, and Mai'a Williams (Binghamton, NY: PM Press, 2016), 11.

2. See Alice Walker's groundbreaking 1972 essay "In Search of Our Mothers' Gardens," in *In Search of Our Mothers' Gardens: Womanist Prose* (New York: Open Road Media, 2011).

3. This theory of radicality mirrors the three parts of the brain—limbic (emotional), reptilic (physical/instinctual), and neocortic (intellectual/reasoning)—described in Thomas Lewis, Fari Amini, and Richard Lannon, *A General Theory of Love* (New York: Vintage Books, 2001), chapter 1.

4. See Eboo Patel's radio broadcast "We Are Each Other's Business," NPR, November 7, 2005. https://www.npr.org/templates/story/story.php?storyId=
4989625

5. On the album *Private Dancer* (Capitol, 1984).

6. Walter Benjamin, "On the Mimetic Faculty," in *Reflections: Essays, Aphorisms, Autobiographical Writings*, edited by Peter Demetz, translated by Edmund Jephcott (New York: Schocken Books, 1978), 333–36.

7. See Appendix A.

8. Astro.com. Personal Portrait. Inputs for the astrological chart: 14 April 1952, 8:00 am, New York City. See Appendix A.

9. Tom Vitale, "Ralph Ellison: No Longer The 'Invisible Man' 100 Years After His Birth." *All Things Considered*, NPR. Aired May 30, 2014. https://www

.npr.org/sections/codeswitch/2014/05/30/317056807/ralph-ellison-no-lon ger-the-invisible-man-100-years-after-his-birth

10. Ralph Ellison, *Invisible Man* (New York: Random House, 1952), 3.

11. For the definition of this term, see Alice Walker, "[Womanist: Definition]," *Buddhist-Christian Studies* 32 (2012): 45. www.jstor.org/stable/2327 4467

12. Toni Morrison, "A Knowing So Deep," *Essence* (May 1985): 230.

13. Morrison in *Essence*, 230.

14. Morrison in *Essence*, 230.

15. Ellison, *Invisible Man*, 41.

16. Here I am not thinking of the type of separatism espoused by the Nation of Islam, for instance, which is itself institutional, but of an intrinsically derived sense of self-worth that minimizes negative external input that values human worth according to racial hierarchy, physical characteristics and abilities, and class categorization.

17. Audre Lorde, *Sister Outsider* (Berkeley, CA: Crossing Press, 1984), 63.

18. Sara Ahmed: "Universities often describe their missions by drawing on the languages of diversity as well as equality. But using the language does not translate into creating diverse or equal environments. This . . . is a gap between a symbolic commitment and a lived reality." *Living a Feminist Life* (Durham, NC: Duke University Press, 2017), 90.

19. Ota Benga's story, in which a white American "trader" kidnapped the youngster from his home in the Congo and presented him at the Bronx Zoo as an exhibition alongside primates, holds particular relevance. See https:// www.bbc.com/news/world-africa-53917733

20. Jordan, "The Creative Spirit," 12.

Chapter 2

1. Instead of the anglicized translation Black Hawk, I will use the Sauk: Mahkatêwe-meshi-kêhkêhkwa.

2. Toni Morrison, *Playing in the Dark: Whiteness and the Literary Imagination* (New York: Vintage, 1992), 13.

3. Kimberlé Williams Crenshaw, "Demarginalizing the Intersection of Race and Sex: A Black Feminist Critique of Antidiscrimination Doctrine, Feminist Theory and Antiracist Politics," *University of Chicago Legal Forum* 1989, art. 8: 150. https://chicagounbound.uchicago.edu/uclf/vol1989/iss1/8

4. See Claudia Rankine, "In Our Way: Racism in the Creative Writing Classroom," *Writer's Chronicle,* October/November 2016. https://www.awpw riter.org/magazine_media/writers_chronicle_view/4120/in_our_way_racism _in_creative_writing

5. See J. Brian Charles, "The *New York Times* 1619 Project Is Reshaping the

Conversation on Slavery. Conservatives Hate It," Vox.com, August 20, 2019. https://www.vox.com/identities/2019/8/19/20812238/1619-project-slavery-conservatives

6. See "Map: Where Critical Race Theory Is Under Attack," *Education Week*, June 11, 2020; updated January 20, 2022. https://www.edweek.org/policy-politics/map-where-critical-race-theory-is-under-attack/2021/06

7. Newt Gingrich tweet, August 18, 2019.

8. Saidiya Hartman writes about the problematic empathy whites in positions of power articulate while watching forced slave performances in "Innocent Amusements: The Stage of Sufferance," in *Scenes of Subjection: Terror, Slavery, and Self-Making in Nineteenth-Century America* (New York: Oxford University Press, 1997), 46.

9. Toni Morrison, *The Origin of Others* (Cambridge, MA: Harvard University Press, 2017), 39.

10. Morrison, *Origin of Others*, 39.

11. For more on "what racial ideology does to the mind, imagination, and behavior of masters," see Toni Morrison, *Playing in the Dark*, 11–12.

12. Herman Melville, *The Confidence-Man: His Masquerade* (Washington, DC: Library of America, 1985), 849. Subsequent quotes are cited in the text.

13. Morrison, *Playing in the Dark*, 24.

14. Hartman, *Scenes of Subjection*, 32.

15. See Victor H. Strandberg, "God and the Critics of Melville," *Texas Studies in Literature and Language* 6, no. 3 (Autumn 1964): 321–33. https://dukespace.lib.duke.edu/items/2561dcd6-f634-49d1-b4d3-810025f76a31

16. "Today, on the second anniversary of the Charlottesville violence that led the president to call neo-Nazis 'very good people,' and as the president's overall approval ratings remain relatively low, many of those who brought him to the dance appear to be dancing more closely than ever." Eugene Scott, "Anger at Being Labeled Racist Is the New 'Cultural Anxiety' for Trump Supporters," *Washington Post*, August 12, 2019. https://www.washingtonpost.com/politics/2019/08/12/anger-being-labeled-racist-is-new-cultural-anxiety-trump-supporters/

17. For more on how reviewers at the time perceived *The Confidence-Man: His Masquerade*, as well as trust and goodness, see Zack Friedman, "Prose and Cons: On Melville's 'The Confidence-Man,'" *Hypocrite Reader*, no. 17 (June 2012). http://hypocritereader.com/17/prose-and-cons

18. Morrison, *Playing in the Dark*, 3.

19. Morrison, *Origin of Others*, 30.

20. Athaly Altay, "It's Time to End 'Fake Claim' Harassment of Disabled People," *The Mighty*, July 6, 2021. https://themighty.com/2021/07/ending-fake-claim-harassment-chronic-illness-disability/

21. Hartman, *Scenes of Subjection*, 35.

22. Although I want to stay with *The Confidence-Man* here, it's important

to note that we could expand the discussion on race to include *Benito Cereno,* even *Moby-Dick,* and that we could examine "Bartleby, the Scrivener" for more on Melville's satire regarding what constitutes "goodness."

23. Frances Ellen Watkins Harper, *Iola Leroy; or, Shadows Uplifted* (Oxford: Oxford University Press, 1988), 83–84. Subsequent quotes are cited in the text.

24. See http://library.cincymuseum.org/aag/bio/garner.html. Note the January 29, 1856, newspaper article's dehumanizing reference to two-year-old Mary Garner as "it."

25. See https://www.smithsonianmag.com/history/the-true-life-horror -that-inspired-moby-dick-17576/

26. Hartman, *Scenes of Subjection,* 4.

27. Hartman, *Scenes of Subjection,* 4.

28. Jessica Wells Cantiello, "Frances E. W. Harper's Educational Reserva- tions: The Indian Question in *Iola Leroy," African American Review* 45, no. 4 (2012): 575–77.

29. Cantiello, "Harper's Educational Reservations," 575.

30. As an aside: In 1981, when I was in first grade and the only Black stu- dent in my class in Los Angeles, I opened our history textbook to an indexed illustration of a pyramid of races. It had a cherubic pair of blonde children at the top, stately Spaniards second below them, caricatured Asians at the third level, indigenous peoples fourth, and a Black man on all fours at the bottom. I complained to my teacher, but to no avail. I took the book home to show my mother, even though we weren't supposed to bring our books home. She raised hell at the school, and that same day the books, which were tattered and falling apart from age, were removed from our curriculum.

31. Hartman, *Scenes of Subjection,* 10.

32. Nazera Sadiq Wright, *Black Girlhood in the Nineteenth Century* (Cham- paign: University of Illinois Press, 2016), 86.

33. Harriet Jacobs, *Incidents in the Life of a Slave Girl* (New York: Penguin, 2000), 7.

34. Wright, *Black Girlhood,* 84.

35. Wright, *Black Girlhood,* 87.

36. See Jeffrey Taylor Pusch, "Moral Performances: Melodrama and Nineteenth-Century American Literature," PhD diss., University of Southern Mississippi, 2011. https://aquila.usm.edu/cgi/viewcontent.cgi?article=1540& context=dissertations

37. Jacobs, *Incidents,* 30.

38. Jacobs, *Incidents,* 32.

39. Kate Chopin, "Désirée's Baby," in *Bayou Folk* (New York: Houghton Mifflin, 1894). While the proper French spelling is Désirée, in this essay I remain faithful to Chopin's spelling. Quotes in the text reference this edition.

40. See Andrew J. Wistrich, Jeffrey J. Rachlinski, and Chris Guthrie, "Heart

Versus Head: Do Judges Follow the Law or Follow Their Feelings?" *Texas Law Review* 93, no. 5 (April 2015): 855–923. http://texaslawreview.org/wp-content /uploads/2015/08/Rachlinski-93-4.pdf

41. Black Hawk (Ma-ka-tai-me-she-kia-kiak), *The Life of Black Hawk, or Ma-ka-tai-me-she-kia-kiak: Dictated by Himself*, edited by J. Gerald Kennedy (New York: Penguin, 2008). Quotes in the text reference this edition.

42. Hartman, *Scenes of Subjection*, 12.

43. In *All About Love: New Visions* (New York: HarperCollins, 2018), writer and intellectual bell hooks discusses love as action, rather than a feeling: "To begin by always thinking of love as an action rather than a feeling is one way in which anyone using the word in this manner automatically assumes accountability and responsibility" (13). I agree, but add the possibility that we can consider feeling and action as aligned in this case—i.e., readers/critics construct belief based on initial feeling, and then take action (arrive at conclusions and communicate their analysis).

44. For more on love, artists' approaches to meaning-making, and more, see James Baldwin in a 1973 interview, particularly on page 41. "The Black Scholar Interviews: James Baldwin," *The Black Scholar* 5, no. 4 (1973): 33–42. http://www.jstor.org/stable/41065644. Accessed 18 Dec. 2023.

Chapter 3

1. I am presumably speaking here about cis women, but for those who would like to parse, when I say women throughout this essay and this book, I mean anyone who identifies as a woman. Trans women are women, whatever the century.

2. There is also strong evidence that her first language is Nahuatl, and that it influenced her poetry. See Caroline Egan, "Lyric Intelligibility in Sor Juana's Nahuatl *Tocotines*," *Romance Notes* 58, no. 2 (2018): 207–18. https:// www.repository.cam.ac.uk/bitstream/handle/1810/287541/Lyric_intelligib ility_rev_final.pdf

3. Nick Ripatrazone, "A Brilliant 17th-Century Nun Is Brought to Life on Netflix," *America Magazine*, February 27, 2017. https://www.americamagazine .org/arts-culture/2017/02/27/brilliant-17th-century-nun-brought-life-net flix

4. Geoffrey Kantaris, University of Cambridge, Centre of Latin American Studies, "The Poetry of Sor Juana Ines de la Cruz: Hybrid Difference," 1992. https://jaifroid.github.io/latam-resources/sorjuana/

5. This poem is often translated with the title "You Foolish Men." See Michael Smith's translation at the Academy of American Poets: https://poets .org/poem/you-foolish-men

6. David Frye, http://www-personal.umich.edu/~dfrye/SORJUANA.html

7. See Frances Ellen Watkins Harper, "A Double Standard." https://www
.poetryfoundation.org/poems/52449/a-double-standard

8. Harper, "A Double Standard."

9. See note 5, "You Foolish Men."

10. Edgar F. Love, "Negro Resistance to Spanish Rule in Colonial Mexico,"
Journal of Negro History 52, no. 2 (1967): 89–103. www.jstor.org/stable/271
6127

11. While the gender I'm speaking of here is female, I am quoting Love,
and he is speaking of both genders; hence *blanco* instead of *blanca*.

12. Love, "Negro Resistance to Spanish Rule," 90.

13. Alexandra Parma Cook and Noble David Cook, *Good Faith and Truthful Ignorance: A Case of Transatlantic Bigamy* (Durham, NC: Duke University
Press, 1991).

14. Kathleen Ann Myers, *Neither Saints nor Sinners: Writing the Lives of
Women in Spanish America* (Oxford: Oxford University Press, 2003).

15. Matthew Restall, "'He Wished It in Vain': Subordination and Resistance among Maya Women in Post-Conquest Yucatan," *Ethnohistory* 42, no. 4
(1995): 577–94. https://www.jstor.org/stable/483144

16. Restall, "'He Wished It in Vain,'" 591.

17. Irene Silverblatt, "Lessons of Gender and Ethnohistory in Mesoamerica," *Ethnohistory* 42, no. 4 (1995): 644–47. https://www.jstor.org/stable/48
3149

18. Silverblatt, "Lessons of Gender and Ethnohistory," 641.

Chapter 4

1. José Ortega y Gasset, *The Dehumanization of Art and Other Writings on
Art and Culture* (New York: Doubleday, 1956), 114.

2. Ortega y Gasset, 114.

3. Natasha Trethewey, *Thrall* (New York: Houghton Mifflin Harcourt,
2012), 9–12.

4. Trethewey, *Thrall,* 12.

5. See The Mary Turner Project, http://www.maryturner.org/

6. Lucille Clifton, *The Collected Poems of Lucille Clifton* (Rochester, NY:
BOA Editions, 2012), 552.

7. Adam Weinstein, "The Trayvon Martin Killing, Explained," *Mother
Jones,* March 18, 2012. http://www.motherjones.com/politics/2012/03/what
-happened-trayvon-martin-explained

8. Trethewey, "Knowledge," in *Thrall,* 28. Subsequent quotations from
this volume are cited in the text, by page number where appropriate, and by
line numbers.

9. William Logan, "Song & Dance," *New Criterion* 31, no. 4 (December 2012): 69–76.

10. Logan, "Song & Dance," 74–75.

11. Logan, "Song & Dance," 74.

12. See p.76 in Edward Said's *Humanism and Democratic Criticism* for more on discussions awareness of racial discourse in education, readership, and frameworks of literary analysis that acknowledge both disclosed and hidden texts.

13. Said, 27.

14. Logan, "Song & Dance," 75.

15. See "Interchange: Genres of History," *Journal of American History* 91, no. 2 (September 2004): 572–93.

16. "Interchange," 581.

17. "Interchange," 581.

18. "Interchange," 586.

19. Natasha Trethewey, *Beyond Katrina* (Athens: University of Georgia Press, 2010), 63. Subsequent citations are given in the text.

20. Natasha Trethewey and Patricia Smith, "Conversation: In the Path of the Storm," Panel, Dodge Poetry Festival, North Star Academy Great Room, Newark, NJ, October 13, 2012.

21. Trethewey and Smith, "Conversation."

22. Trethewey, "Congregation," in *Beyond Katrina*, 79, lines 1–6. Subsequent quotations are cited in the text.

23. Jerry W. Ward Jr., "Beyond Katrina: A Meditation on the Mississippi Gulf Coast," *Southern Quarterly* 49, no. 1 (Fall 2011): 133.

24. Natasha Trethewey, "Incident," in *Native Guard* (New York: Houghton Mifflin, 2006), 41. Subseqent in-text references are to this work.

25. See Kevin Powell, "The Insanity of White Justice and Black Forgiveness," *The Progressive*, October 4, 2019. https://progressive.org/latest/insanity -of-white-justice-black-forgiveness-powell-191004/

26. Natasha Trethewey, "Elegy for the Native Guards," in *Native Guard,* 44, lines 12, 14, 17.

27. Natasha Trethewey, "We Have Seen," *Smithsonian Magazine* 47, no. 5 (September 2016): 53, 4. Subsequent quotations are cited in the text.

28. Trethewey, *Beyond Katrina*, 33.

29. Octavio Paz, "Seeing and Using: Art and Craftsmanship," in *Convergences: Essays on Art and Literature* (New York: Harcourt Brace Jovanovich, 1987), 53.

30. Natasha Trethewey, *Bellocq's Ophelia* (Minneapolis: Graywolf Press, 2002), 47, lines 10–14.

31. Amy Fleury, "What is Boundless: A Conversation with Edward Hirsch about Ekphrastic Writing," *Interdisciplinary Humanities* 20, no. 1 (Spring 2003): 49.

32. Nicolas Bourriaud, *Relational Aesthetics*, translated by Simon Pleasance and Fronza Woods, with the participation of Mathieu Copeland (Dijon and Paris: Les presses du réel, 2002), 18.

33. Natasha Trethewey, "Vignette," in *Bellocq's Ophelia*, 47. Subsequent quotations are cited in the text.

34. Octavio Paz, "The New Analogy: Poetry and Technology," in *Convergences*, 120.

35. Trethewey, "Letters from Storyville," in *Bellocq's Ophelia*, 20–21.

36. "In the art-form of the European nude the painters and spectator-owners were usually men and the persons treated as objects, usually women. This unequal relationship is so deeply embedded in our culture that it still structures the consciousness of many women. . . . But there was little to replace it except the 'realism' of the prostitute—who became the quintessential woman of early *avant-garde* 20th century painting." John Berger, *Ways of Seeing* (London: British Broadcasting Corporation and Penguin Books, 1972), 63.

37. Édouard Glissant, *Poetics of Relation*, translated by Betsy Wing (Ann Arbor: University of Michigan Press, 1990), 8.

38. Muriel Rukeyser, *The Life of Poetry* (Amherst, MA: Paris Press, 1996), xi.

39. Bourriaud, *Relational Aesthetics*, 98.

40. Rita Dove, Introduction to Natasha Trethewey, *Domestic Work* (Minneapolis: Graywolf Press, 2000), xi.

41. See Matthew Bolton, "Gwendolyn Brooks and the Epic Tradition," in *Critical Insights: Gwendolyn Brooks*, edited by Mildred R. Mickle (Armenia, NY: Salem Press, 2009).

42. Fleury, "What Is Boundless," 49.

43. Coco Fusco, "Lorna Simpson," *Bomb*, no. 61 (Fall 1997), pp. 50–55.

44. Natasha Trethewey, "Hot Combs," in *Domestic Work*, p. 29, lines 1–3. Subsequent references in the text are to this poem.

45. The closing two lines deliver a punch that recalls Bourriaud's final lines: "The poetic function, which consists in re-forming worlds of subjectivization, possibly would not have any meaning if it, too, were not able to help us to negotiate" (104) life's trials in their public-historic contexts—what Guattari calls the "ordeals of barbarism, the mental implosion and chaosmic spasms looming on the horizon, and transform them into riches and unforeseen pleasures." Félix Guattari, *Chaosmosis: An Ethico-Aesthetic Paradigm*, translated by Paul Bains and Julian Pefanis (Bloomington: Indiana University Press, 1995), 134.

46. Natasha Trethewey, "What the Body Can Say," in *Native Guard*, 9.

47. See "In Mississippi, a Feeling of Neglect," Associated Press, September 4, 2005. http://www.nbcnews.com/id/9190498/ns/us_news-katrina_the_lo ng_road_back/t/mississippi-feeling-neglect/

48. Trethewey, *Beyond Katrina*, 33.

Chapter 5

1. "Book designers call these two pages by the Latin terms 'recto' for the right-hand page and 'verso' for the reverse or left-hand page. This usage may help you remember that each new section always starts on the recto or right-hand page, not on the 'reverse.'" See "Publishing and Book Design Basics: Elements of Page Design," Michigan State University, n.d. https://libguides .lib.msu.edu/c.php?g=97090&p=908734

2. Erica L. Johnson, "Building the Neo-Archive: Dionne Brand's *A Map to the Door of No Return*," *Meridians: Feminism, Race, Transnationalism* 12, no. 1 (2014): 150.

3. Dionne Brand, *The Blue Clerk* (Durham, NC: Duke University Press, 2018), 210. Subsequent citations are given in the text.

4. Dionne Brand, *A Map to the Door of No Return* (Toronto: Vintage Canada, 2002), 64.

5. Calvin Warren, "Black Time: Slavery, Metaphysics, and the Logic of Wellness," in *The Psychic Hold of Slavery: Legacies in American Expressive Culture,* edited by Soyica Diggs Colbert, Robert J. Patterson, and Aida Levy-Hussen (New Brunswick: Rutgers University Press, 2016), 56.

6. Warren, "Black Time," 58–59.

7. Warren, "Black Time," 62.

8. Warren, "Black Time," 61.

9. Warren, "Black Time," 61.

10. Warren, "Black Time," 66, 65.

11. Warren, "Black Time," 66, 65.

12. Katherine McKittrick, "Commentary: Worn Out," *Southeastern Geographer* 57, no. 1 (2017): 98.

13. Hortense Spillers, "Mama's Baby, Papa's Maybe: An American Grammar Book," *Diacritics* 17, no. 2 (1987): 65, 67.

14. Michelle Wright, *Physics of Blackness: Beyond the Middle Passage Epistemology* (Minneapolis: University of Minnesota Press, 2015), 38.

15. Wright, *Physics of Blackness*, 39.

16. Wright, *Physics of Blackness*, 41.

17. Saidiya Hartman, "Venus in Two Acts," *Small Axe* 12, no. 2 (2008): 4.

18. Warren, "Black Time," 66.

19. McKittrick, "Worn Out," 97–98.

20. McKittrick, "Worn Out," 98.

21. Roland Barthes, *The Pleasure of the Text* (New York: Hill & Wang, 1975), 14.

22. BBE Music. *Charles Mingus—Pithecanthropus Erectus (Long version)*, 2018. https://www.youtube.com/watch?v=xd8PcqxgzTo

23. Hank Shteamer, "Review: Charles Mingus' 'Jazz in Detroit' Sheds Light on an Overlooked Era," *Rolling Stone*, November 2, 2018. https://www.rolling

stone.com/music/music-album-reviews/album-review-charles-mingus-jazz
-in-detroit-strata-concert-gallery-46-selden-750144/

24. Shteamer, "Review: Charles Mingus' 'Jazz in Detroit,'" para. 2.

25. See also Prince's iconic song "Joy in Repetition," on *Music from Graffiti
Bridge* (Paisley Park and Warner Bros. Records, 1990).

26. James Snead, "On Repetition in Black Culture," *Black American Literature Forum* 15, no. 4 (Winter 1981): 146–54.

27. Snead, "On Repetition," 148.

28. Snead, "On Repetition," 149.

29. Snead, "On Repetition," 150.

30. Snead, "On Repetition," 153.

Chapter 6

1. In examining intuition's role in thinking, *A General Theory of Love*
offers the result of a 1996 meteorological prediction study: "In tasks similar
to weather prediction, one study found that conscious attempts at problem-
solving got in the way of burgeoning intuition and actually impaired subjects'
performance" (Thomas Lewis, Fari Amini, and Richard Lannon, *A General
Theory of Love* [New York: Random House, 2000], 109). Another study from
1992, in which subjects correctly intuited an invented grammatical structure,
showed similar results: "What the subjects *couldn't* do was specify how they
were reaching their correct determinations. Once again, they had mastered
the inner workings of an intricate system in a way that they could not render
specific. They could only say they were using their intuition" (111, emphasis
in the original).

2. Akasha Gloria Hull, "Bringing Beauty from Above: Spirituality and
Creativity," in Hull, *Soul Talk: The New Spirituality of African American Women*
(Rochester, VT: Inner Traditions, 2001), 122.

3. "It is worthy of note that nearly all that has been done for the improve-
ment of the steam engine has been accomplished, not by men educated in
colleges or technical schools, but by laborers, mechanics, and engine-men.
There seem to be instances where the mechanical instinct takes precedence
over the higher powers of the mind, in efficiency in harnessing the forces of
nature and causing them to do our work." Francis Edgar Stanley, inventor of
the Stanley Steamer. In the paper "Stephenson and Transportation" (1916),
collected in Francis Edgar Stanley, *Theories Worth Having and Other Papers*
(1919), 66–67.

4. https://www.merriam-webster.com/dictionary/channel

5. Hull, "Bringing Beauty from Above," 125.

6. "'Reason is the substance of the universe,' Hegel crowed in an age
when science still expected to explicate everything. But these memory stud-

ies have intuition leading comprehension by a country mile; they reveal our lives lit by the diffuse glow of a second sun we never see. . . . Aristotle drew the distinction between knowing *that* something is so and knowing *why*. The restless desire of the Athenians to seek causes marked the first unsteady steps of scientific exploration. Their explanations have metamorphosed into myth, but their hierarchy of knowing endured: real knowledge, true knowledge comes from knowing *why*." *A General Theory of Love*, 112, emphasis in the original.

7. See Plato's *Ion*, *Foucault's Archaeology of Western Culture: Toward a New Science of History*, the dread pirate Heidegger's *Being and Time*, etc.

8. Edward Said, *Humanism and Democratic Criticism* (New York: Columbia University Press, 2003), 18.

9. Said, *Humanism and Democratic Criticism*, 25.

10. Said, *Humanism and Democratic Criticism*, 26.

11. Colleen Flaherty, "Not the Queen's English Department," *Inside Higher Ed*, February 14, 2021. https://www.insidehighered.com/news/2021/02/15/english-departments-rethink-what-call-themselves

12. Grace L. Dillon, ed. *Walking the Clouds: An Anthology of Indigenous Science Fiction* (Tucson: University of Arizona Press, 2012), 10, emphasis in the original.

13. Said, *Humanism and Democratic Criticism*, 25.

14. Gerald Vizenor, "The Ruins of Representation: Shadow Survivance and the Literature of Dominance," *American Indian Quarterly* 17, no. 1 (1993): 7.

15. Black Hawk (Ma-ka-tai-me-she-kia-kiak), *The Life of Black Hawk, or Ma-ka-tai-me-she-kia-kiak: Dictated by Himself*, edited by J. Gerald Kennedy (New York: Penguin, 2008), 49, emphasis in the original. Subsequent citations are given in the text.

16. Elissa Washuta and Theresa Warburton write in the introduction to the anthology *Shapes of Native Nonfiction* (Seattle: University of Washington Press, 2019): "The writers and anthropologists who wrote Native life-stories were motivated by an impulse to capture *everything* about Native life before the complete vanishing they saw as inevitable . . . The lyric essay's associative leaps . . . def[y] the diminishing into nonexistence through which settlement is structured" (9, emphasis in the original).

17. The phrase "sentence work" is taken from the poet Sueyeun Juliette Lee, stated in informal conversation.

18. "I surveyed the country that had cost us so much trouble, anxiety, and blood, and that now caused me to be a prisoner of war. I reflected upon the ingratitude of the whites, when I saw their fine houses, rich harvests, and every thing desirable around them; and recollected that all this land had been ours, for which me and my people had never received a dollar, and that the whites were not satisfied until they took our village and our grave-yards from us, and removed us across the Mississippi" (Black Hawk, *The Life*, 87).

19. After educating himself on the slavery issue, he offered up a combination of indenture, purchase, and freedom according to age and gender, with removal to free states, adding: "If the free states did not want them all for servants, we would take the balance in our nation, to help our women make corn!" (Black Hawk, *The Life,* 97).

20. Katherine McKittrick, *Dear Science and Other Stories* (Durham, NC: Duke University Press, 2020), 2.

21. Tiffany Lethabo King, *The Black Shoals: Offshore Formations of Black and Native Studies* (Durham, NC: Duke University Press, 2019), x.

22. Christina Sharpe, *In the Wake: On Blackness and Being* (London and Durham, NC: Duke University Press, 2016), 20.

23. Toni Morrison, *A Mercy* (New York: Vintage International, 2008), 68.

24. Toni Morrison, *A Mercy,* 58–59.

25. Toni Morrison, *A Mercy,* 71.

26. King, *The Black Shoals,* xi.

27. Toni Morrison, *A Mercy,* 64.

28. Toni Morrison, *A Mercy,* 114.

29. Toni Morrison, *A Mercy,* 72.

30. Toni Morrison, *A Mercy,* 54.

31. Toni Morrison, *A Mercy,* 56–57.

32. While I use the term Native here, other terms do appear throughout. I've also used the nation identifier specific to individuals where appropriate. See the National Museum of the American Indian for a basic discussion of proper terminology: https://americanindian.si.edu/nk360/faq/did-you-kn ow#:~:text=What%20is%20the%20correct%20terminology,by%20their%20s pecific%20tribal%20name

33. Tom Holm, Ben Chavis, and J. Diane Pearson, "Peoplehood: A Model for the Extension of Sovereignty in American Indian Studies," *Wicazo Sa Review* 18, no. 1 (Spring 2003): 12.

34. Holm, Chavis, and Pearson, "Peoplehood," 18.

35. Holm, Chavis, and Pearson, "Peoplehood," 18.

36. Holm, Chavis, and Pearson, "Peoplehood," 18.

37. Leslie Marmon Silko, *Ceremony* (New York: Penguin/Random House, 2016), 177. Subsequent citations are given in the text.

38. Simon Ortiz, *From Sand Creek* (Tucson: University of Arizona Press, 1981).

39. Simon Ortiz, "Towards a National Indian Literature: Cultural Authenticity in Nationalism," *MELUS* 8, no. 2 (Summer 1981): 11.

40. For a long time after my discharge from the service, I was also treated at VA hospitals because my medical treatment is free there. The substandard, slow care and the dismal atmosphere meant I only went when I absolutely had to, and as soon as I could afford outside insurance, I signed up.

41. Ortiz, *From Sand Creek,* 83.

42. Holm, Chavis, and Pearson, "Peoplehood," 8. Subsequent citations are given in the text.

43. Ortiz, *From Sand Creek,* 67. Subsequent citations are given in the text.

44. Said, *Humanism and Democratic Criticism,* 26.

45. Muriel Rukeyser, *The Life of Poetry* (Amherst, MA: Paris Press, 1996), 8.

46. Silko, *Ceremony,* 179.

Chapter 7

1. Muriel Rukeyser, *The Life of Poetry* (Middletown, CT: Paris Press/Wesleyan University Press, 1996), ix. Subsequent citations are given in the text.

2. Rukeyser's allusion to roots also echoes Glissant's theory of the rhizome discussed in the Preface.

3. Adrienne Rich, "Introduction," in *A Muriel Rukeyser Reader,* edited by Jan Heller Levi (New York: W. W. Norton, 1994), xi.

4. This seems to be shifting, though by no means fully shifted—Rukeyser is not quite canon yet. See W. Scott Howard and Broc Rossell, eds., *Poetics and Praxis 'After' Objectivism* (Iowa City: University of Iowa Press, 2019), as well as Sam Huber's "Muriel Rukeyser: Mother of Everyone," *Paris Review,* May 30, 2018, https://www.theparisreview.org/blog/2018/05/30/muriel-rukeyser-mother-of-everyone/.

5. Rich, "Introduction," xi.

6. Dara Barnat, "'Women and Poets See the Truth Arrive': Muriel Rukeyser and Walt Whitman," *Studies in American Jewish Literature* 34, no. 1 (2015): 96. https://muse.jhu.edu/article/577309

7. Rich, "Introduction," xiii.

8. Jane Cooper, "Foreword: Meeting-Places," in Rukeyser, *The Life of Poetry,* xxviii.

9. According to her FBI record, Rukeyser and another individual were "held for 'inciting the Negroes to insurrections,' but were released" (FBI Vault, 81; https://vault.fbi.gov/Muriel%20Rukeyser/Muriel%20Rukeyser%20Part%201%20of%201/view)

10. J. Edgar Hoover signs a note on November 4, 1942, noting enclosure of a "summary of the pertinent information pertaining to Miss Muriel Rukeyser as reflected in the files of this bureau" (FBI Vault, 6).

11. In a "Memorandum to Director" date-stamped August 20, 1974, an unnamed SAC (Special Agent in Charge) writes: "Due to an apparent lack of extremist activity re subject, this case is being placed in closed status. In the event that additional information of a positive nature is obtained re subject, appropriate action will be initiated" (FBI Vault, 121).

12. Al Filreis analyzes the writings of both Baldwin and Rukeyser, among others writing in the aftermath of WWII and in the thick of 1950s conserva-

tism, in his book *1960: When Art and Literature Confronted the Memory of World War II and Remade the Modern* (New York: Columbia University Press, 2021).

13. Sarah Chadfield writes about Rukeyser's trip in her entry "Muriel Rukeyser and the Spanish Civil War" for the Library of Congress's John W. Kluge Center blog *Insights*: "In 1936, the young poet Muriel Rukeyser went to Spain to report on the People's Olympiad being held in Barcelona. Intended as an alternative to the Nazi Olympic Games in Berlin, the Olympiad never took place as days before the opening ceremony, the Nationalists staged a coup on the Republican government and the Civil War began" (January 8, 2015, https://blogs.loc.gov/kluge/2015/01/muriel-rukeyser-and-the-spanish -civil-war/)

14. American involvement in this attempt—which Rukeyser traveled to Spain to report on—to provide an alternative to the Hitler-led Nazi Germany participation in the Olympic Games is explored by Rachel Aileen Searcy in "The Olympics That Never Were: The People's Olympiad," *The Back Table*, February 7, 2014, https://wp.nyu.edu/specialcollections/2014/02/07/the-oly mpics-that-never-were-the-peoples-olympiad/.

15. Muriel Rukeyser, *Savage Coast* (New York: The Feminist Press, 2013), 298. Subsequent citations are given in the text.

16. Chapters of the novel contain quotes and epigraphs, sometimes lengthy. Chapter 4, for example, begins with an excerpt of the *Communist Manifesto* which discusses class, closing with the characterization of work-ing people as "the revolutionary class" and, as such, "the class that holds the future in its hands" (55).

17. Rowena Kennedy Epstein, introduction to *Savage Coast*, xxx.

18. Again, in the introduction to *Savage Coast*, Kennedy-Epstein points out that the novel, "written before Hemingway, Orwell, or Malraux's major works on the subject, is one of only a handful of novels written by foreign women on the war," and gives readers a better sense of women's public and interior lives (x).

19. Rowena Kennedy-Epstein, "'Her Symbol Was Civil War': Recovering Muriel Rukeyser's Lost Spanish Civil War Novel," *Modern Fiction Studies* 59, no. 2 (2013): 462.

20. Kennedy-Epstein, "'Her Symbol Was Civil War,'" 419.

21. Rukeyser's focus on people—particularly women and families—contrasts heavily with the violence-focused, hypermasculine content of her contemporaries Malraux, Orwell, and Hemingway.

22. In her essay "Muriel Rukeyser and the Security of the Imagination: Poetry and Propaganda in 1940s America," *Modernist Cultures* 14, no. 4 (November 2019): 439, Eleanor Careless writes that the poet "prioritize[s] the *informative* rather than the *promotional* function of propaganda, to edify rather than control the masses and to disseminate war news with a view to supplying an intelligent American public with sound and substantial infor-

mation, a stance in line with that of poet Archibald MacLeish, the assistant director of the OWI."

23. Rich, "Introduction," vii.

24. Rich, "Introduction," xiii.

25. Muriel Rukeyser, *The Outer Banks* (Greensboro, NC: Unicorn Press, 1967), viii. Subsequent citations are given in the text.

26. Muriel Rukeyser, *The Gates* (New York: McGraw-Hill, 1976), 71. Subsequent citations are given in the text.

27. Rich, "Introduction," xii.

28. Saidiya Hartman, *Scenes of Subjection: Terror, Slavery, and Self-Making in Nineteenth-Century America* (Oxford: Oxford University Press, 1997), 18.

29. Hartman, *Scenes of Subjection*, 18–19.

30. Hartman, *Scenes of Subjection*, 18–19.

31. Muriel Rukeyser, *Houdini: A Musical* (Middletown, CT: Paris Press/Wesleyan University Press, 2002), 15. Subsequent citations are given in the text.

32. Rich, "Introduction," xv.

33. Rich, "Introduction," xv.

Chapter 8

1. A cartoonist, Dani Donovan, made a poster that reflects the process of storytelling for people with ADHD vs. neurotypical people. For the latter, a box labeled "start of story" leads directly along a straight arrow to another box, labeled "end of story." For the flowchart titled "ADHD Storytelling," however, there are *twelve* boxes; not all of them connect, and some of them lead to multiple outcomes—most often not in straight lines, but with arrows that bend in stairstep fashion. The last box is not the end of the story; it's an apology. But I refuse to include that. See https://www.adhddd.com/shop/adhd-storytelling-poster/

2. I speak here of mostly anecdotal confidences, but there is much research and discussion of the obstacles that Black faculty and staff of all genders face in academia. See, for example, https://www.washingtonpost.com/education/2021/06/16/penn-state-black-faculty-racism/

3. My second book, *Black Peculiar*, was written during my three-semester stint in a visual arts MFA program.

4. Hanif Abdurraqib, "In *I'm So Fine*, Khadijah Queen Casts Her Eye on Toxic Masculinity and Celebrity Culture," *New Yorker*, November 16, 2017, https://www.newyorker.com/books/page-turner/im-so-fine-khadijah-queen-toxic-masculinity-celebrity-culture

5. Often, a person does not *need* a clinical diagnosis to know they're neurodivergent, since diagnoses have their own fiery hoops of proof to

jump through. I was lucky to have timely evaluation and treatment through the Veterans Affairs hospital. For women especially, gender bias precludes prompt and accurate diagnosis. See the American Psychological Association's 2003 article "ADHD: A Women's Issue," https://www.apa.org/monitor/feb03/adhd

6. Henry Ford Health Staff. "Why ADHD Is Often Underdiagnosed In Women." September 7, 2023. https://www.henryford.com/blog/2023/09/why-adhd-is-often-underdiagnosed-in-women#:~:text="Women%20with%20untreated%20ADHD%20can,back%20some%20self%2Desteem"

7. Kenneth Blum et al., "Attention-Deficit-Hyperactivity Disorder and Reward Deficiency Syndrome," *Neuropsychiatric Disease and Treatment* 4, no. 5 (October 2008): 893–918. https://www.ncbi.nlm.nih.gov/pmc/articles/PMC2626918/

8. David Shepardson, Rajesh Kumar Singh, and Jeff Mason, "U.S. Will No Longer Enforce Mask Mandate on Airplanes, Trains after Court Ruling," *Reuters*, April 19, 2022, https://www.reuters.com/legal/government/us-judge-rules-mask-mandate-transport-unlawful-overturning-biden-effort-2022-04-18/

9. Zachary B. Wolf, "Biden Declares the Pandemic Over. People Are Acting Like It Too," CNN, September 19, 2022, https://www.cnn.com/2022/09/19/politics/biden-covid-pandemic-over-what-matters/index.html

10. Deidre McPhillips, "Hospitals in the US Are the Fullest They've Been throughout the Pandemic—but It's Not Just Covid," CNN, December 9, 2022, https://www.cnn.com/2022/12/08/health/hospitals-full-not-just-covid/index.html

11. U.S. Department of Health and Human Services, "New Surgeon General Advisory Sounds Alarm on Health Worker Burnout and Resignation," May 23, 2022, https://www.hhs.gov/about/news/2022/05/23/new-surgeon-general-advisory-sounds-alarm-on-health-worker-burnout-and-resignation.html

12. Lauren L. O'Mahoney et al. "The Prevalence and Long-Term Health Effects of Long Covid among Hospitalised and Non-hospitalised Populations: A Systematic Review and Meta-analysis," *Lancet* 55 (January 2023), https://www.thelancet.com/journals/eclinm/article/PIIS2589-5370(22)00491-6/fulltext

13. Hassan M. Otifi and Balkur K. Adiga, "Endothelial Dysfunction in Covid-19 Infection," *American Journal of the Medical Sciences* 363, no. 4 (April 2022): 281–87. https://www.ncbi.nlm.nih.gov/pmc/articles/PMC8802031/

14. "Inflammation and Intussusceptive Angiogenesis in COVID-19: Everything In and Out of Flow," *European Respiratory Journal* 56, no. 5 (November 2020): 2003147. https://www.ncbi.nlm.nih.gov/pmc/articles/PMC7530910/

15. Ethan Davitt et al. write: "Both the innate and adaptive immune systems experience dysregulation in COVID-19." Noted in "COVID-19 Disease

and Immune Dysregulation," *Best Practice and Research Clinical Haematology* 35, no. 3 (September 2022): 101401. https://www.ncbi.nlm.nih.gov/pmc/artic les/PMC9568269/#

16. Mayo Clinic, "COVID-19: Long-Term Effects," June 28, 2022, https:// www.mayoclinic.org/diseases-conditions/coronavirus/in-depth/coronavir us-long-term-effects/art-20490351

17. Damir Huremović, "Brief History of Pandemics (Pandemics through-out History)," *Psychiatry of Pandemics* (May 16, 2019): 7–35. https://www.ncbi .nlm.nih.gov/pmc/articles/PMC7123574/

18. Daniel Ackerman, "Before Face Masks, Americans Went to War against Seat Belts," *Business Insider*, May 26, 2020, https://www.businessinsider.com /when-americans-went-to-war-against-seat-belts-2020-5

19. Centers for Disease Control. "People with Certain Medical Condi-tions." Updated May 11, 2023. https://www.cdc.gov/coronavirus/2019-ncov /need-extra-precautions/people-with-medical-conditions.html#:~:text=Li ke%20adults%2C%20children%20with%20obesity,very%20sick%20from%20 COVID%2D19

20. Katie Robertson, "Nikole Hannah-Jones Denied Tenure at Univer-sity of North Carolina," *New York Times*, May 19, 2021, updated July 15, 2022, https://www.nytimes.com/2021/05/19/business/media/nikole-hannah-jon es-unc.html

21. Ford Foundation, "Meet the Disability Futures Fellows," 2022, https:// www.fordfoundation.org/work/investing-in-individuals/disability-futures -fellows/2022-disability-futures-fellows/

22. Centers for Disease Control, "Interim Infection Prevention and Con-trol Recommendations for Healthcare Personnel during the Coronavirus Dis-ease 2019 (COVID-19) Pandemic," September 23, 2022, https://www.cdc.gov /coronavirus/2019-ncov/hcp/infection-control-recommendations.html

23. See Rick Webster, "The ADHD Tax Is Draining—Financially and Emo-tionally," *ADDitude Magazine*, January 10, 2023.

24. See Ed Yong, "The Final Pandemic Betrayal," *Atlantic*, April 13, 2022, https://www.theatlantic.com/health/archive/2022/04/us-1-million-covid -death-rate-grief/629537/

25. An AARP calculator for long-term care costs in the U.S. is available by zip code at https://www.aarp.org/caregiving/financial-legal/long-term-care -cost-calculator.html

26. William Haseltine, "Carbon Dioxide Levels May Predict Covid Risk in Your Immediate Surroundings," *Forbes Magazine*, June 23, 2022, https://www .forbes.com/sites/williamhaseltine/2022/06/23/carbon-dioxide-levels-may -predict-covid-risk-in-your-immediate-surroundings/?sh=6bd53d1f108b

27. For a comprehensive article on the pace of work post-tenure and the cost of overwork, see James Mulholland, "Slow Down: On Dealing with Mid-career Burnout," *Profession*, Winter 2020. https://profession.mla.org/slow-do wn-on-dealing-with-midcareer-burnout/

28. For one example, see Emma Brockes, "The Pretense of Normality Is Contagious—Even for a Covid Realist Like Me," *Guardian*, July 21, 2021, https://www.theguardian.com/commentisfree/2021/jul/16/normality-cov id-holiday-risk-florida-sun

29. Adam Serwer, "The Cruelty Is the Point: President Trump and His Supporters Find Community by Rejoicing in the Suffering of Those They Hate and Fear," *Atlantic*, October 3, 2018, https://www.theatlantic.com/ideas /archive/2018/10/the-cruelty-is-the-point/572104/

30. *Stolen Hours* (1963), directed by Daniel M. Petrie, screenplay by Jessamyn West, 36:01–38:25. Subsequent references to this film are given in the text.

31. In late October 2019, I flew home from London feeling like I was so sick I might be dying. I thought at first it was an allergy to soy, but I could not get out of bed; my skin hurt. I couldn't eat. I was delirious. All I could do was sleep, and only on my stomach, because lying on my back made me feel like I couldn't breathe. I was still sick two months later and never regained the same level of energy I had before getting sick. Reuters has reported that COVID-19 likely originated sooner than previously thought. See David Stanway, "First COVID-19 case could have emerged in China in Oct 2019—study," June 25, 2021. https://www.reuters.com/world/china/first-covid-19-case-cou ld-have-hit-china-oct-2019-study-2021-06-25/

In September 2022, a white woman coughed a wet, nasty cough on me while I was dining outside with poet Mary Jo Bang as I was visiting Washington University St. Louis—we were outside, trying to be safe. The woman went out of her way to cough on me, leaning forward, open-mouthed. I felt the warm and disgusting cloud of it. She looked at me and smirked. My SARS-CoV-2 test—taken the next day, my nose violently swabbed by a clinic van— was inconclusive.

32. More accurately, I mostly love watching Formula One because of seven-time world champion Lewis Hamilton, the first and only Black F1 driver, who races for the Mercedes-AMG Petronas team representing Great Britain and is tied with Michael Schumacher for the record number of world drivers' championships ever.

33. The history of eugenics when it comes to disability is well-known and ongoing. See Michael Rembis, Catherine Kudlick, and Kim E. Nielsen, eds., *The Oxford Handbook of Disability History* (Oxford Academic, online ed., July 10, 2018), https://doi.org/10.1093/oxfordhb/9780190234959.013.6

34. Toni Morrison, *The Source of Self-Regard* (New York: Knopf, 2019), 3.

35. For more about "the neurotypical as the building block of human existence," and a disability-focused critique of "the idea that certain forms of human life are more worthwhile than others," see Erin Manning, *The Minor Gesture* (Durham, NC: Duke University Press, 2016), 135.

36. Canadian attorney Silvia Yee, in her article "Where Prejudice, Disabil-

ity and 'Disabilism' Meet," writes that "individuals and society as a whole must advocate not only for a bare tolerance of difference, but for a celebration of diversity, intrinsic worth and human ability in all its forms." Disability Rights Education & Defense Fund, n.d., https://dredf.org/news/publications/disability-rights-law-and-policy/where-prejudice-disability-and-disabilism-meet/

37. See Tacitus's The *Annals*, 109 CE.

38. See Lianne Mandelbaum, "Want Food Allergy 'Jokes' to Stop? Call Them Out," *Allergic Living*, March 9, 2022, https://www.allergicliving.com/2022/03/09/want-food-allergy-jokes-to-stop-call-them-out/

39. "What Data Analysis Shows About Campus Shootings." PBS NewsHour, February 14, 2023. https://www.pbs.org/newshour/nation/what-data-analysis-shows-about-campus-shootings

40. *Tombstone* (Hollywood Pictures 1993), directed by George P. Cosmatos, written by Kevin Jarre, 1:38:22–28.

41. "By the dawn of the 19th century, tuberculosis—or consumption—had killed one in seven of all people that had ever lived." *The Forgotten Plague: Tuberculosis in America*, PBS, aired February 10, 2015, https://www.pbs.org/wgbh/americanexperience/films/plague/

42. See Brown's blog entry "Ableism/Language," created July 2012 and last updated September 14, 2022, https://www.autistichoya.com/p/ableist-words-and-terms-to-avoid.html

43. Philip Bump, "When the battle over American freedom was centered on seat belt laws," *The Washington Post*, September 16, 2021. https://www.washingtonpost.com/politics/2021/09/16/when-battle-over-american-freedom-was-centered-seat-belt-laws/

44. Octavia E. Butler, *Parable of the Sower* (New York: Grand Central Publishing, 2000), 3.

Chapter 9

1. Toni Morrison, *Song of Solomon* (New York: Houghton Mifflin, 1995), 179.

2. Quoted in Toni Morrison's essay "The Site of Memory," p. 91 in William Zinsser's *Inventing the Truth: The Art and Craft of Memoir* (Houghton Mifflin, 1995).

3. See the definition of gaslighting via the National Domestic Violence Hotline: https://www.thehotline.org/what-is-gaslighting/

4. While the organization is now defunct and original statement is no longer available at http://www.vidaweb.org/statements-against-silence/ there are separate letters written in solidarity just days after "Statements Against Silence." They can be found in *Luna Luna Magazine*: http://www.lu

nalunamagazine.com/blog/vida-statement-of-silence and in *Apogee Journal*: https://apogeejournal.org/2016/04/13/to-become-louder-even-still-respon ses-to-sexual-violence-in-literary-spaces/

5. Domestic workers organized to fight workplace abuses in the late 1990s. See https://www.pri.org/stories/2016-03-19/unsung-black-heroines -launched-modern-domestic-workers-movement-powered-their-own

6. Actress Gabrielle Union points out the differences between abuse reports by white women and those of Black women and other women of color. See https://www.washingtonpost.com/news/arts-and-entertainment /wp/2017/12/08/gabrielle-union-on-metoo-the-floodgates-have-opened -for-white-women/

7. "I resent the idea that people would blame the messenger for the mes- sage, rather than looking at the content of the message itself."—Anita Hill, during congressional hearings regarding the nomination of Clarence Thomas to the Supreme Court, as reported by Richard L. Berke in "Thomas Nomina- tion: Thomas's Accuser Assails Handling of Her Complaint." *New York Times*, October 8, 1991. https://www.nytimes.com/1991/10/08/us/the-thomas-no mination-thomas-s-accuser-assails-handling-of-her-complaint.html

8. I will not name the reporter, either, because she used that article— which critiqued the writing style of survivor testimony, and questioned their autonomy and authority over their own safety—to catapult her career. When I read it, I got physically sick for a full week.

9. I told a friend and fellow writer about my work with the Collective to remove him from literary spaces, and she confided in me about being abused by Sherman Alexie. I offered some of our approaches and she worked hard to implement them, though ultimately only three of the dozens upon dozens of victims she spoke with would go on record, or even allow their anonymous testimony to be made public. They were too afraid of personal and profes- sional backlash. See https://www.npr.org/2018/03/05/589909379/it-just-fe lt-very-wrong-sherman-alexies-accusers-go-on-the-record

10. This is the point, in reading this essay aloud as mentioned in the note above, when I began to weep in front of an audience of at least 150 of my peers, students, and strangers. But I kept going. Afterward, I felt alone and destroyed, despite thank yous and notes of appreciation, despite dinner after- ward with the Collective. People went on with their conference activities, and I felt used and discarded. I went out to try and lighten up, but saw two apologists at the bookfair (one of whom had referred to me as a "child bride" when my abuser and I were together because she said she was jealous), and retreated. I went back to my room and cried, watching that night's powerfully moving episode of *Grey's Anatomy*—which happened to be about how hospi- tals and police treat victims of rape (callously), and the empowering, kind, patient, deeply humane alternative that the fictional Grey-Sloan Memorial

staff provided in supporting every need the patient voiced, often intuited by the female doctor—also a rape survivor.

11. Read the US Dept of Health & Human Services, Office on Women's Health, definition of coercion: https://www.womenshealth.gov/relationshi ps-and-safety/other-types/sexual-coercion

12. See Camille Aroustamian, "Time's up: Recognising sexual violence as a public policy issue: A qualitative content analysis of sexual violence cases and the media," for further context. *Aggression and Violent Behavior*, Volume 50 (2020): 101341, https://doi.org/10.1016/j.avb.2019.101341

13. Of course, everyone defines ease for themselves. I'm asking in a social sense, in a way that challenges us—as a species—to rethink our assumptions, to eschew veneers of propriety and create real systems of empowerment that work in practice and are easily accessible. We have the tools. Where is the will? I do *not* ask these questions to shame folks who are trapped in cycles of abuse. They are doing the best they can, in the midst of social systems that offer no sustainable, effective protection.

14. Sample sites to visit: https://www.timesupnow.com/#resources-an chor, https://www.salon.com/2018/01/16/when-sexual-assault-victims-sp eak-out-their-institutions-often-betray-them_partner/, and https://www.cn bc.com/2017/10/26/5-ways-men-can-address-and-help-prevent-sexual-ha rassment-at-work.html and https://www.americantrainingresources.com /ptv-228.aspx

15. See Bishop's poem "One Art," performed beautifully by Miranda Otto in the 2013 film *Reaching for the Moon*: https://www.youtube.com/watch?v=w kQf8ArHOCo

16. *The Cancer Journals*, 13.

17. Video of poet and essayist Vanessa Angélica Villarreal teaching her son Joaquin about personal authority over his body. January 11, 2018 on Insta-gram. https://www.instagram.com/p/Bd1jS00nYmo/?taken-by=vv_angelica

18. Bettina Judd. Text message to author. 26 October 2016.

19. See "Big Name Problems for Academe": https://www.insidehighered .com/views/2017/11/07/will-academe-ever-truly-hold-big-name-professo rs-more-accountable-sexual-harassment

20. See Michelle Goldberg's 2014 article in *The Nation*, "Why the Campus Rape Crisis Confounds Colleges": https://www.thenation.com/article/why -campus-rape-crisis-confounds-colleges/

21. https://www.rainn.org/statistics/criminal-justice-system

22. https://www.rainn.org/statistics/victims-sexual-violence

23. More on the BTC at https://ndsmcobserver.com/2014/03/look-black -took-collective/

24. "In Support Of: A Statement Against Abusive Behavior in Our Creative Community": http://vinylpoetryandprose.com/2016/03/in-support-of-a-sta tement-against-abusive-behavior-in-our-creative-community/

25. "The precise role of the artist, then, is to illuminate that darkness, blaze roads through that vast forest, so that we will not, in all our doing, lose sight of its purpose, which is, after all, to make the world a more human dwelling place."—James Baldwin, quoted in *Brainpickings*, https://www.brainpickings.org/2014/08/20/james-baldwin-the-creative-process/

26. See Thierry Steimer, "The biology of fear- and anxiety-related behaviors." https://www.ncbi.nlm.nih.gov/pmc/articles/PMC3181681/

27. *The Revolution Starts at Home: Confronting Partner Abuse in Activist Communities*, edited by Ching-In Chen and Leah Lakshmi Piepzna-Samarasinha. http://criticalresistance.org/wp-content/uploads/2014/05/Revolution-starts-at-home-zine.pdf

28. For the complete poem, please find Jordan's reading of it at https://www.youtube.com/watch?v=XUSTxhYu7-4

29. Tarana Burke. Cultural Events Board speaker, Macky Auditorium, University of Colorado, Boulder, CO, April 15, 2019. See also Burke's organizational website: https://metoomvmt.org

30. Burke.

31. Read more at https://margaretprice.wordpress.com/access-statement-for-presentations/

References

"In Support Of: A Statement Against Abusive Behavior in Our Creative Community." March 26, 2016. *Vinyl Poetry & Prose.* http://vinylpoetryandprose.com/2016/03/in-support-of-a-statement-against-abusive-behavior-in-our-creative-community/

Abdurraqib, Hanif. 2017. "In *I'm So Fine*, Khadijah Queen Casts Her Eye on Toxic Masculinity and Celebrity Culture." *The New Yorker.* November 16, 2017. https://www.newyorker.com/books/page-turner/im-so-fine-khadijah-queen-toxic-masculinity-celebrity-culture

Ackerman, Daniel. 2020. "Before Face Masks, Americans Went to War against Seat Belts." *Business Insider.* May 26, 2020. https://www.businessinsider.com/when-americans-went-to-war-against-seat-belts-2020-5

Ahmed, Sara. 2017. *Living a Feminist Life.* Durham: Duke University Press.

Ahmed, Sara. 2004. "Collective Feelings: Or, the Impressions Left by Others." *Theory, Culture & Society* 21, no. 2 (2004): 28.

Anonymous. March 6, 2016. "Reports from the Field: Statements Against Silence." VIDA: Women in Literary Arts. http://www.vidaweb.org/statements-against-silence/

Astrodienst AG/Astro.com. n.d. "Personal Portrait." Inputs: 14 April 1952, 8:00am, New York City.

Baldwin, James. 1973. "The Black Scholar Interviews: James Baldwin." *The Black Scholar* 5, no. 4 (1973): 33–42. www.jstor.org/stable/41065644

Barnat, Dara. 2015. "'Women and poets see the truth arrive': Muriel Rukeyser and Walt Whitman." *Studies in American Jewish Literature* 34 no. 1 (2015): 94–116. muse.jhu.edu/article/577309. Project MUSE.

Barthes, Roland. 1975. *The Pleasure of the Text.* New York: Hill & Wang.

Bellocq, E. J. 1912. *Storyville Portrait.* Fraenkel Gallery. https://www.artsy.net/artwork/e-j-bellocq-storyville-portrait-7

Benjamin, Walter. 1978. "On Mimetic Faculty." In *Reflections: Essays, Aphorisms, Autobiographical Writings.* Edited by Peter Demetz. Translated by Edmund Jephcott. New York: Schocken Books.

Benjamin, Walter. 1968. Illuminations. Edited by Hannah Arendt. Translated by Harry Zohn. New York: Schocken Books.

Black Hawk (Mahkatêwe-meshi-kêhkêhkwa). 2008. Life of Black Hawk, or Ma-ka-tai-me-she-kia-kiak: Dictated by Himself. Edited by J. Gerald Kennedy. New York: Penguin.

Blum, Kenneth, et al. 2008. "Attention-Deficit-Hyperactivity Disorder and Reward Deficiency Syndrome." *Neuropsychiatric Disease and Treatment* 4, no. 5 (October 2008): 893–918. https://www.ncbi.nlm.nih.gov/pmc/articl es/PMC2626918/

Bourriaud, Nicolas. 2002. *Relational Aesthetics.* Translated by Simon Pleasance and Fronza Woods, with the participation of Mathieu Copeland. Dijon and Paris: Les presses du réel.

Brand, Dionne. 2002. *A Map to the Door of No Return.* Toronto: Vintage Canada.

Brand, Dionne. 2018. *The Blue Clerk.* Durham: Duke University Press.

Brooks, Gwendolyn. 1971. "Paul Robeson." In *Family Pictures.* Detroit: Broadside Press.

Butler, Octavia. 2000. *Parable of the Sower.* New York: Grand Central Publishing.

Cantiello, Jessica Wells. 2012. "Frances E. W. Harper's Educational Reservations: The Indian Question in *Iola Leroy." African American Review* 45, no. 4 (2012): 575–92.

Careless, Eleanor. 2019. "Muriel Rukeyser and the Security of the Imagination: Poetry and Propaganda in 1940s America." *Modernist Cultures* 14, no. 4 (Nov 2019): 421–45. http://sro.sussex.ac.uk/id/eprint/98483/

Chadfield, Sarah. January 8, 2015. "Muriel Rukeyser and the Spanish Civil War." *Insights: Scholarly Work at the Kluge Center.* Library of Congress. https://blogs.loc.gov/kluge/2015/01/muriel-rukeyser-and-the-spanish-ci vil-war/

Chen, Ching-In, Dulani, Jai, and Piepzna-Samarasinha, Leah Lakshmi, eds. 2016.

The Revolution Starts at Home: Confronting Intimate Violence Within Activist Communities. Oakland: AK Press.

Chopin, Kate. 1894. "Désirée's Baby." In *Bayou Folk.* New York: Houghton Mifflin.

Cixous, Hélène. 1976. "The Laugh of the Medusa." Translated by Keith Cohen and Paula Cohen. *Signs* 1, no. 4 (Summer 1976): 883. https://www.jstor.org /stable/3173239

Clifton, Lucille. 1993. *Book of Light.* Port Townsend, WA: Copper Canyon Press.

Clifton, Lucille. 2012. *The Collected Poems of Lucille Clifton.* Rochester: BOA Editions.

Cook, Alexandra Parma, and Noble David Cook. 1991. *Good Faith and Truthful Ignorance: A Case of Transatlantic Bigamy.* Durham: Duke University Press.

Cosmatos, George P., dir. *Tombstone.* 1993. Hollywood Pictures.

Crenshaw, Kimberlé. 1989. "Demarginalizing the Intersection of Race and

Sex: A Black Feminist Critique of Antidiscrimination Doctrine, Feminist Theory and Antiracist Politics." *University of Chicago Legal Forum*, vol. 1989, issue 1, article 8: 139–67. https://chicagounbound.uchicago.edu/uclf/vol19 89/iss1/8

Davitt, Ethan, et al. 2022. "COVID-19 Disease and Immune Dysregulation," *Best Practice and Research Clinical Haematology* 35, no. 3 (September 2022): 101401. https://www.ncbi.nlm.nih.gov/pmc/articles/PMC9568269/#

de la Cruz, Sor Juana. 1999. "Poema 92. Sátira filosófica/Poem 92. Philosophical Satire." Translated by David Frye. https://public.websites.umich.edu/~dfrye/SORJUANA.html

de la Cruz, Sor Juana. 2004. "You Foolish Men." Translated by Michael Smith. Academy of American Poets. https://poets.org/poem/you-foolish-men

de Villoldo, Isidro. 1539. *The Miracle of the Black Leg*. Museo Nacional de Escultura de Valladolid, Spain. https://www.culturaydeporte.gob.es/mnescultu ra/en/visitanos/prepara-tu-visita/audioguia/sala12.html

DMX, featuring Jay-Z and The Lox (Jadakiss, Styles P, and Sheek Louch). 1998. "Blackout." *Flesh of My Flesh, Blood of My Blood*, Ruff Ryders/Def Jam. Track 13.

Dillon, Grace L., ed. 2012. *Walking the Clouds: An Anthology of Indigenous Science Fiction*. Tucson: University of Arizona Press.

Donovan, Dani. 2022. "ADHD Storytelling." https://www.adhddd.com/shop /adhd-storytelling-poster/

Dziech, Billie Wright. 6 November 2017. "Big-Name Problems for Academe." *Inside Higher Ed.* https://www.insidehighered.com/views/2017/11/07/wi ll-academe-ever-truly-hold-big-name-professors-more-accountable-sexu al-harassment

Elliott, J. H. 2006. *Empires of the Atlantic World: Britain and Spain in America 1492–1830*. New Haven: Yale University Press.

Ellison, Ralph. 1952. *Invisible Man*. New York: Random House.

Fleury, Amy. 2003. "What is Boundless: A Conversation with Edward Hirsch about Ekphrastic Writing." *Interdisciplinary Humanities* 20, no. 1 (Spring 2003): 47–53.

Ford Foundation. 2022. "Meet the Disability Futures Fellows." https://www .fordfoundation.org/work/investing-in-individuals/disability-futures-fell ows/2022-disability-futures-fellows/

Freire, Paulo. 2006. *Pedagogy of the Oppressed*. Translated by Myra Bergman Ramos. London, New York: Continuum.

Fusco, Coco. 1997. "Lorna Simpson." *Bomb Magazine*, no. 61 (Fall 1997): 51-55.

Gazit, Chana, dir. 2015. *The Forgotten Plague: Tuberculosis in America*. PBS. Aired February 10, 2015. https://www.pbs.org/wgbh/americanexperience /films/plague/

Glissant, Édouard. 1990. *Poetics of Relation*. Translated by Betsy Wing. Ann Arbor: University of Michigan Press.

Goldberg, Michelle. June 5, 2014. "Why the Campus Rape Crisis Confounds Colleges." *The Nation*. https://www.thenation.com/article/archive/why-campus-rape-crisis-confounds-colleges/

Goldenberg, Naomi. 1985. "Archetypal Theory and the Separation of Mind and Body: Reason Enough to Turn to Freud?" *Journal of Feminist Studies in Religion* 1, no. 1 (1985): 55–72.

Goulimari, Pelagia. 2014. *Literary Criticism and Theory: From Plato to Postcolonialism*. New York: Routledge.

Gumbs, Alexis Pauline, China Martens, and Mai'a Williams, eds. 2016. *Revolutionary Mothering: Love on the Front Lines*. Binghamton: PM Press.

Harper, Frances Ellen Watkins. 1895. "A Double Standard." In *Atlanta Offering: Poems*. Philadelphia: George S. Ferguson Co.

Harper, Frances Ellen Watkins. 1988. *Iola Leroy; or, Shadows Uplifted*. Oxford: Oxford University Press.

Harshav, Benjamin. 2007. *Poetics of Exploration*. Stanford: Stanford University Press.

Hartman, Saidiya. 1997. *Scenes of Subjection: Terror, Slavery, and Self-Making in Nineteenth-Century America*. Oxford: Oxford University Press.

Hartman, Saidiya. 2008. "Venus in Two Acts." *Small Axe* 12, no. 2 (June 2008): 1–14.

Haseltine, William. June 23, 2022. "Carbon Dioxide Levels May Predict Covid Risk in Your Immediate Surroundings." *Forbes Magazine*. https://www.forbes.com/sites/williamhaseltine/2022/06/23/carbon-dioxide-levels-may-predict-covid-risk-in-your-immediate-surroundings/?sh=6bd53d1f108b

Holm, Tom, J. Diane Pearson, and Ben Chavis. 2003. "Peoplehood: A Model for the Extension of Sovereignty in American Indian Studies." *Wicazo Sa Review* 18, no. 1 (Spring 2003): 7–24.

hooks, bell. 2018. *All About Love: New Visions*. New York: HarperCollins.

hooks, bell. 1994. *Teaching to Transgress: Education as the Practice of Freedom*. New York: Routledge.

Howard, W. Scott, and Broc Rossell, eds. 2019. *Poetics and Praxis 'After' Objectivism*. Iowa City: University of Iowa Press.

Hull, Akasha. 2001. *Soul Talk: The New Spirituality of African American Women*. Rochester, VT: Inner Traditions.

Huremović, Damir. 2019. "Brief History of Pandemics (Pandemics throughout History)." *Psychiatry of Pandemics* (May 16, 2019): 7–35. https://www.ncbi.nlm.nih.gov/pmc/articles/PMC7123574/

Jacobs, Harriet. 2000. *Incidents in the Life of a Slave Girl*. New York: Penguin.

Johnson, Erica L. 2014. "Building the Neo-Archive: Dionne Brand's *A Map to the Door of No Return*." *Meridians: Feminism, Race, Transnationalism* 12, no. 1 (2014): 149–71. https://muse.jhu.edu/article/541875

Jordan, June. 2005. "Poem About My Rights." Reprinted from *Directed By Desire: The Collected Poems of June Jordan*. Port Townsend, WA: Copper Can-

yon Press. https://www.poetryfoundation.org/poems/48762/poem-about
-my-rights

Kantaris, Geoffrey. 1992. "Difference and Indifference: The Poetry of Sor Juana Ines de la Cruz." University of Cambridge, Centre of Latin American Studies. http://www.latin-american.cam.ac.uk/culture/SorJuana/SorJuana5.htm

Kennedy-Epstein, Rowena. 2013. "'Her Symbol Was Civil War': Recovering Muriel Rukeyser's Lost Spanish Civil War Novel." *Modern Fiction Studies* 59, no. 2 (2013): 416–39, 462. https://search-proquest-com.du.idm.oclc.org/docview/1406196117?accountid=14608

King, Tiffany Lethabo. 2019. *The Black Shoals: Offshore Formations of Black and Native Studies*. Durham: Duke University Press.

Levi, Jan Heller, ed. 1986. *A Muriel Rukeyser Reader*. New York: W. W. Norton.

Lewis, Thomas, Fari Amini, and Richard Lannon. 2000. *A General Theory of Love*. New York: Random House.

Logan, William. 2012. "Song & Dance." *New Criterion* 31, no. 4 (December 2012): 69–76.

Lorde, Audre. 1984. *Sister Outsider*. Berkeley: Crossing Press.

Love, Edgar F. 1967. "Negro Resistance to Spanish Rule in Colonial Mexico." *Journal of Negro History* 52, no. 2 (1967): 89–103. www.jstor.org/stable/2716127

Mack, David. 2016. "Vision Quest: Echo." *Moonshot: The Indigenous Comics Collection, Volume 1*. Hope Nicholson, ed. Toronto: Alternate History Comics, Inc.

Manning, Erin. 2016. *The Minor Gesture*. Durham: Duke University Press.

McKittrick, Katherine. 2020. *Dear Science and Other Stories*. Durham: Duke University Press.

McKittrick, Katherine. 2017. "Commentary: Worn Out." *Southeastern Geographer* 57, no. 1 (2017): 96–100.

Melville, Herman. 1985. *The Confidence-Man: His Masquerade*. Washington, D.C.: Library of America.

Michigan State University Libraries. n.d. "Publishing and Book Design Basics: Elements of page design." https://libguides.lib.msu.edu/c.php?g=97090&p=908734 (Accessed November 19, 2018).

Miltko, Caelin. 2014. "A Look at Black Took Collective." *The Observer*. March 18, 2014. https://ndsmcobserver.com/2014/03/look-black-took-collective/

Mingus, Charles. 2018. "Pithecanthropus Erectus." *Jazz in Detroit/Strata Concert Gallery/46 Selden*. BBE Music.

Morrison, Toni. 1985. "A Knowing So Deep." *Essence Magazine* (May 1985): 230.

Morrison, Toni. 2008. *A Mercy*. New York: Vintage International.

Morrison, Toni. 1992. *Playing in the Dark: Whiteness and the Literary Imagination*. New York: Vintage.

Morrison, Toni. 1995. *Song of Solomon*. New York: Houghton Mifflin.

Morrison, Toni. 2017. *The Origin of Others*. Cambridge, MA: Harvard University Press.

Morrison, Toni. 2019. *The Source of Self-Regard*. New York: Penguin Random House.

Myers, Kathleen Ann. 2003. *Neither Saints nor Sinners: Writing the Lives of Women in Spanish America*. Oxford: Oxford University Press.

NPR. 2019. "Widening the Lens on a More Inclusive Science." *Science Friday*. September 6, 2019. https://www.sciencefriday.com/segments/indigenous-science/

Ortega y Gasset, José. 1956. *The Dehumanization of Art and Other Writings on Art and Culture*. New York: Doubleday.

Ortiz, Simon. 1981. "Towards a National Indian Literature: Cultural Authenticity in Nationalism." *MELUS* 8, no. 2 (Summer 1981): 7–12.

Ortiz, Simon. 1981. *From Sand Creek*. Tucson: University of Arizona Press.

Otifi, Hassan M., and Balkur K. Adiga. 2022. "Endothelial Dysfunction in COVID-19 Infection." *American Journal of the Medical Sciences* 363, no. 4 (April 2022). https://www.ncbi.nlm.nih.gov/pmc/articles/PMC8802031/

Paz, Octavio. 1987. *Convergences: Essays on Art and Literature*. New York: Harcourt Brace Jovanovich.

PBS. 2008. *Walt Whitman: American Experience*. Aired April 14, 2008. https://www.pbs.org/wgbh/americanexperience/films/whitman/#transcript

Petrie, Daniel M., dir. *Stolen Hours*. 1963. Mirisch Company/Barbican Films.

Porter, Lavelle. 2019. "Should Walt Whitman be #Cancelled?" April 17, 2019. *JSTOR Daily*. https://daily.jstor.org/should-walt-whitman-be-cancelled/

Price, Margaret. n.d. "Access Statement." https://margaretprice.wordpress.com/access-statement-for-presentations/ (Accessed March 1, 2018).

RAINN (Rape, Abuse & Incest National Network). "The Criminal Justice System: Statistics." 2019. https://www.rainn.org/statistics/criminal-justice-system

Restall, Matthew. 1995. "'He Wished It in Vain': Subordination and Resistance among Maya Women in Post-Conquest Yucatan." *Ethnohistory* 42, no. 4 (1995): 577–94. https://www.jstor.org/stable/483144

Rowell, Charles, ed. 2004. "Interchange: Genres of History." *Journal of American History* 91, no. 2 (September 2004): 572–593.

Rukeyser, Muriel. 1976. *The Gates*. New York: McGraw-Hill.

Rukeyser, Muriel. 1948. *The Green Wave*. New York: Doubleday.

Rukeyser, Muriel. 2002. *Houdini: A Musical*. Amherst: Paris Press.

Rukeyser, Muriel. 1996. *The Life of Poetry*. Amherst: Paris Press.

Rukeyser, Muriel. 1981. *More Night*. New York: Harper & Row.

Rukeyser, Muriel. 1967. *The Outer Banks*. Greensboro: Unicorn Press.

Rukeyser, Muriel. 2013. *Savage Coast*. New York: The Feminist Press.

Said, Edward. 2004. *Humanism and Democratic Criticism*. New York: Columbia University Press.

Scott, Eugene. 2019. "Anger at Being Labeled Racist Is the New 'Cultural Anxiety' for Trump Supporters." *Washington Post*. August 12, 2019. https://www.washingtonpost.com/politics/2019/08/12/anger-being-labeled-racist-is-new-cultural-anxiety-trump-supporters/

Shafer, Ronald G. 2022. "Whitman's 'Leaves of Grass' was banned—and cost him his federal job." *Washington Post*. April 30, 2022. https://www.washingtonpost.com/history/2022/04/30/walt-whitman-leaves-grass-interior-department/

Sharpe, Christina. 2016. *In the Wake: On Blackness and Being*. London and Durham: Duke University Press.

Shteamer, Hank. 2018. "Review: Charles Mingus' 'Jazz in Detroit' Sheds Light on an Overlooked Era." *Rolling Stone*. November 2, 2018. https://www.rollingstone.com/music/music-album-reviews/album-review-charles-mingus-jazz-in-detroit-strata-concert-gallery-46-selden-750144/ (Accessed November 19, 2018).

Silko, Leslie Marmon. 2016. *Ceremony*. New York: Penguin/Random House.

Snead, James A. 1981. "On Repetition in Black Culture." *Black American Literature Forum* 15, no. 4 (Winter 1981): 146–54.

Spillers, Hortense. 1987. "Mama's Baby, Papa's Maybe: An American Grammar Book." *Diacritics* 17, no. 2 (1987): 64–81.

Staff, *BrooklynVegan*. 2016. "Larkin Grimm Accuses Swans' Michael Gira of Rape and Harassment, and Thomas Sayers Ellis of Sexual Harassment." *BrooklynVegan*. February 26, 2016. www.brooklynvegan.com/larkin-grimm-ac/

Stanley, Francis Edgar. 1919. *Theories Worth Having and Other Papers*. Boston: private papers.

Steimer, Thierry. 2002. "Abstract: The biology of fear- and anxiety-related behaviors." *Dialogues in Clinical Neuroscience* 4, no. 3 (September 2002): 231–49. https://www.ncbi.nlm.nih.gov/pmc/articles/PMC3181681/

Tate, Claudia, ed. 1985. *Black Women Writers at Work*. New York: Continuum.

Trethewey, Natasha. 2002. *Bellocq's Ophelia*. Minneapolis: Graywolf Press.

Trethewey, Natasha. 2010. *Beyond Katrina*. Athens: University of Georgia Press.

Trethewey, Natasha. 2000. *Domestic Work*. Minneapolis: Graywolf Press.

Trethewey, Natasha. 2006. *Native Guard*. Boston and New York: Houghton Mifflin.

Trethewey, Natasha. 2012. *Thrall*. Boston and New York: Houghton Mifflin.

Trethewey, Natasha. 2016. "We Have Seen." *Smithsonian Magazine* 47, no. 5 (September 2016): 4, 53.

Vitale, Tom. 2014. "Ralph Ellison: No Longer The 'Invisible Man' 100 Years After His Birth." NPR (National Public Radio). May 30, 2014. http://www

.npr.org/sections/codeswitch/2014/05/30/317056807/ralph-ellison-no
-longer-the-invisible-man-100-years-after-his-birth

Vizenor, Gerald. 2008. "The Aesthetics of Survivance: Literary Theory and Practice." In *Survivance: Narratives of Native Presence, edited by Gerald Vizenor*, 1–23. Lincoln and London: University of Nebraska Press.

Vizenor, Gerald. 1993. "The Ruins of Representation: Shadow Survivance and the Literature of Dominance." *American Indian Quarterly* 17, no. 1 (1993): 7–30. www.jstor.org/stable/1184777 JSTOR.

Ward Jr., Jerry W. 2011. "Beyond Katrina: A Meditation on the Mississippi Gulf Coast." *Southern Quarterly* 49, no. 1 (Fall 2011): 128–33.

Warren, Calvin. 2016. "Black Time: Slavery, Metaphysics, and the Logic of Wellness." In *The Psychic Hold of Slavery: Legacies in American Expressive Culture. Edited by Soyica* Diggs Colbert, Robert J. Patterson, and Aida Levy-Hussen. New Brunswick: Rutgers University Press.

Washuta, Elissa, and Theresa Warburton. 2019. *Shapes of Native Nonfiction*. Seattle: University of Washington Press.

Webster, Rick. 2023. "The ADHD Tax Is Draining—Financially and Emotionally." *ADDitude Magazine.* January 10, 2023. https://www.additudemag.com/adhd-tax-financial-wellness-money-problems/

Wolf, Naomi. 2004. "The Silent Treatment." *New York Magazine*. February 20, 2004. http://nymag.com/nymetro/news/features/n_9932/index.html

Wolf, Zachary B. 2022. "Biden Declares the Pandemic Over. People Are Acting Like It Too." CNN. September 19, 2022. https://www.cnn.com/2022/09/19/politics/biden-covid-pandemic-over-what-matters/index.html

Wright, Michelle. 2015. *Physics of Blackness: Beyond the Middle Passage Epistemology*. Minneapolis: University of Minnesota Press.

Wright, Nazera Sadiq. 2016. *Black Girlhood in the Nineteenth Century*. Champaign: University of Illinois Press.

Yancy, George, and bell hooks. 2015. "bell hooks: Buddhism, the Beats and Loving Blackness." *New York Times.* December 10, 2015.

Yee, Silvia. n.d. "Where Prejudice, Disability and 'Disabilism' Meet." Disability Rights Education & Defense Fund. https://dredf.org/news/publications/disability-rights-law-and-policy/where-prejudice-disability-and-disabilism-meet/

Yong, Ed. 2022. "The Final Pandemic Betrayal." *The Atlantic.* April 13, 2022. https://www.theatlantic.com/health/archive/2022/04/us-1-million-covid-death-rate-grief/629537/

Zander, Thea, Michael Öllinger, and Kirsten G. Volz. 2016. "Intuition and Insight: Two Processes That Build on Each Other or Fundamentally Differ?" *Frontiers in Psychology* 7, 2016. https://www.frontiersin.org/articles/10.3389/fpsyg.2016.01395/full

Zinsser, William, ed. 1995. *Inventing the Truth: The Art and Craft of Memoir*. New York: Houghton Mifflin.